"You're lying, Billy, and we know it. You lied about how you found them. You lied about the route you took back. You lied about the blood on your pants. You've been lying all day.

"You killed those girls," Bell continued, pointing his finger at the boy. "We know you killed those girls. We've got the proof. You lied and now you're caught. Just admit it."

Billy lifted his head. "I need to talk to my dad," he whispered.

The two officers left the room, leaving Billy and his father alone. Shutting the door behind them, the policemen stationed themselves directly outside.

"Billy, did you kill those girls?" They could hear Ed Keenan's voice clearly through the thin bedroom door. Billy's response was muffled.

Then Ed Keenan spoke again. "Oh no," the father cried softly. "Why?"

LOSS OF INNOCENCE

A TRUE STORY
OF JUVENILE MURDER

ERIC J. ADAMS

AVON BOOKS NEW YORK

LOSS OF INNOCENCE: A TRUE STORY OF JUVENILE MURDER
is an original publication of Avon Books. This work has never before
appeared in book form.

AVON BOOKS
A division of
The Hearst Corporation
105 Madison Avenue
New York, New York 10016

First Avon Books Printing: May 1991

AVON TRADEMARK REG. U.S. PAT. OFF. AND IN OTHER COUNTRIES, MARCA
REGISTRADA, HECHO EN U.S.A.

Printed in the U.S.A.

RA 10 9 8 7 6 5 4 3 2 1

To the sweet memories of
Kristy and Sherry Janson

Author's Note

All events and characters in this book are based on fact. Conversations were reconstructed using court and personal documents and the recollections of those involved. Though some scenes have been dramatized, all events and descriptions are based on verifiable sources. Some names have been changed, including the names of Billy Keenan and his family.

Acknowledgments

There are, of course, many who assisted in this project: neighbors, family members, police officers, investigators, psychologists, lawyers, judges, experts in the field of juvenile law and rehabilitation, school friends, and teachers. A special thanks to Investigator Mike Bell; Psychologist Christopher Berry, Ph.D.; District Attorney Victor Reichman; *Durango Herald* Editor Barry Smith; Editor-at-Large Nancy Beckus; Julie Fallowfield; Robert Mecoy; and Judge James D. Childress for his defense of First Amendment rights.

This project could not have been completed without the patient assistance of Joe and Vickie Janson, who deserve much more than thanks.

Contents

Prologue: The Find

The call to Emergency Dispatch came in at 3:57 on the afternoon of April 25, 1983. The slow-rolling reels of the police tape recorder dutifully recorded the conversation.

"Emergency?"

"Yes?"

"Okay. My name is Ed Keenan. I've got my son on the telephone on another line that I'm holding in my other hand over here. We live up on Wallace Gulch, out towards Bayfield."

"Yes." The voice carried the unmistakable quiver of all serious calls.

"Now, he has just advised me on the phone that one or two of our little girl neighbors have been evidently cut up and are layin' up in the woods between their home and ours. He said that they've been cut up and are layin' on a path out in the woods. The kids are terrified. I need an officer up there immediately."

"Okay, where's the location of the kids exactly?"

Keenan gave the address. "It's Bayfield. Hang on just a minute please."

The caller paused to speak to his son holding on another line. The dispatch tape recorded Mr. Keenan's half of the conversation.

"Son, calm down. I'm right here; I'm talking to the police."

1

The dispatcher continued her inquiry. "Is anybody with the little girls right now?"

"No, and my son and my daughter are home alone, and the fastest I can get there will be ten or fifteen minutes, or twenty if I go like the devil out there."

"Now, where exactly are they? Do you have any idea?"

"All right, my children are at the house." The caller gave the dispatcher the phone number. "But I'm keeping them on an open line."

He paused again briefly to listen to an instruction from his son. "All right, now. All right."

Then Keenan returned his attention to the dispatcher. "There's one of your officers over there in the area."

"Is that behind the high school?"

"No, no. It's up in Wallace Gulch."

"What county road is Wallace Gulch?"

"All right. It's up on County Road 502, right down at the end of County Road 503."

"Does he know what cut them up?"

"He thinks there's somebody out there that has done this—I'm right here, son, I'm right here."

"Okay. I'm going to get the ambulance rolling up that way . . . Can you send anyone out there to meet them?"

"All right. There aren't any adults up there to my knowledge at this point. I'm going just as rapidly—"

"How old are the children?"

"My boy is thirteen and my daughter is eleven, and the other two kids are about, uh, thirteen and nine, I think."

"Are they together that you know of?"

"Yeah, uh, no. The ones that have been hurt or killed are layin' out there in the woods."

"Okay. I'm going to get someone out there," the dispatcher said.

"And please send someone that's armed out there."

"Okay, I sure will."

The dispatcher signaled with three long beeps to

identify the call as an emergency. Her shaky voice followed:

"Upper Pine Rescue, Mercy Ambulance, Sheriff's Department, I need you to respond to County Road 503 by Wallace Gulch. We have a report of some children molested. We don't know at this time if it's Code Frank. Two small children who have been molested on County Road 503 by Wallach Gulch. Stand by for more information."

"Code Frank" meant a death was possible.

When Captain Nick Boyd received the call over his patrol Jeep radio, he thought it an extraordinary coincidence that he had patrolled the subdivision just minutes before. Over one thousand miles of roads traced La Plata County and he was the only officer on duty behind a wheel, yet he was just minutes from the scene.

"I'm three miles east of there on 502," Boyd radioed in. "What's the exact address on 503?"

The dispatcher responded.

Boyd spun his vehicle around and floored the accelerator as he flipped on his lights and siren. He knew what Code Frank meant.

"What's the problem with the children?"

"Apparently they've been molested in some way. They have cuts all over them and are bleeding at this time and not moving. They're on a footpath. The reporting party is Ed Keenan at that address, and apparently two of his children were with these two girls earlier."

The Homestead subdivision was tucked away at the end of a dead-end road that circled through Wallace Gulch. Its dozen or so houses hid behind stands of tall pines and scrub oak.

As Boyd rumbled over the gravel, he spotted the street address on a leaning mailbox in front of a low ranch-style home halfway around the loop.

Boyd checked his watch. Four minutes had passed.

The nearest sheriff's deputy was fifteen to twenty minutes away. Boyd patted his service revolver, waiting snugly in his belt holster. He glanced at the 12-gauge shotgun lying unlocked and loaded on the floor of the new Jeep Cherokee.

Then he hit the siren and screeched to a halt, hoping the commotion would catch the attention of whoever was in the house.

The house remained still.

Boyd saw that the front glass door of the house was shut but the solid wooden door behind it was partially open. As the captain went to knock, the door opened before him.

A young girl stood there whimpering. Her hand rested limply on the doorknob. Boyd figured she was eleven or twelve. He couldn't make out her words.

The captain knelt down to meet the girl's eyes. "Do you know where the girls are?" Boyd asked. The young girl muttered, then pointed toward another part of the house.

"The girls? Do you know where the girls are?" he pleaded again. Again she raised her finger and pointed.

Boyd followed her lead. He saw a slender boy leaning against the dining room wall, crying, talking on the telephone. The boy was older, taller.

"What's your name?" Boyd asked.

"Billy. Billy Keenan."

"Where are the girls?"

The boy didn't respond. His thin brown bangs shielded his wide-set eyes. "The police are here," he said softly into the phone. "I have to go—"

Boyd grabbed the receiver and hung it up.

"The girls," Boyd asked sternly. "Where are the girls?"

Billy raised his eyes and looked up briefly at the officer. Then the boy returned his gaze to the floor, dirtied with mud from his hiking boots.

"Up on the hill," he said. "One's in the kitchen and one's on the path between here and there."

"Can you show me?" Boyd asked.

"Yes." Billy nodded.

Boyd walked behind the children as he led them to his truck. He opened the back door for the girl, whom Boyd assumed was Billy's sister. He didn't ask. The boy rode in the front passenger seat.

"This way," Billy told Boyd when they reached the end of the driveway. Boyd turned right and traveled a good half mile back down the gravel road past the hidden houses.

"Turn here."

Boyd swung the truck around and drove down a narrow driveway marked by a sign that read in big letters HILL HOLLOW RANCH, and in smaller letters THE JANSONS. Another sign read PRIVATE ROAD. The driveway led to a two-story house wrapped with a redwood deck.

"She's in there," Billy said.

Boyd looked at the children. "Stay here."

He parked the truck, took the keys, and jogged the thirty feet to the front of the deck. He walked up the stairs to the landing. The front door was closed but not shut tight.

A wind chime sounded at the end of the porch. Boyd glanced back at the two children in his truck. They stared back.

Boyd withdrew his service revolver. Then with a push of his shoulder he slapped the door open.

He heard no sounds. The furniture rested in place. Pictures hung square on the wall. The magazines on the coffee table lay undisturbed.

Boyd proceeded down a hallway and glanced into two bedrooms. Nothing unusual. He turned back toward the front door. He made a left into the living room area. Nothing. Then farther, into the kitchen.

He stopped cold.

A body lay sprawled on the kitchen linoleum. A child's body. Boyd wasn't sure if it was a boy or a girl. He drew back, then knelt down near it.

It was a girl. She had red hair and freckles.

Her throat had been slit and her face slashed. There

were other stab wounds to her body, too many to count. Boyd touched the girl's cheek. Cool but not cold. He shook her slightly. The body wobbled then rested still again.

The girl wore no sign of terror. Her body was not contorted. She lay supine with her arms at her sides, almost as if she were sleeping.

The blood on the face had nearly dried. Boyd turned and saw that the sliding door leading to the porch was open and a light breeze ruffled the curtains.

Boyd quickly checked the other rooms on the ground floor but found nothing. He made pains not to put fingerprints on the doorknobs and walls as he walked silently on the wall-to-wall carpeting. The afternoon light streamed in from the sliding glass door.

On the living room walls hung authentic and replica revolvers and rifles, and antlers and hides of deer and elk. The wall in the hallway was covered with snapshots of smiling children and family members with arms around each other.

In the kitchen on the counter, Boyd saw a cutting board with crackers, several slices of cut cheese, and a knife undisturbed. Crumbs of orange cheese stuck to the knife blade. There were no traces of blood.

Nor were there signs of a struggle anywhere, no tracks or drops of blood on the carpet. All was unremarkable except for the dead girl in the kitchen and the small puddle of blood that circled her head like a halo.

Boyd hustled out to the waiting children. He did not check the upstairs; the second victim was reportedly outside on a path.

The kids in the truck hadn't moved. Boyd didn't say a word. He pulled the walkie-talkie from his belt and moved away from the Jeep.

"Dispatch. This is 530."

"Go ahead, 530."

"I have one Code Frank, adolescent."

Another officer radioed in and asked for directions. Boyd responded, then turned to the Jeep.

"Where's the other girl?" he yelled.

Billy pointed. "Over there. In the yard."

Boyd looked to where the boy motioned but saw nothing. He walked quickly.

He crested a small rise to see what looked like a pile of clothing in a clearing some seventy-five yards away. His trot turned into a run.

It was a body, another child, a younger child. She lay on her stomach with her arms hidden beneath her body. Her bloodstained face rested on the dry pine needles. A few feet away lay a butterfly net. She was no older than seven or eight years old. Her hair was red but not as red as the girl's in the kitchen. She had more freckles. Her face was covered by a shock of curly hair.

Boyd knelt down and touched her face. No sign of life, no sign of warmth. The girl had been stabbed several times in the back. Her throat was also slit. By the scuff marks on the ground, it looked as if she had been running as she fell.

Boyd pulled out his radio and called in to Dispatch a second time. "Code Frank, adolescent," he said again. He requested backup from the detective unit and all available patrol deputies. Another deputy radioed back requesting directions. This time the dispatcher obliged.

Boyd returned to his Jeep, where Billy and his sister stared back still. He paused in the driveway in earshot of the children. His head spun slightly, overwhelmed by his discoveries.

Other than the knife by the cutting board, Boyd had not seen a possible weapon or obvious evidence. There wasn't a knife near either of the girls, no torn or ripped clothing clutched in the girls' hands, no traces of blood indicating a body had been drug across a floor. There was no sign of robbery. The guns on the walls were not touched. And there was no sign of molestation. Both girls were fully dressed in jeans, blouse, and sneakers.

There was no sign of anything but murder.

There was another curiosity. In his eight years as a cop, Boyd had seen his share of car accident and murder victims. Each time, the bodies were covered with and surrounded by huge pools of blood. Oddly, there was relatively little blood around each girl. Yet each girl had had her throat slit, the surest way to spill blood fast.

The blood from the younger girl, out in the clearing, could have soaked into the porous ground. But the older girl, in the kitchen, was lying on a cold linoleum floor. Blood should have flooded it but the pool was small.

There was no explanation unless the girls had been killed elsewhere and transported to the scene. Yet, neither was there evidence of that. Boyd plainly saw the scuff marks where the little girl had fallen after running in the clearing. And in the kitchen the mess was concentrated near the body and nowhere else.

Boyd scanned the dirt driveway. Besides his own tire tracks he couldn't detect any that particularly stood out. The cars parked on the edges of the gravel driveway were dusty, and it was obvious they hadn't moved all winter.

Could the intruder or intruders have come on motorcycles? On foot from the highway? The main road was four miles overland or twelve miles over unpaved roads, then it required two turns and a hidden driveway to get here. En route, Boyd had passed a few vehicles but none seemed suspicious. Neither were there any cars stalled on the roadside.

Why didn't the girls fight? Who could find this home? Who would stab to death two girls, and why?

The officer looked again at the two children in the Jeep. They looked frightened as they gazed through the window glass.

It was well past 4:00 and already the tall pines obscured the sun's light.

A search through the woods was obviously priority number one. The killer might be nearby. Next door. He could be killing again, now, at this moment.

Priority two, preserve the scene. Three, gather evidence. Four, question neighbors. Five, stop the media. Six, prepare for parents.

Boyd knew what happened at crime scenes. In a matter of moments, others would arrive: rescue workers, sheriff's deputies, detectives, police dogs, city police, frightened neighbors, horrified parents. The woods would be flooded by officers packing loaded guns and searching for a killer. Detectives would photograph footprints and rope off bodies. Sirens would wail, walkie-talkies crackle, and the smell of trampled pine needles and boot leather fill the air.

Darkness, too, would arrive soon. Colorado's sun sets quickly. The air thins and grows cold. Under the cover of night the killer could easily reach the main road and flee in any direction. Darkness was a little more than an hour away.

Within two hours, the killer could take refuge in any of four states. By morning the trail would be as cold as February.

But now, on the gentle western slope of Wallace Gulch, Nick Boyd was alone with two scared but very much alive children and two children who had not been so lucky. The wind carried the musty, fragrant scent of sage. Aside from the breeze there was silence.

Boyd paused and listened. He tasted in his mouth the infectious adrenaline that accompanies shock. His tongue swelled and his fingertips numbed. Boyd had felt it before.

If the murder had occurred in town, neighbors would have raced out to gawk. Crowds would form and mothers howl. Police officers would arrive in seconds, bark out orders, and quickly draw that fragile line that separates pandemonium from order.

Yet by some quirk of fate, Boyd had been the first to reach this scene and he was all alone.

Now he heard an approaching siren.

Yet his fear did not relent. As the siren grew louder, Boyd realized that his fear stemmed not so much from his aloneness or the sight of death as from the profound and overwhelming sense of the unknown.

PART 1

———

"Code Frank"

———

"There came another [messenger], and said,
'Your children . . . are dead . . .'
Then Job arose and rent his robe . . .
and fell down upon the ground."

—*Job 1:18–20*

1

As usual, Sherry was the last one to wake up at the Janson home. She didn't hear her older sister's alarm as it rang a few feet from her bed. It was Monday morning after an exhausting weekend playing in the April warmth. Yesterday had been spent outside, at last, where the ground cover of pine needles captured the sun's heat and warmed the air, and the isolated patches of snow were slowly melting.

As Sherry slept, her older sister, Kristy, slipped quietly into the clothes she had prepared by her bedside the night before. Kristy brushed her hair, washed her face, tidied the bed, then tiptoed down the stairs to kiss her parents good-morning.

Sherry continued her slumber, oblivious to the first pleading of her mother to get ready for school, and the second, and the third.

Vickie Janson gave up trying to rouse her eight-year-old and continued her morning chores. Then once again she yelled up the carpet-covered stairs toward the girls' loft bedroom. Vickie heard faint rumblings of Sherry rising.

It was Monday, Vickie's day to work in town rather than at home. Monday meant that the kids *had* to be ready for the bus, which invariably honked its horn at 7:00 A.M. sharp. Fortunately for Sherry, the driver was good enough to blast the horn a second time, after she rounded the mile loop that circled through the subdivision in Wallace Gulch. Vickie looked at the kitchen clock. It was 6:30. The girls, rather Sherry, would be late again.

"Joe, please wake your youngest daughter."

Joe set down the spatula and strode to the landing, gripping the wooden railing with his right hand.

"Sherry Janson. Thirty seconds," Joe bellowed. At the sound of her father's voice, the youngster threw on some clothes and tumbled downstairs, sleepy-eyed but ready for the breakfast Joe had waiting. Sherry was forever late, always keeping the family waiting.

Kristy, on the other hand, was entering the teenage years ruled by the dual gods of punctuality and image. She set her clock every evening. She wouldn't be late, that would be embarrassing. And every day she made sure her clothes matched her socks and shoes. It was another sign of the conscientiousness that her parents were proud to have instilled in her, but it sometimes got out of hand. She was a member of the school council, worked as an aide in the principal's office, and participated weekly in Girl Scouts and the 4-H club. She excelled in school and loved church, and she knew that made her different. Some kids taunted her with calls of "Goody two-shoes" or "Teacher's pet" because of her excellent grades. It hurt her. She was also embarrassed about how she looked, her freckles and shocking red hair, and how, because of her tall, lanky body, she loomed over the boys her age.

Sherry didn't worry much about school, her age, or anything. She was good in school but not excellent. She was of average height, had light reddish brown hair, immense blue eyes, and just enough freckles to tantalize every eight-year-old boy in Bayfield and most of their older brothers, too.

But, then, Sherry had other qualities. She was the passionate child. To her father's delight, she enjoyed hunting. She absolutely would not go to bed until the deer they had bagged was quartered and hanged in the cold garage and the hide ready for tanning. Only then could Joe carry his sleepy little hunter to bed. It was all part of what the parents had discovered was Sherry's voracious curiosity and her almost dangerous fearlessness.

Sherry never minded that she shrieked with delight. Kristy, while outgoing, was reflective and tactful. Sherry plunged. Kristy pondered. Kristy was the smart one and Sherry the cute one. Both understood and slightly resented that this perception was, for the most part, correct.

Despite their differences in temperament and age, the two were inseparable. They never tired of baking pies, visiting the neighbors with little presents they had made, or staging drama shows complete with curtain calls for their parents. Sherry was Kristy's shadow, attempting whatever her sister tried, regardless of the difficulty, oblivious to the gentle laughter of the adults when she failed or succeeded in pure Sherry style.

At night, before their mother and father kissed them good-night, the two girls would kneel by their beds and pray. Each one of them created her own prayers based on the day's happenings. One night, Kristy started to cry.

"What's the matter, Kristy?" her mother asked. "What's wrong?"

"Are we rich?" Kristy asked.

"No, we're not rich. We have the things we need, but we're not rich." Still, Kristy was sad. "What is it?"

"It's about Tricia Brown."

"What about Tricia?" Vickie knew that in the early afternoons after the bus dropped Tricia off, the young girl would remain alone until far past dark when her mother got home from the two jobs she worked. Tricia's father had moved away some time ago.

Kristy began crying again. "It's just that we have so much and she has so little."

Vickie looked at Kristy with quiet pride. "I guess all we can do is pray for her, Kristy, just pray."

And she did.

Sherry didn't think to worry about Tricia, though if someone had told Sherry that Tricia was sad, Sherry would have been happy to pick flowers for her.

As seven o'clock approached, Sherry was still dallying. Joe and Kristy waited impatiently in the car, ready to drive to the bus stop. Vickie stood sentry at the front door, imploring her youngest to hurry. The bus driver honked, which meant she was starting the loop to pick up the other children and would return for the girls in just a few minutes. Finally, with a stern look on her face, Vickie hunted Sherry down in the house and lovingly hounded her all the way to the car.

The family made it to the bus stop moments before the bus arrived. In the grand finale of the morning rush, Sherry and Kristy leaned over the front seat, kissed their mom and dad good-bye, then climbed into the yellow bus with a wave.

There was no time for a long hug or a meaningful "I love you." The parents didn't watch the bus make the right turn toward school in Bayfield or see their girls rubbing the dew from the bus window to wave and smile one last time. Instead, Joe and Vickie turned left toward the little city that was Durango and work, grateful this latest minor crisis was over.

The parents drove down a series of gravel back roads, which depending on the season were either dusty, muddy, or snowy. The twenty-mile ride rarely took less than thirty minutes, but that didn't bother Joe and Vickie. They enjoyed traveling through the hills dotted with brush oak, sagebrush, and tall cottonwoods, aspen, and pines. The lonely La Plata Mountains stood stoically to the west, still covered with winter snow.

It was beautiful country. The streams sent their cold waters flowing through the seasons and the invariable summer afternoon thunder bursts kept the countryside green and lush.

In the winter, weeks of sunshine were interrupted

only briefly by heavy snowstorms. But the snow was light, insulating, and dazzling under the bright sun.

Now it was spring and the green hills were bursting with blue, pink, yellow, and purple wildflowers. Wild strawberries hid under their leaves and tiny shoots of asparagus sprouted near the stream banks. On their way to and from town, the Jansons often saw elk herds, bald eagles, purple skies, yellow moons, and more stars than their children could dream about in a lifetime.

It was this idyllic isolation that had brought Joe and Vickie here from the never-ending metropolis of Southern California. Quickly they found a place they told friends was a slice of heaven. It was ten miles northwest of the little town of Bayfield and twenty miles east of Durango, the county seat and the center of the universe in southwestern Colorado. The homestead was one of a dozen or more parcels carved out of the mighty Bellflower Ranch, once one of the largest and most prestigious ranches in Colorado.

Joe and Vickie named their new place Hill Hollow Ranch because it sat on a hill overlooking a hollow called Wallace Gulch. Joe painted a sign and tacked it on a pine tree at the entrance. The girls loved it.

It wasn't all paradise. The move to Colorado had meant a great sacrifice of income for the thirty-nine-year-old Joe, though nothing severe enough to make him regret leaving behind the perils of city life. His wavy reddish blonde hair, thick mustache, and sideburns showed signs of gray, but his smiling, turquoise eyes and the laugh lines around them reflected a boyish youthfulness that wouldn't submit to age. And, like a boy, he played with hot rod cars, boats, guns, anything mechanical. His ruddy complexion revealed his English-Norwegian heritage and his thick hands were those of a man who worked with his hands.

Joe had left behind a job as an aerospace engineer for Rockwell International in Southern California. He had helped design the J2 engines for NASA's Apollo program and later the vertical ascent engines used in the space shuttles.

In Durango, Joe found work designing factory equipment for a nonprofit manufacturing plant that employed the handicapped. Sherry called the workers "people locked in funny bodies." The position was lower paying, less demanding, and less exciting than rocket design, but Joe didn't miss the smog and traffic. He was content because Vickie was happier than she had ever been.

The two had known each other since they were thirteen-year-olds singing together in their hometown Catholic church choir. But Vickie attended parochial school and Joe public school, and the romance never strayed past the church grounds. After a while they lost touch.

Years later, when Joe was in the air force and he swore he was the loneliest enlistee in the armed forces, he wrote every girl he had ever dated. It was the same letter; he just changed the names. "Hi, this is Joe. How are you? Remember me? Please write." Vickie got one, and unlike the other girls, she replied.

The wedding took place in May of 1965, a big Catholic wedding attended by all of Vickie's nine brothers and sisters, Joe's five siblings, both sets of parents, and every relative and friend in Southern California. The air force limited the honeymoon to a week before Joe had to fly back to Travis Air Force Base near San Francisco.

The couple waited until Joe had been out of uniform for nearly five years to have their first child. Kristine Anne arrived on December 18, 1969, with a head of hair redder than her father's.

Five years later, on June 20, 1974, their second child, Sherry Lee, was born.

But her birth was disastrous.

The couple hadn't known, no one had told them, that they were RH incompatible, a condition that grew progressively more serious with each child. Sherry's kidneys functioned poorly, almost not at all. In her first twenty-four hours of life, doctors pumped three complete blood transfusions through her veins. They almost pronounced her dead.

With all the concern over Sherry, Vickie's internal bleeding went unnoticed. With Kristy at his side, Joe waited for days in the hospital, not sure if tomorrow he would be without his wife, his newborn daughter, or both.

But Vickie and Sherry pulled through, slowly. Vickie's mother and mother-in-law moved in temporarily to help with the newborn. It was two months before Vickie was strong enough to resume her motherly duties. Shortly after the crisis, an obstetrician took Joe and Vickie into his office and advised them that having a third child could be fatal. The parents had no intention of reliving the nightmare of the past few months. Sherry and Kristy's love was plenty.

Though the crisis with Sherry was over, she was not well. As a result of the transfusions, her natural immune system had weakened considerably. Her recovery was slow and punctuated with complications. The Los Angeles smog tormented her breathing. It was the flu, followed by a cold, followed by an asthma attack, followed by the flu. Sherry's health was one more reason Joe and Vickie knew it was time to move to Colorado.

The move worked. Sherry gained strength in the mountains. The frequent trips to the doctors decreased then ultimately ceased. The only remnants of her troubles were a feisty will to fight back and a unquenchable thirst for life.

Vickie recovered completely, as well, and as the years passed her only problem was finding enough time to be a mother, business owner, and wife. Everyone could help with the chores at home, but Vickie's medical bookkeeping and billing service was surpassing expectations and demanding more time than she could spare. A petite woman with green soulful eyes, delicate hands, and high cheekbones, Vickie complemented her husband's boisterousness with a serene, but never haughty, sophistication.

Vickie managed to do most of her business work at home, but recently a friend had asked Vickie to cover for her as a receptionist at a dentist's office. It was only on Mondays and only for a few months. One day a week in Durango couldn't be too bad.

With the girls now getting older, Vickie didn't mind leaving them alone one afternoon a week. As isolated as their home was, what could happen? And should, God forbid, anything happen, the neighbors were there.

Several of the nearby families had children Kristy's and Sherry's ages. They would often get together for barbecues or to help each other with woodcutting, deck building, and baby-sitting. Somebody was always giving somebody else's kids a ride to town and back. Everyone was helpful and friendly. They were good people.

Joe and Vickie were happy with the neighborhood, the schools, and the Presbyterian church they had joined after leaving the Catholic church. They felt safe and appreciated here. It was hard to explain to relatives and friends in Southern California that the move was a celebration of a simpler life, not a retreat into isolation. They explained that they had all the modern amenities—it was the modern hassles they lived without.

The Jansons' sentiments were shared by many of their neighbors on the loop. Most families had escaped the big cities, happy now to live in this out-of-the-way paradise where less was more. There were the Chews, the Cromeys, the Rudolfs, the Surprenans, and others.

And there were the Keenans. Ed and Phyllis Keenan lived on the other side of the loop from the Jansons, a half mile by road but just a few hundred yards by way of a hilly footpath. The two families shared remarkable similarities. Ed and Phyllis also had two children, thirteen-year-old Billy and eleven-year-old Laura. And like the Jansons, the Keenans had moved from Southern California to Bayfield, just six months after the Jansons had moved. They, too, fell in love with a multiacre parcel in Wallace Gulch on the old Bellflower. Bayfield was a natural choice because Ed's parents lived in town, and the extended family often gathered there for family vacations.

In California, Ed Keenan had held several prestigious accounting positions with major corporations. A balding man with a history of heart trouble, he told friends that he just got tired of the three-piece suits, ties, and the rat race. So he took a job as business manager for Durango's daily newspaper, the *Herald*. Phyllis found work as a receptionist with a Durango dentist.

The Jansons and Keenans got along well at first. Kristy and Billy were the same age. When the two families first moved to Bayfield, the children spent many hours together. It was always the four of them—Kristy, Sherry, Billy, and Laura—trekking off on some trail or playing the games children do.

But as they grew older, the children saw less and less of each other. Kristy was going to church more and excelling in school. Billy was hunting more, ignoring his schoolwork, watching scary videos, and acting more like a "boy." Laura was just too old to play with Sherry, who was three years her junior. And there were a few fights between the children that added to the distance.

Billy threw a dead rabbit down a well once and Kristy told her dad, who bawled Billy out. Kristy teased Billy for being such a poor student. He didn't take kindly to it and started picking on Sherry, who said some mean things to Laura, who said mean things back. By the winter of the seventh grade for Kristy and Billy, the four had lost their bond. The children merely put up with one another.

But that was to be expected. They were children and children sometimes didn't get along. It was no big deal. There was plenty of woods separating the two houses. Maybe as they grew older they would find common ground again. And if not, that would be fine, too.

2

On the early afternoon of April 25, Louise Fisher lined up her bus at the entrance of Bayfield Middle School to take the morning-shift children home as usual. It was another in a string of warm days and the kids had spring fever. School would be out in less than a month and the distractions of summer were already bewitching them. Today, despite the fact that it was Monday, the children were further entranced by the unusual warmth and the lingering sun.

Billy was one of the first students to board the yellow bus, and he was fighting mad. He stomped up the bus steps swinging his elbows side to side in a fashion overly dramatic even for a thirteen-year-old. He brushed by Louise without the slightest acknowledgment, stormed to a seat in the back of the bus, and sat down in a huff. With his arms crossed and lips pursed, he stared out the window at his classmates chasing one another as they shrieked with delight.

Billy's behavior didn't seem at all strange to Louise. She had been driving a bus for the district for eight years and she had never dealt with a child as ill-mannered as this one. The boy was just plain troublesome, and it looked like today would be no different.

Louise prided herself on running a strict bus. It was tough driving down rural roads through all kinds of weather with one eye fixed on the road and the other on a mirror full of screaming kids. If for no other reason than safety, Louise demanded good behavior.

Every year, however, it seemed the children became more difficult to handle. Louise had watched several generations of children grow up during her sixty-odd years, and children today were more unruly than she could ever remember.

In Louise's view, children needed discipline as much as they needed love, and she was ready to give both.

She made it a point to spend time talking with all her kids and to introduce herself to their families. Louise was their neighbor—she passed her own house twice daily—and no matter what was happening in the rest of the country, in Bayfield it was your duty and pleasure to seek out and introduce yourself to the folks next door.

She knew Billy's parents and she had had occasion to speak with the Keenans several times concerning his behavior. She told them how much trouble Billy caused on the bus, told them about the fights, the missing sunglasses and notebooks. He was forever in trouble, forever agitating people, forever instigating.

Louise did her best to keep a sharp eye on Billy, but he would execute his mischief down low, behind the seats. When the bus got rolling, Louise could never quite see what he was up to. Then suddenly a fight would erupt. And, usually, Billy was at the heart of the commotion. If Louise slowed down the bus, or worse, stopped it, Billy immediately hid his mischief or pulled back from the fight. Louise's reprimands would reverberate down the bus aisle and Billy would answer with a polite "Yes, ma'am" or a "No, ma'am." But as soon as the trip resumed Billy disregarded Louise's admonitions and began dealing in deviousness again. Louise had told Billy's parents what she thought, but she'd tempered it a bit. It wasn't her business to tell them how to raise their children.

She didn't say that she thought Billy was a spoiled child. She didn't mention how he had bragged to her about manipulating his parents to get them to do what he wanted. If he wanted to go hunting with his grandfather, he would promise good grades for the week. At the first sign of improvement, his parents would let him go. But as soon as he returned from the weekend excursion, it was back to failing. He wouldn't do well until his parents offered him something tangible. They always did. And he bragged to Louise all about it.

Nor did Louise explain how Billy treated his sister, Laura. Louise feared for Laura, feared that Billy would hurt her terribly one day. On the bus, Louise could tell when Billy was about to pounce on his sister. And Laura knew it too. Billy would get up and tower over her, his fist wavering in the air and his face turning red from his held breath. Laura would shrink into her seat. If Louise didn't intervene quickly, Billy would punch Laura in the arm or slap her atop her head, messing her hair. Laura was afraid to sit in the back of the bus, and out of fear of Billy she often took a seat directly behind Louise. Louise wondered how parents allowed such behavior to continue. Sometimes Billy would hurt Laura just to prove he was a big shot in front of other kids. Louise would say, "Billy, leave your sister alone." And Billy would answer back, "She's my sister, I can do what I want with her."

Laura protested sometimes, but she couldn't do much to stop her brother. She was a pretty girl, Louise thought, with her dark curly hair and wide smile. So much more mature and well-behaved than Billy. Louise feared that Laura was being mistreated by Billy at home. And with the mood Billy was in today, Laura was in store for another episode of Billy's wrath.

It had not been a good day for Billy. First, the girls in his last class had teased him with pictures of dress patterns. They told him how nice he would look in each dress.

Then Mr. Winter, Billy's math, physical education, and shop teacher, told Billy that if his math grades didn't come up he could flunk the year. It was a scolding, and it was the second time in two weeks Billy had been threatened with failing. His parents would really punish him if he flunked. Billy seethed through his last class and stormed out of the building toward the bus, past Louise, and to his usual seat in the back.

While they waited for the other students to board, Louise heard a ruckus and turned to see Billy pestering someone. Yet as she watched him she realized she had never seen him this upset, never this "out of it" before. One moment he was sulking in the back, the next he was loud, telling students "Get the hell away; I don't want to sit with you." He drew an imaginary line with his belligerence and dared everyone to cross it. Then he crossed it himself to hassle others. Most of the kids, long wise to Billy's tricks, found new seats. After Billy scattered everyone, he propped up his feet on the seat in front of him and looked glumly out the window.

"Get your feet down, Billy," Louise shouted back as she peered in the mirror. Billy did, slowly, then turned again toward the laughing crowd outside.

The day had been grand for Sherry, who got on the bus after walking the short distance from the elementary school. Louise could see that Sherry was all excited.

"What is it?" Louise asked.

In her squeaky voice, Sherry told Louise that she was excited over a 4-H project she was starting. It was a butterfly collection she was going to share with the class. And she couldn't wait to get started right after they got home today. There was more to Sherry's excitement, Louise discovered.

Since it was nearing Mother's Day, the whole class had been working on a Mother's Day project. Each second-grader had chosen a photograph or small drawing to varnish onto a wooden cutout of a teapot. The final product was a hot plate. Sherry had chosen a photo of an antelope and had varnished her hot plate in the early afternoon. She was so excited because it only needed drying before she could bring it home. To top it off, she was going out to collect butterflies. What a beautiful day.

Laura got on the bus and took her usual seat behind Louise.

Through her rearview mirror, Louise could see Billy taunting Sherry. Why did he have to pick on someone so much younger? she thought.

"Louise," Sherry said. "Can I move up and sit near Laura?" On Louise's bus, students had to ask permission to move once they had chosen a seat. "Of course you may," Louise replied.

Finally, Kristy climbed onto the bus. She was carrying a neat pile of textbooks. Her routine of classes had gone without a hitch. It had been another day of excellent marks and "well dones." She had helped at the principal's office and hung out with some friends. She found a seat near Billy but not too near.

Just as Louise released the brake and began moving, Billy kicked something or pushed somebody, Louise wasn't sure what. But she knew that if she didn't speak up now there would be serious trouble once the bus got rolling. She slowed to a halt.

"Billy Keenan," Louise yelled back, "if you don't straighten up, young man, you can just get off the bus and have your father pick you up." The threat made Billy quiet down. Louise unhitched the brake and began the trip once again. The ride following the mild reprimand was fairly uneventful.

Sherry held fast to her butterfly net in the seat behind Louise. The children weren't supposed to talk to the bus driver, but Sherry's enthusiasm got the best of her.

"You know what?" she asked Louise.

"What, sweet child?" Louise said with a smile.

"If I catch more than one of the same kind of butterfly I think I'll let it go." That was typical Sherry, Louise thought, never wanting to harm a thing.

Billy walked up to Kristy and whispered something in her ear. Kristy turned and gave him a look of disgust.

She rose and found a new seat. She didn't ask for permission.

Louise slowed down near the top of County Road 503, the Jansons' stop. There was a little trail not more than twenty feet long that started just a little farther down from where the girls usually embarked. Sherry loved to be dropped off at the trailhead rather than by the road that led to her driveway. It wasn't at all much of a trail, but it meant so much to Sherry to be dropped off there.

"Can you please drop us off at the trail?" Sherry asked. Louise said certainly. She liked to make Sherry happy.

The young girl had given Louise a little sticker that said "Up with Jesus!" which Louise stuck on the visor above the driver's seat. Louise looked at it now. Sherry and Kristy were always doing little things like that to make you happy. A birthday card, a Christmas present—nothing much, but always thoughtful.

When the bus stopped and the door opened, Sherry stepped up and gave Louise a kiss on the cheek.

"I love you," Sherry said.

"I love you, too."

As Louise pulled away, she saw the sisters meander down the short path, Kristy with her books, Sherry waving her butterfly net in the air, skipping in the breeze. Louise pushed the bus into second gear and headed down to Laura and Billy's stop.

It was 1:10 in the afternoon when Cindy Barker decided it was just too nice to be cooped up inside. She put shoes on her two little boys and began strolling along the road fronting her house. Cindy didn't always like company, especially when Luke and Jake laid down for their naps. But it got lonely sometimes during the day, what with Ben teaching in Durango and most of the neighbors at work. So Cindy was glad when she saw the yellow bus rumbling down the gravel road. It would be nice for the boys to meet the kids coming off the bus. They loved it so.

The bus squeaked to a stop, the door opened, and out stepped the neighbor children, Billy and Laura Keenan. "Hi," Cindy said.

"I got so much homework to do," Billy said in a sulk, almost before he stepped down from the bus stairs.

Cindy was in no mood to hear Billy's complaints and turned to Laura. "What are you going to do today?" Cindy asked.

Laura said she was going to watch television. Then Billy said he was going to check his live game traps.

"Oh," Cindy said. "What do you do when you catch a live animal?"

"I let it go," Billy said.

"What happens when you catch a skunk?"

"I guess I'll think of that when the time comes," Billy said with his usual indifference.

Cindy had never liked Billy's attitude. It seemed as if his parents did everything to make it easy for him to do well in school. Billy wasn't dumb, either. He was fairly smart. Cindy knew that from the times she had tutored him in math. If you made the subject interesting Billy was right there, ahead of you even. But if you sat Billy down with a paper and pencil, his concentration scurried out the door like a scorned puppy. Once Cindy took Billy into the hills and turned a geometry lesson into an animal tracking demonstration. Billy loved it. If Billy was failing math now, Cindy couldn't take the blame. She had done her best. Billy just hadn't stuck with it, just like he didn't stick with anything.

When the roar of the school bus could no longer be heard, Cindy could see that the Keenan kids were anxious to get away. She said good-bye and continued her stroll with the boys until she reached home just before 2:00 P.M.

Cindy Barker hardly had time to put down her boys for a nap when she heard the front porch step creak. She was in the kitchen and thought nothing of it; the old wood planks always creaked when warmed by the sun.

Then she heard someone trying to open the screen door, very gently, no more than a slight tug. An eye-hook latch held the screen door shut. Cindy turned and saw a dark figure behind the screen mesh.

It was Billy standing motionless.

A moment passed before Billy knocked.

"Can I come in?" he asked.

"Billy, what is it?"

"Where are the boys?" Billy's hands were in his back pockets.

"What do you want the boys for?" Cindy asked, as she let Billy in.

"To play."

"They're in taking naps and they're just getting to sleep," Cindy said. "And anyway, they're a little young for you to play with, don't you think?"

Billy shrugged. Then he said, "Oh yeah, everybody's asleep over there." Cindy didn't know what he meant.

Then Billy added, "Is your phone out of order?"

It wasn't unusual for the phones to go out in the neighborhood, but Cindy hadn't had any problems today.

"No, I don't think so," she said.

"Well, ours is out of order," Billy said.

"Did you need to use the phone?"

"Well yeah, but it can wait," Billy said calmly.

Cindy walked over to the phone and picked up the receiver. It was working fine.

"I really need you to leave, Billy. I don't want the boys waking up." Cindy had a way of imposing her will and she used it now with Billy.

Billy said good-bye, turned, and walked out the door.

Cindy closed the door behind him and fastened the latch.

Her boys never did get to sleep.

At the Jansons', Sherry's butterfly-collecting enthusiasm led her straight outside to wander the trails surrounding the house. Kristy remained inside doing her homework. Then she made her usual mid-afternoon phone call to her mother.

"Hi, Mom," Kristy said. "We're home."

"How's your day going?" Vickie asked.

"Just fine. Sherry's catching butterflies."

"That's nice," Vickie said.

"Can I fix something for dinner?" Kristy asked. Kristy loved to cook for the family and often had meals waiting when her parents arrived home on Monday evenings.

"Sure, what do you want to fix?" Vickie asked.

"I'll surprise you," Kristy said.

"Okay," Vickie said. Just then a patient walked into Dr. Caldwell's office.

"I've got to go," Vickie told her daughter.

"Okay, bye. I love you, Mom."

"I love you too, dear."

The patient had an appointment with Dr. Caldwell at 2:30. She was five minutes early.

At the Keenans', Billy called his mother and spoke to her briefly. He told her that Tubby, the Jansons' dog, had wandered down to their house. Billy said he was going to take the dog back to the Jansons. His mother said that was a good idea.

It was 2:55.

Billy told Laura he was going to take the dog back to the Jansons. Laura said okay. "The Richard Simmons Show" came on.

It was 3:00.

At 3:30, just as "The Richard Simmons Show" was ending, Billy came running back to Laura.

Billy got on the phone to his father. He had trouble getting through the first time. Then he tried again.

It was 3:43 before he finally made the connection.

At the *Durango Herald,* credit manager Boots Holyoak was preparing to leave for the day. Her parents had just flown into town, and her boss, Ed Keenan, had given her the afternoon off.

Boots' office was in the basement of the Herald Building along with the rest of the financial department. She was gathering her belongings when she heard another employee on the telephone.

"Billy, calm down, I'm trying to find your dad. Just calm down."

Boots knew Billy well. He, Laura, and Phyllis were in the office regularly. Boots also knew that Billy spoke with his dad every afternoon, so his call was not unusual, it was just that her co-worker was so upset.

"What's the matter?" Boots asked.

"Something's wrong with Billy and I can't find Ed."

Boots knew Ed was somewhere in the building. She had just seen his truck in the parking lot.

"Let me run upstairs and see if I can find him," Boots said. But when the co-worker pleaded with Billy to calm down once more, Boots knew something was very wrong and she picked up the phone.

"Billy, this is Boots. What's the matter?"

"My friends, their arms, their legs, there's blood all over. I found them! I found them!" Billy was hysterical.

"Who?" Boots asked.

"My friends. I found them! They're all cut up!"

"What happened?"

"My dad, I got to speak to my dad."

"Okay, hold on."

Boots hustled upstairs and spotted Ed across the room. She caught his eye and signaled that he had a phone call. She saw Ed pick up the phone.

Several minutes later, with Billy still on the line, Ed Keenan called 911 and reported that his neighbor's girls were cut up and lying on the trail between his house and theirs. Ed stayed on the line with his son until Captain Boyd arrived at the Keenan house. The officer took the phone from Billy's hand and hung it up. It was 4:03.

Boots could see across the room that Ed was distressed, but she had to get going. Her parents were coming in soon. She drove the twenty miles to her house thinking about nothing but Billy and that phone call.

When Boots got home she dialed Ed at work, but he had already left. So she called some friends who lived in the same subdivision as the Keenans.

No one answered at the Janson home.

She waited a few minutes. Then Boots called the Keenans again. This time Billy's grandmother answered.

"Oh my God, Boots, it's the Janson girls. They're dead. Ed is up there now."

Grandma Keenan gave the sketchy details. "Everything is okay. The police are here. We don't know what killed them." Then she said, "Boots, I've got to go. It's pretty hectic up here."

Boots hung up the phone, hoping it was all a mistake. As she drove to the airport all she could do was pray. She prayed that someone had got their story terribly confused and that Kristy and Sherry were as alive as ever. But then, Billy had sounded so distraught on the phone. He must have seen something terrible. Billy never got that upset.

Suddenly it dawned on Boots why nobody had answered the phone at the Janson home. Her heart sunk.

Several hours passed before Boots returned from the airport. When she arrived home there was no need to call anyone. A special bulletin on the radio reported two girls had apparently been killed or molested out by

Bayfield. The details were sketchy. All reports were secondhand. No names were given. Nothing was confirmed.

But Boots knew, and she wept.

3

Nick Boyd didn't speak with Billy or Laura as the three waited for backup units to arrive. The children sat quietly in the Jeep. Billy would be going into shock soon. Boyd didn't know if Laura had seen the bodies. She hadn't said. Boyd hadn't asked.

Out of earshot of the children, Boyd radioed back to Dispatch the details of his discoveries. The radio channels were jammed with officers requesting directions. The remote location of the scene caused some confusion, and more than once speeding police car passed speeding police car traveling in the opposite direction.

Boyd was glad to hear the sound of a distant siren nearing. It grew louder and louder until an Upper Pine River Valley Search and Rescue ambulance rumbled over the top of the hill and careened down the driveway. The truck came to a halt in front of Boyd. Two volunteer firemen jumped out.

Their entrance had laid down a fresh set of tracks on the driveway. A trained officer would have known to park up top.

Despite their error, Boyd appreciated their presence. It jogged him from his ghoulish mood. He ordered the firemen to back up their ambulance to beyond the top of the driveway.

"Before you go," he said, "take the kids and put them in the back of the truck. They're scared out of their wits.'' The men did as Boyd ordered, and without hesitation the children obeyed.

Moments later, Sheriff's Deputy Dave Allmon came running down the driveway waving a revolver in one hand and holding on to his cap with the other. Allmon would have been the first to arrive if Boyd had not by chance been in the area.

Allmon slowed to a stop. ''What do we got?'' he asked. It was a question Boyd would hear many times during the evening to come.

Boyd escorted Allmon to the body in the kitchen. The blood on the girl's face was dry now, and the body had cooled considerably.

''We got another one out in the yard,'' Boyd said. ''But we should check the second floor first.''

Boyd led the way as the two crept up the stairs. He kicked open the master bedroom door. Allmon burst through with his pistol in outstretched arms ready to shoot. Nothing. No suspects, no victims, no sign of anything.

Their approach was somewhat comical, Boyd thought. A killer in hiding certainly would have heard the sirens, the commotion, and Boyd and Allmon's discussion in the kitchen. Their training manual tactics weren't surprising anyone.

The men took the thirty-second jog to the second victim. She was lying on her stomach, so the men couldn't see her face in full. As they searched the grounds for a weapon, they heard the cacophony of sirens bringing more officers from Durango. Then, topping the horizon, they saw scores of policemen advancing like a posse on a band of outlaws.

The double Code Frank had been radioed in during a shift change at the sheriff's department, which meant that twice the usual number of officers were available to respond. Police from other jurisdictions were on their way as well.

The overwhelming response meant Boyd would spend precious minutes briefing others. Each arriving ranking officer felt it necessary to inspect the victims. As soon as Boyd led one officer on the circuit from the house to the body in the field, another officer arrived and requested the tour. Boyd resented the role of tour guide.

He did not mind, however, briefing Undersheriff Mike Bell. A career investigator with seventeen years of experience in various Southern California police departments, Bell had overseen many murder investigations. A quiet man with a ruddy complexion, Bell was a man of few words. He had little to say today.

Bell's background had not prepared him for the sight of the victims when Boyd led him on "the tour." The murder, or murderers, had killed without a hint of mercy. Bell had witnessed the aftermath of many repulsive murders in the city, but none matched this one for chilling ruthlessness. Bell had two daughters nearly the same ages as the victims. He allowed his thoughts too many liberties.

Neither was Detective Jim Harrington, also a seasoned cop, prepared for the gruesome sight. A towering man dressed impeccably in Western apparel complete with large silver belt buckle and black Western boots, Harrington was Hollywood's image of a Western lawman. His graying mustache hung over his mouth as he spoke in his deep Western drawl. He viewed the slashed bodies with his typical stoic silence.

Without looking too closely, Harrington saw that the girls had been cut up pretty badly, both their faces and torsos.

The men, over three dozen now by Bell's count, instinctively fanned out into the woods surrounding the house in search of the elusive perpetrator. The slight wind died to nothing as the sun waned below the horizon. The early evening chill descended, and the diminishing sunlight added a sense of urgency to the activity.

Despite the abundance of officers there was no idle chatter, none of the typical morbid wisecracks that allow police officers to retain a semblance of sanity while facing fear or death. Whatever talk there was came in hushed tones.

The first rumor pegged the killer or killers as members of a roving motorcycle gang. Someone suggested a cult killing, a satanic sacrifice; there had been talk in Bayfield lately of Satan worship.

Fingers hung loosely on triggers. Men bumped into each other at every trail crossing. The search parties crossed paths twice, three times, discovering only each other. The first sign of life was discovered at a nearby home less than one hundred yards from the Jansons'. The neighbor there told police he had been using power tools to build a greenhouse. He had heard nothing until the sirens.

Most of the other neighborhood houses were empty, and soon the fear of discovering other victims subsided. Meanwhile, deputies kept pouring over the hill like cavalry reinforcements. Somehow, the sleepy Durango media were missing the action.

Bell knew that the men thrashing through the woods were trampling evidence. He set up a command post at the bottom of the driveway and ordered a squad of officers to rope off the areas along the trail that led from the house to the young girl's body in the yard. He ordered another squad to stand guard around the perimeter of the property. Two other deputies were told to search the house again. He cut the search teams in half and radioed a request for a bloodhound and the coroner. He asked Sue Naholnik, wife of the Bayfield marshal, to stay with Billy and Laura in the ambulance at the top of the driveway. Finally, at the insistence of Sheriff Al Brown, he requested forensic help from the Colorado Bureau of Investigation. Then Bell and Harrington walked into the house again to see what they had missed.

Harrington pointed to hair and blood in the sink. Someone had washed his hands of the murder. A kitchen counter drawer was open. It was filled with kitchen knives. On the counter above they saw the cutting board and slab of cheese with the knife resting nearby.

The two men walked outside through the sliding glass door and down the trail to the second body.

A deputy had identified a trail of footprints near the victim and roped it off. It was the only evidence so far, and Bell and Harrington could not be sure that the prints did not belong to a deputy. Sue Naholnik came up and spoke with Harrington. Harrington left with her to talk to Billy, "the boy who found the bodies."

The taste of the air became sweeter as twilight descended. In one hour it would be too dark for the search teams to gather evidence. Bell recalled his reaction upon seeing the girl in the kitchen, the banality, the pure and palpable evil of it. This was not your ordinary killer. This was far worse, whoever or whatever it was. The mystery intensified now that it appeared the murderer had succeeded in vanishing without a trace. Was the killer as devious as he was wicked? That was the question Bell pondered most. Would they catch him, or would this be the quizzical case that Bell would take to his grave? The lawman feared the answer.

When Ed Keenan burst through the door into Dr. Caldwell's office, Vickie Janson knew that something was terribly wrong. It was approximately twenty minutes after four, and a few patients waited quietly in the reception area reading dated magazines.

Ed rushed up to Vickie sitting behind the reception desk. His face was so pale that she swore he was suffering a heart attack.

"Are you okay?" Vickie asked.

"Vickie," Ed yelled. "I'm taking you home. There's something wrong up on our hill."

Ed spoke loudly. His breathing was labored. Beads of perspiration dotted his forehead and collected in his wrinkles. His eyes implored wildly. Unconsciously he loosened his tie while talking.

The patients turned their heads to watch, ever so mindful not to appear intrusive.

"Billy found one of your girls all cut up on a trail. He's talking to the police right now."

Vickie grabbed the arms of her chair. Her pulse jumped. For a instant she imagined Kristy or Sherry lying motionless on a wooded trail. "Lord no!" She closed her eyes and gripped the chair tighter.

"Where's Joe?" Ed demanded. "We've got to call Joe!"

Joe, Vickie thought, where was Joe? Vickie remembered that he had had a meeting scheduled for 4:00. But it wasn't in his office. It was somewhere else and Vickie could not remember where. She looked at the clock. Could they still catch him? "God, please, be there Joe. Be there."

Vickie fumbled the phone with her shaking hands. "The number, the number. God, help me remember the number."

Ed yanked the receiver from her hands. "What's the number?" he asked. Vickie blurted out the number, an act more of rote than of consciousness. One prayer answered.

"Hello. Get me Joe Janson," Ed shouted. "This is an emergency. Get me Joe Janson, now!"

Vickie touched her temples. "Please be there, Joe. Please be there." She opened her eyes and felt slightly embarrassed when she noticed the patients staring. She shut her eyes again.

"Joe. This is Ed Keenan. One of your girls is cut up. You better get up there right now. I got Vickie with me. We'll meet you up there. Get going. Now!"

Prayer number two answered. Now just one more, that the girls were safe. "Please God."

Vickie hurried to the coatroom and found her purse and coat.

As she turned to leave, she dropped her coat on the floor and buckled to her knees.

Air, there wasn't enough air.

Ed yelled from the reception area. "Let's go, Vickie. Let's go."

But Vickie couldn't move. "Oh, God," Vickie prayed. "Whatever it is, you have to get me through this. It's up to you, Lord Jesus. It's up to you."

She stood up, picked up her coat, and breathed deeply. She calmed down and walked quickly to the reception area and Ed.

Dr. Caldwell emerged from his examining room.

"What's wrong?" he asked.

"I've got to go," Vickie pleaded. "Sorry. The girls, something is wrong with the girls."

Some of the patients were standing now, trying to help Vickie out the door.

"Let's go! Let's go!" Ed ordered.

Dr. Caldwell watched as Ed hurried Vickie down the hall.

Ed whisked Vickie to his Chevrolet Blazer, where Phyllis stood waiting. His wife worked for the dentist next door and Ed had summoned her first.

Vickie was glad to see her.

"Get in," Ed ordered. Vickie climbed into the cab between Ed and Phyllis. Vickie felt the couple's bigness engulf her. Ed backed up the truck and tore through town toward Bayfield.

Ed and Phyllis each lit a cigarette.

It was nearing rush hour. The traffic was getting heavier.

"Get out of my way," Ed yelled at motorists.

"Slow down!" Phyllis cried. "You're going too fast!"

Vickie whispered to herself. "God. It's up to you, God. It's up to you."

Phyllis lit another cigarette and handed it to Ed.

Ed cursed.

Phyllis took Vickie's hand and held it. It felt good.

When they reached the gravel roads, the truck rumbled and skidded around the curves. On the straightaways the truck swayed back and forth. Ed's foot hung heavy on the accelerator. Vickie thought he was going too fast but she didn't care. "My babies."

There was no talk, just the sound of gravel pounding the underside of the truck and the race of the engine. A cloud of dust trailed along.

Phyllis lit another cigarette.

Vickie shrunk between the two, feeling like a child. "Lord Jesus, you have to give me the strength to endure whatever it is I'm about to encounter. Lord Jesus."

Ed got to the subdivision in what seemed to Vickie like no time. They turned the final corner and saw the assembly of police cars lining the roadway up and down the hill. Vickie's heart plunged.

A neighbor stopped the Blazer, bent down, and looked into the cab. She saw Vickie but said nothing.

Ed jumped out of the truck and hustled over to several officers standing nearby. He spoke for a few moments, then returned to the waiting women.

"We're going to go down to my house. And Vickie, I want you to stay there."

Vickie didn't question his authority. He had gotten her this far. They raced down the loop and veered into the Keenans' driveway, where more police cars waited.

Grandma Keenan came running out of the house.

"Where are the children?" she cried. "Where's Laura and Billy?"

"They're safe," Ed said. "Don't worry."

He turned to Phyllis and Vickie. "You stay in the truck," he said.

He grabbed a pistol from the glove box, kicked the front door open, and ran into the house. A few moments later he returned to the waiting women.

"Go in the house, both of you, in the house. And Mom, you too. And stay here until I come back."

Inside, the women found Cindy Barker sitting on the edge of the living room couch. Her two little boys played on the carpeted floor in front of her.

Earlier, Cindy had seen the police cars whiz into the Keenan driveway. She dressed her children quickly and came over to investigate, certain it was just another "Billy prank." But now, when Cindy saw the expressions on the faces of Phyllis and Vickie, she knew it was more than Billy playing tricks.

The women sat down.

"Vickie," Phyllis said. "I'm going to bring you a glass of wine. You drink it, now."

Vickie didn't answer. "Lord Jesus. Lord Jesus."

The other women eyed one another. Cindy could sense that Phyllis knew what was happening. When Vickie rose to go to the bathroom, Phyllis pulled Cindy aside.

"Cindy," Phyllis whispered. She turned to make sure Vickie wasn't around to hear what she was about to say.

"The girls are dead," Phyllis continued. "Kristy and Sherry. Both of them. Dead."

Cindy instinctively turned to find her children. They were safe, watching television now.

"What happened?"

"Killed. Stabbed or something. All cut up. And Vickie doesn't know it yet. Billy found them."

Billy, Cindy thought. Did Billy do it? But Billy was just at my house. How could he have done it?

Cindy wondered why Vickie wasn't demanding to go to her house right away. Cindy thought that if it were her children nothing could prevent her going to them. Finally she thought about Kristy and Sherry.

Vickie returned from the bathroom and sat down. The women broke up their clutch and sat next to her, chatting idly, passing time. Vickie didn't hear a word.

Instead she prayed that all this was a misunderstanding, a practical joke that had gone too far. She prayed that soon the girls would emerge with tearful "I'm sorry"'s for the worry they had imposed, ready to receive punishment for their misdemeanor.

Vickie stared out the window and up the trail that

led to her home, hoping to see Kristy, Sherry, Billy, and Laura strolling amiably toward the house.

Instead, Vickie saw a group of police officers following a dog on a leash. The dog was black and big, his nose was to the ground, and the leash was taut. The scent he followed was leading the men here, to the front porch of the Keenan home.

Joe Janson didn't think much of Ed Keenan's phone call. Ed was forever exaggerating small crises and this most probably was the latest episode. Joe envisioned one of the girls scraped and crying from a bicycle fall. By now they were probably playing again and had completely forgotten the bruised knee, or whatever it was. His girls were tough.

Joe looked at his watch. He already had been running late for his four o'clock meeting and now he would have to miss it altogether. He wasn't pleased. Joe had joined with several friends to plan a new company, one that would manufacture three-quarter-size vintage airplanes. The subjects of timeliness and absenteeism had been raised at board meetings before, largely by Joe, and now he was in danger of practicing what he had preached against.

But he had no choice, so he jumped in his truck and started down the road. Only then did it dawn on him to call home and ask the girls themselves what was going on.

He stopped and dialed his number. No answer.

Joe spotted a State Patrol car and flagged it down. He explained the situation and asked for an escort.

The patrolman agreed but didn't race Joe home. Instead, the officer crawled at thirty-five miles per hour. Joe wanted to pass the patrol car; he could go faster himself. But he didn't. When they neared his home, the patrolman slowed to a stop, stepped from his car, and signaled to Joe not to pass.

"I want you to wait here a few minutes. We got a problem down there."

"Okay," Joe said.

One minute passed. Another. Then another. Joe checked his watch. Four minutes. Five minutes. He could see activity around his house. Why couldn't he go up there? It was his house. His girls.

The officer told him to hold on again.

"Look," Joe told the officer, "I'm going up to my house and there is nothing legally you can do to stop me. Either arrest me or let me go through."

The patrolman let Joe pass, then quickly got on his radio as Joe walked the short distance to the road above his driveway. Joe saw the scores of police cars parked at odd angles, with doors left open, radios squawking, emergency lights silently revolving.

Jim Harrington jogged down to meet the father. The tall lawman knew this was to be the toughest assignment of the day.

"Mr. Janson?" Harrington said with a slight rise in inflection.

"Yes."

"I'm sorry, but your girls are dead."

"Dead?"

"Dead."

"Both of them?"

"Yes, both of them. I'm sorry."

The father paused, not knowing what to say or think.

"Were they sexually molested?" Joe asked. Why were these the first words from his lips? Joe wondered.

"No, there's no evidence of that," Harrington said.

"Were they mutilated?" Again Joe wondered where the question came from.

Harrington paused.

"No. Not really. I'm sorry."

Joe swayed. "The girls, dead? It can't be. It can't be." He spoke more to himself than to Harrington.

Harrington nodded.

"But I just saw them. I just put them on the bus this morning. Are you sure?" Joe implored. "Are you sure?"

"I'm sorry," Harrington said.

Joe staggered up the driveway toward the house. Nick Boyd saw him coming and met him on the road.

"Have you been up to the house?" Joe asked. "Are you sure it was my girls? Red hair, curly. Two of them. Thirteen. Eight."

"Yes," Boyd said. "I was the first one up here. It's them."

"What do they look like?" Joe asked again, still disbelieving it could ever be his children.

Boyd repeated the descriptions.

Joe buried his face in his hands. "I want to go down and see my kids," Joe said.

Boyd positioned his body between Joe and his home. The father didn't need to see the children in the state they were in.

"I wish you wouldn't do that," Boyd said. "There's no need."

Joe protested, then stopped. He wiped his forehead and shook his head.

"Okay," Joe said. "You do whatever has to be done. But I don't want anybody to see the kids. It'll be a closed coffin."

"We'll take care of everything, Mr. Janson," Boyd said.

Joe turned toward his car. Then turned around and called out to Boyd.

"I know you guys do a good job," Joe said, his finger wavering at the officer. "But *you* find him, or *I* will. You understand? If you don't, I will."

Joe turned once more to leave. He met Ed Keenan coming up the road. The two men embraced.

"Someone's killed the kids," Joe said.

Ed place his arm around Joe's shoulder. "I know. I'm sorry, Joe. I can't believe this thing happened. I'm sorry."

There was silence.

"Joe," Ed said, "Vickie's down at our house."

Joe nodded and walked to his car. He waited to turn

on the ignition, then he drove slowly the half mile around the loop to the Keenans' house.

Vickie. How would Vickie take this? She wouldn't survive.

As he pulled in the short driveway, Joe looked for the girls, hoping the police officers were wrong, hoping it was all one big mistake.

Instead, he saw Vickie slap open the screen door and run toward him. Her face was traced with tears, her arms spread open wide.

4

The dog's name was Babe, a female coonhound as gentle as her name. Through dust, mud, and blizzard, she was considered the best tracker in the county. But when her trainer, Terry Woods, put her on a lead at the threshold of the Janson home, she didn't immediately find Kristy's body lying on the kitchen floor. First she smelled the living room couches and the upholstered chairs. Then she sniffed her way into the kitchen, putting her nose to the countertop. Only then did she turn and discover Kristy's body.

Babe shied back. She wrapped her tail between her legs and trembled slightly, causing her claws to chatter lightly on the linoleum floor. The dog had seen warm corpses before without showing fright and her reaction puzzled Woods. Babe sniffed once more, then arched her tail above her back, a sign to Woods that she had cast a scent. Woods switched over to a harness, letting Babe know they were ready to work.

"Get 'em," Woods commanded.

With her nose three inches from the ground, Babe guided Woods out the front door at a run. Woods tugged back but Babe would not slacken her pace. She raced in the direction of the second body. But the moment Babe saw Sherry lying dead, the dog veered away. She led Wood south to a barbed wire fence at the edge of the Janson property some forty feet from the second body.

Babe circled back north, past some footprints, then west until the team returned to the house where they had started. Babe led Woods into the Janson garage, sat down, and looked up dutifully at her master. Woods noted Babe's movement in his notebook. What it meant he did not know.

Woods walked Babe on a lead to Sherry's body in the clearing. She sniffed around, this time showing little fear. When she arched her tail, Woods refitted the harness, again indicating to her it was time to work a trail. From Sherry's body, Babe headed south down the hillside, stopping near another footprint of a shoe with a deep lugged sole. With her harness taut, she continued along the slope, pulling hard until she reached the road about one hundred yards from an unidentified house. Woods would later learn that it was the Keenan house.

Babe paused at the road, sniffed left, sniffed right. Then she dropped her tail.

Babe looked up at Woods. She had lost the scent.

Woods fastened the lead and walked the dog back to the Keenans'. Babe again cast a scent and traveled north. But near a small snowbank tucked in the shade, Babe lost the scent once more. Woods was growing frustrated. Babe, the best sniffer in the county, couldn't sniff it out this time.

But Rotten could.

A huge male rottweiler with a thick chest and brown accents on his short black coat, Rotten immediately cast a scent at the house. He led his trainer, Mike Hooker, to a sewage evaporation pond about one hundred feet southeast of the Janson house. Rotten moved swiftly south along the hill until he reached the Keenan house via a footpath. It was not the path Babe had taken. After touching the Keenan house with his nose, Rotten pulled north again via a neighbor's property toward the Janson home. He pulled hard until he came upon Sherry.

Hooker recorded Rotten's movements, then found Harrington in the sea of policemen.

"I think the murder weapon is in the pond," Hooker said. "And whoever did it went down to a house below that hill." He pointed toward the trail that led to the Keenan home.

Harrington knew the pond. It wasn't large at all, perhaps ten feet in diameter. Earlier Harrington had noticed a dense wooden object shaped like a bowling pin floating on the surface of the muddy water. He'd thought nothing of it. Now the pond would have to be drained in the morning.

Rotten got a pat on his head and jumped into the bed of his master's pickup truck. As Hooker drove away, Rotten watched the men and their movements until his master turned a corner and the house was out of sight.

Sue Naholnik didn't mind sitting in the ambulance with Billy and Laura. She was happy to help. Her husband was the Bayfield marshal, a large man who had set many locals against him by his ironfisted rule. He was out of his jurisdiction now, since this was not Bayfield proper, far from it. But Marshal Naholnik felt responsible for the eastern half of La Plata County, enough to deputize his wife and take her with him on serious calls.

Laura and Billy seemed like nice kids, Sue thought. They had calmed down now and were sitting near each other on the padded benches of the ambulance looking out the windows. It was quiet inside looking out, detached from the rumblings outside. The evening wind had started to blow. Billy sat with his elbows on his knees, resting his chin in his hands.

Sue started talking, small chatter, just to keep the children's thoughts off the murders. She asked their names and if they were warm enough. Did they want anything to drink? Did they have any questions?

Laura said, "It's hard to believe that the two girls are dead because I had just—they were just on the bus this afternoon and were laughing and talking. It's just hard to believe that they're dead.''

Sue agreed. She said it had happened so suddenly.

There was a pause in the conversation as the three watched several officers rush by. Then Laura added that she was glad that she hadn't seen the girls dead.

After a while, Billy said that Kristy had been in the kitchen. Kristy got it first. Then Sherry walked in. They got her out on the trail.

Sue listened intently. How odd it was, she thought, that Billy could know the order of the deaths, since he found the girls presumably when they were dead. Either one of the victims could have been killed first. How would Billy know?

Then Laura said wasn't it funny that Billy had just talked to Kristy moments before she must have died. He had called to tell Kristy he was coming to return Tubby, the Jansons' dog, who had wandered down to the Keenan home.

When her brother came back, Laura said, he was screaming that the Janson girls had been cut up. Ten minutes couldn't have passed.

Sue listened politely, not letting on what she was thinking. After a few minutes she left the truck, found Jim Harrington, and told him what the children had said.

She returned and sat with the children again.

"Where are you from?" Sue asked.

"From California," Laura said.

"Well, it's someplace I'd like to go. I've never been there," Sue said.

Billy said California was "okay, but it's real hot there."

"Well," Sue said, "you can always go down to the beach and cool off there."

"Oh," Laura said, "we weren't allowed to go to the beach."

"What do you mean you couldn't go to the beach?" Sue asked.

Laura said that her mother had grounded them from going to the beach.

Sue asked why.

Laura said it was because, when they were little, Billy used to tear up her dolls all the time. And one particular time, he got hold of a doll and tried to tear the smile off its face, and so her mother grounded them.

Billy objected. "Well, that was when I was real little. I was about five."

"No," said Laura, "because I would have only been about two then, and I know I was old enough to remember it."

Billy shrugged. The three fell silent.

They heard footsteps outside the ambulance. The door opened. It was Detective Harrington. He had come from examining the footprints found near Sherry's body and on the hillside beyond it.

Harrington maneuvered his six-foot-four-inch frame through the back door of the ambulance. He smiled at the children.

Billy sat with his hands between his knees, nervous but composed. Harrington knelt in front of the boy. In his baritone voice he began his questioning. Billy looked up only briefly at the detective.

The investigator asked how was it Billy found the bodies? At about what time? Which body had he discovered first? Did he see anyone? How was he feeling?

Billy mumbled responses but Harrington wasn't listening very closely. Instead, he was examining the boy's shoes, hoping to get a glance at the soles.

As he did, Harrington spotted something else. He saw on the boy's blue jeans an almost imperceptible spray of blood above and below the knee. It wasn't much, just a four-inch trail of spatters, each no more than one-sixteenth of an inch in diameter. The blood hid well on the blue denim, appearing as dark brown on the dark blue.

"Look here," Harrington said, pointing to the spatters. "Where did the blood come from?"

Billy looked down at the spray, somewhat surprised. "I guess I must have brushed one of the girls' bodies when I found them," he said.

Harrington knew that blood spatters didn't come from incidental contact with motionless victims. Not spatters like these. He also knew that many murder convictions relied on little more than a forensic expert's analysis of spatters. According to his experience, the blood on Billy's pants came from blood moving at a high rate of speed.

The conversation in the ambulance took less than two minutes. Harrington did not pause to ask the girl any questions. He thanked the children and smiled again. As he turned to leave he snatched a look at the soles of Billy's shoes. They matched the pattern of the imprint found near Sherry's body.

Harrington walked back toward the crime scene. He rounded up Boyd, Bell, and Sheriff Al Brown. He led the men away from the other deputies.

"I think the boy did it," Harrington said. "I just talked to him and saw spatters of blood on his pants. He's the one."

For Nick Boyd, even though the thought had never crossed his mind, Harrington's revelation made perfect sense. For Brown, too, the explanation seemed plausible. No wonder they had had no luck uncovering any trace of a killer. The killer was in their midst, protected by the very men searching for him.

"Let's get him out of there," Harrington continued. "Get him isolated. Get him talking. Get a story. Find out what happened, because he's the one who did it."

Only Mike Bell had his doubts. He couldn't believe a thirteen-year-old boy could so savagely murder two girls. He had seen Billy in the ambulance. He was just a kid.

Yet even with his doubts, Bell changed the focus of the investigation. The search was off for a mad-dog killer or a motorcycle gang on the run. Bell was now looking for evidence linking Billy to the murders.

Bell called the search parties back. They had been searching for well over an hour now and had turned up nothing. He ordered the deputies to stay away from the scene at all costs. He sent a police photographer to take pictures of the bodies, the kitchen, the sliding glass door, and the path between the house and Sherry's body and the footprints around the body. A deputy carefully scraped into plastic bags samples of the blood on the walls and the hair in the sink. If the boy was the killer, they needed evidence. And so far, it didn't look like there was much to find.

Vickie Janson was not the only one who saw her husband slowly drive up the Keenan driveway. In the fading afternoon sunlight, Cindy, Phyllis, and Grandma Keenan could also see Joe's car pulling in. The three women slipped out the back door of the Keenan home, leaving Vickie alone.

Joe rolled the car to a stop and slowly opened the driver's door.

Vickie ran out of the house to meet him. She froze when she saw Joe's face.

Oh, God, no, she thought.

Her eyes closed. Her knees trembled.

Joe walked the short distance to Vickie standing at the bottom of the porch stairs. He took her in his arms and buried his face in her hair. His eyes filled with tears and his throat choked off the words before they reached his lips.

Then he gathered his strength and cupped Vickie's face in his hands. He met her eyes with his. "Vickie," he said, "we lost them. We lost them both."

Joe wrapped his heavy arms around his wife to keep her from melting. With her eyes she implored him to tell her something different. But he couldn't.

"No, no, no. My babies!" Vickie cried. "My babies!" She beat her fists against Joe's chest.

"Shhh, sweetheart."

"How? Why?" Vickie asked.

''Hush, honey.''

''What have they ever done? Oh, God, no! Please, God, no! Jesus.''

Then something strange happened.

Vickie felt herself leaving her body and floating upward. She no longer looked up at Joe's face, rather, she looked down on him as she circled above both him and herself. She was floating above the house and the yard, above her pain and the moment. She possessed no weight, no emotion, just consciousness as pure and uncluttered as light. She circled above like an astral voyeur, looking down, feeling pity for this woman bound to the earth in pain, this woman whose greatest curse was to exist on the material plane.

Yet Vickie was also that anguished crying mother with her feet on the ground and only her husband's arms holding her upright. She was that suffering woman fainting in a dizzying whirl of emotion. She felt her body protesting its own will to live. She felt a terror so consuming there was no choice but to surrender to it.

She felt all this and she felt nothing.

She was two beings, the one above and the one below. It was as if, by some act of God, her world, like the Red Sea, had separated, and suddenly there were two worlds. One was a nightmare and one was a dream, and Vickie felt the pain and oblivion of each.

Joe led Vickie up the stairs to the swinging bench on the porch. The swing creaked under the weight of the parents as they rocked gently, unconsciously. They held each other. Cried. Their tears and hands intermingled as they touched each other's faces. There were no words.

The sky turned from blue to purple. The few clouds that lingered were colored peach, then faded to gray. The green of the trees turned to dark green, then black. Slowly, the last vestige of light slipped away.

It was the end of consciousness for Vickie.

Soon the trembling began, the pounding heart, the steady flow of torment erupting from a place she never knew existed. It was a trembling Vickie couldn't control and medication would fail to diminish.

It would be two weeks before the trembling would stop and years before Vickie could summon the courage to remember this moment. This moment when she rocked gently on the porch swing, the light fading softly, and she inhabited two worlds as disparate as life and death.

Night was falling rapidly. The word spread among the officers that it was the boy. Many were convinced of Billy's participation not so much based on the evidence against him but rather on the utter lack of evidence against anyone else, seen or unseen. Bell thanked the officers from the other departments and politely asked them to leave. The parking jam at the top of the county road eased. Officers drove off in silence, listening to the crunch of pebbles beneath their wheels.

Bell knew that the investigation from now on had to adhere to strict criminal guidelines. Moreover, it had to adhere to strict juvenile guidelines, and nobody was really sure what those guidelines were. It was understood, at least, that Billy's father was to be present for any questioning.

Bell, Harrington, Brown, and Assistant District Attorney Victor Reichman laid out their strategy during an impromptu conference under the darkening pines. Billy would be driven to town with Mike Bell and Al Bell, another investigator not related to Mike. The two would interrogate Billy once they arrived. Investigators Cliff Cox and Ralph Newberry would speak to Laura separately. Harrington would stay behind and preserve the scene.

Under no circumstance was Billy or his parents to know that Billy was a suspect. Bell needed to get the boy's story in full, so that investigators might contradict it later when the corroborating evidence was in. If the Keenans suspected the police's motive, they could stop the interrogation at any moment. Bell couldn't have that. Not now.

It took about five minutes for Mike Bell to find Ed Keenan. He was standing near the parking area talking to officers. Bell asked him if he and his family would be good enough to come to Durango for questioning. Ed said of course, anything to help find the killers.

No one understood the delicacy of the situation better than Vic Reichman. As he drove the gravel roads back to Durango, he thought of the ramifications of Billy's age. Legally, it was a mess. Billy was thirteen or fourteen, Reichman had discovered. Laws pertaining to juveniles were among the most arcane and archaic on the books. Reichman had no idea what he was facing. It wasn't his area. He didn't know what charges could be brought against the boy, what the police could or could not do during the course of the interrogation, what special provisions applied because of the youth's age. Reichman was sure, however, that even the slightest deviation from the law could be enough to spring Billy from the charge, if indeed he was the killer.

Then Reichman pondered the political pitfalls. What if Billy was not the killer? How could he explain to the community that the police and his office had botched the biggest criminal investigation in La Plata County history? How could he admit that investigators had interrogated and traumatized a young neighborhood boy already traumatized by the brutal sight of his neighborhood friends butchered to death? What do you say: "Sorry, young man. You can go home now."? No one would forgive the police if they had let the real killer or killers get away. No one would forgive them if Billy Keenan was not the murderer.

If the investigators were wrong, if in their haste they had overlooked some logical explanation for that thin spray of blood on Billy's pants, it meant the end of the political careers of every top law enforcement official in the county. It was a tortuous thought for Reichman, who planned on running next year against his boss for the top spot in the D.A.'s office. There was no room for error.

Jim Harrington had no such fears. He was sure it was Billy, and he was determined to find evidence to prove it. It was not only the blood spatters that told him so, but a feeling that Harrington had picked up in the short interview with the boy. If Harrington was to lose sleep tonight it wouldn't be from uncertainty over the boy's guilt. Finding evidence to corroborate his intuition, however, would have to wait until morning.

It was getting dark and Harrington stationed deputies at critical points on the Janson property. There was little more that could be done tonight.

Sheriff Brown told Harrington not to disturb or cover the bodies of the girls. They were to remain untouched until agents from the Colorado Bureau of Investigation arrived in the morning. Brown wanted the CBI in on the case as soon as possible. If there were any screwups, the CBI could shoulder half the blame.

As he drove to Durango, Mike Bell looked through his rearview mirror at Billy sitting pensively in the back seat. He didn't ask the boy many questions. That would wait until they arrived in Durango and Bell could see Billy's reactions clearly under the bright lights.

The Keenans' Blazer followed behind. Ed Keenan was driving. Phyllis sat beside him. Bell wondered what was being said. Were the parents as busy mapping out an interview strategy as were the investigators?

Bell reviewed what he had so far. It was nightfall and no murder weapon had been found. The footprints appeared to match Billy's shoes, but then Billy admitted to finding the girls, so matching footprints were not incriminating. The dog tracking had been a partial success. Again, there was nothing incriminating about a track to Billy's house. The dogs, however, had not picked up any other trail, only Billy's. That was good. There was Sue Naholnik's conversation with the two children. Not bad, but would it stand up in court? The only solid evidence was the blood spattered on Billy's clothing. In all, there wasn't much to go on.

Bell understood that his best bet was a confession. He glanced again at his rearview mirror. It was his only play and it had to be played perfectly.

Bell turned into the back parking lot of the La Plata County Courthouse in downtown Durango. The Keenans followed and parked beside him. Politely, Bell escorted Billy and his father up the back stairs to Reichman's office.

Bell sat the father and son down in two big chairs facing the desk, as if they were clients in a fancy law office. Billy sent darting looks to his father, then looked up fearfully at the officers.

Bell turned to Billy. ''Would you like a soda pop, Billy? Some coffee, Ed?''

When everyone settled in their places, Al Bell closed the door behind them and the conversation began.

5

The phone calls to the sheriff's office began pouring in shortly after 6:00 P.M. and didn't stop until early the following morning. Word had spread quickly through Bayfield that neighborhood kids had been murdered and it was a vicious killing. The callers pleaded for information. Who got killed? Had the killer been caught? What in the devil was going on?

Police, though, would say little. They acknowledged that a killing or killings had taken place in rural Bayfield near County Road 502 but refused to identify victims or say if police had a suspect in custody.

In truth they did not. Billy Keenan was being questioned as a witness. The last thing investigators needed now was for Billy's parents to discover that their son was the prime suspect by listening to a radio news flash.

But in the countryside, where living close to your neighbor meant seeing his porch light dimly through the trees, and the long stretches of back roads kept the police at least fifteen minutes away, people were terrified.

The telephone party lines were jammed. Word got out that it was the Janson girls. Dead. Cut up. Mutilated. The work of a satanic cult. A motorcycle gang. A crazed killer on foot.

There was even a rumor that it was the boy next door, the Keenan boy. But few believed it. The sketchy reports coming in from the wives of the deputies told of too gruesome a scene for it to be anything a young boy might have done. What's the boy's name, Billy? Couldn't have done it. Good kid, troubled sometimes, but good.

For the neighbors who lived in the small subdivision, the nightmare was more real. The murders had taken place one or two houses away, on their road, in their neighborhood, which until then had been a shelter from calamity. Coming home from work, they had driven past the scene and glimpsed with disbelief the police cars too numerous to count. They had observed the drawn faces of the deputies guarding the perimeter. They had been stopped by other deputies asking questions.

Parents gathered their children. Men unlocked their gun cabinets and loaded up rifles and handguns, whatever they had. Windows and doors were bolted, porch lights kept on. The children were ordered upstairs to sleep or try to sleep. The dog was sent outside to act as sentry. Then, with their boots on and their hands never straying from the cold metal of their rifles, the men sat and waited.

Some of the husbands talked about getting a posse together. If the law couldn't catch the culprit, they would. The older locals, especially, distrusted the law or any authority. Lawmen hadn't been needed when Bayfield was settled and there wasn't much need for them now.

The posse, however, never rode. It was decided it would be better to let police handle the case. This was a different kind of killing, a different kind of killer.

As the night took hold, families began receiving calls from local reporters. Police were keeping the press in the dark and there was nothing the press hated more. Reporters were hoping to tap into the well-established grapevine that branched through Bayfield and its outlying areas. This time, all the grapevine could provide was plenty of rumors, rumors that varied too wildly to incorporate into news reports. The media were at a loss, and the biggest story of the year, at this point, was also the biggest mystery.

The radio stations, too, were bombarded with calls from locals. Soon it became obvious that news reports had to go out on the air. But the reports, made up of little more than rumors and innuendos, only served to increase the panic and prompted more calls.

For Joe and Vickie, the knowledge of what had happened was more terrifying than any mystery. With the Keenans in town talking with police, only the Jansons and a few others remained at the Keenan home. The parents huddled on the living room couch. Joe clasped Vickie's hand. He searched for words to comfort her but couldn't find any. Nor could he find words to comfort himself. No one dared tell Vickie how the girls had been killed. Vickie had the sense not to ask.

Suddenly something flashed on Vickie from earlier in the afternoon: the police dogs coming straight at her as she peered out the Keenan front window. Why were the police dogs coming here to the Keenan home? What did they want? What did they know? Her apprehension told her that someone here, someone connected with this house, had something to do with the murder of her girls. The thought sent a burst of fear racing up her spine. All she wanted was to get out of the house. Now.

Sometime later, the pastor from the First Presbyterian Church, along with a church elder, arrived at the Keenans'. Bob Shanks, the church elder, offered the Jansons a place to stay for as long as they needed, be it one night or several months. Joe accepted the offer. Vickie was helped from the couch to a waiting car and was driven away from Wallace Gulch.

Down the trail through the woods that separated the Keenan and Janson homes, Jim Harrington was in command. The crime scene was peaceful now. The only traces of the earlier commotion were the flattened weeds and sagebrush, crushed under the squads of police cars that had invaded the area, and the pretty yellow ribbon that fluttered in the wind as it traced the path from the Janson house to Sherry's body in the woods.

What bothered Harrington most was the lack of a murder weapon. Billy's movements were limited to the trails between his house and the Jansons'. The search dogs had verified that. Yet sixty deputies turning up every stone could find nothing.

Except for the spray of blood on his clothing, Billy's story was entirely plausible. Perhaps a jury would convict an established criminal based on a four-inch spray of blood, but no jury, none in this county anyway, would convict a boy based on such paltry evidence. The case rested on that elusive sliver of steel that hid somewhere in the pines, underbrush, or isolated snowbanks of Wallace Gulch.

In the house, Harrington paused to gaze at the hallway wall. From ceiling to floor, the wall was covered with photographs of Sherry and Kristy: the girls smiling, kissing, hugging, playacting, dressed up for Halloween, hugging the dog, on horseback, on Joe's shoulders, in Vickie's lap, with friends.

Some of the photos near the kitchen entrance had been splattered with blood in the same arching pattern that stained Billy's clothing.

Harrington turned and looked again at the girl sprawled face up on the kitchen floor. Her head was awkwardly tilted to the right, and her arms were hardening in a bent position. Her right foot held open a cupboard door about three inches. The most obvious stab wounds were to her stomach, her throat, and across her nose. There were more, but Harrington didn't take the time to count.

Harrington looked up and discovered blood spatters on the ceiling above Kristy's body. She had been killed here, Harrington had no doubts.

Yet he puzzled over the same mystery Boyd had earlier. Why wasn't there more blood? There should have been more blood.

Harrington turned away and walked outside.

Several deputies with flashlights were still scouring

the grounds near the house looking for the knife. Another team was busy making castings of the footprints.

Though it was dark, Harrington walked the distance to the sewage pond. Since Rotten's scent had brought him here, Harrington had ordered a pump truck brought in for tomorrow.

Harrington watched the moonlight play on the pond's surface.

"It's in here," Harrington said to a deputy standing by.

"What's in here?" the deputy said.

"The weapon."

Next Harrington took the stroll through the darkness to Sherry's body. The exposed corpse lay hidden under the blanket of night, illuminated only by the shine of a flashlight.

Throughout the evening, the deputy assigned to guard the body had checked it occasionally for signs of movement, knowing full well the thought was foolish. But from his station the house was out of view, and it was dark and lonely.

Harrington aimed his flashlight at the little girl as he squatted on his haunches. Though she was lying on her stomach, Harrington could plainly see at least three deep facial cuts and one cut to the back. He stood up and walked the few feet to the blue butterfly net that pointed toward the house. He estimated that her right foot had drug for a distance of four feet five inches before the girl hit the ground facedown.

There was nothing more Harrington could do. A shift change had been arranged for later in the night, the evidence collected, the scene secured. Except for the occasional rush of wind through the pine trees and the distant bark of a far-off dog, the night was still and quiet. Harrington headed for the station. The morning light would bring the next opportunity for revelation. Perhaps, then, Harrington would uncover the answer to the most perplexing question of all . . . Why?

Nick Boyd had left the scene well before Harrington but long after dark and long after he was of any use to anyone. As he took the long ride back to Durango, he thought of his own daughter, Shannon, and how he loved her. He also thought about his first daughter, who had died of Sudden Infant Death Syndrome. He recalled again the unbearable horror of discovering her breathless body in her crib.

Boyd flashed on Joe Janson and the corrosive anguish he would experience from now to eternity. It would be far worse than Boyd's encounter with death. To have your only two children murdered brutally at your home. Boyd yearned to comfort the father.

The La Plata County Courthouse, like so many other courthouses and schools built in the 1950s and early 1960s, was a squat, unadorned red-brick structure topped with a flat roof. The inside walls were lined with enameled pale green cinder blocks, just a few shades lighter than the green linoleum tiles that covered the floor. Overhead, the white acoustic ceiling tiles and naked fluorescent lights cast an antiseptic glare upon the halls and offices of the building. The place even had its own peculiar smell, as if a phantom custodian forever roamed its halls. It was the kind of atmosphere that made people feel edgy, uncomfortable. Like they wanted to get out. Like they were guilty.

In one of the offices, Cliff Cox and Ralph Newberry spoke with Laura Keenan and her mother. The events of the day had clearly taken their toll on the girl. She cried occasionally, dabbing the tears away gently with a handkerchief. She was frightened, upset, and fearful of the men and the strange surroundings.

Her dark hair was thick and curly, and her eyes brown and sorrowful. She looked like a little gypsy girl. On the threshold of puberty, it was obvious that she would soon blossom into a very pretty girl.

Phyllis looked too old to be Laura's mother. Her face was lined with wrinkles and her arms were thick and heavy. She wore her graying hair short, in matronly fashion. She looked at the men with suspicion. The interview was a blatant violation of her family and she let the men know it.

Laura didn't have much to say. She told the investigators that she had been watching TV when Billy left to take Tubby back, and that she was still watching TV when her brother came running back screaming that Kristy and Sherry had been cut up. She told the officers which television shows she had watched and what the shows were about. The men were glad to hear that she knew the shows' contents. They didn't want to think of her as an accomplice. The men jotted the information down. It would help them time the events of the day. Laura said that Billy seemed very upset after he had returned home, but he didn't say anything about who did it. Before she knew it, Laura said, the police arrived.

In an adjacent office, Mike Bell drew open a window shade, but the view looked out onto the back wall of the jail just two or three feet away. He turned around and faced Billy Keenan and his father.

Billy leaned forward with his arms dangling between his legs. He wore a brown T-shirt with an emblem of a lion on the back. Bell could not make out the spray of blood on Billy's pants but he detected another spray on the boy's shirt. If Bell had had any doubts of the boy's guilt, they were erased now that he knew there were spatters on both Billy's shirt and pants.

"Before we go on," Bell told Billy, "as I told your mom and dad earlier, I'm going to have to read you your Miranda rights. It's just a technicality that protects us more than anything."

Billy agreed with a nod. Bell recited the rights from heart. Throughout, Billy nodded his head obligingly.

Bell looked over the lanky kid. It was the first time he'd gotten a good look at the suspect. Billy was bigger than Bell had realized. Though he was only thirteen, Billy's shoulders were already broad and his biceps well developed. His voice had changed, and though it wasn't deep, it was not the squeak of younger boys. If Bell had seen Billy on the street, he would have guessed the boy was fifteen, perhaps sixteen years old.

Billy's limp hair hung slightly over his brown eyes. Each time Bell attempted to make eye contact, Billy looked away. When Bell looked elsewhere, he could feel Billy's gaze. When he looked toward the boy again, Billy would avert his stare once more.

"Now, tell me again, Billy, how you found the girls."

"Like I said. When I got home from school I watched some TV, played outside, and then found Kristy's dog at our place."

Billy explained how Tubby often wandered down to the Keenans' and how he would have to lead the dog back. Bell didn't remember seeing a dog loose near the scene.

"Then what happened?"

"I called my mother and asked if I could bring Tubby back. Then I called Kristy and told her I was coming over."

Ed Keenan sat silently. He neither encouraged nor discouraged his son.

"What happened then?" Bell asked.

"I walked the trail to the house with Tubby. When I walked in the kitchen I saw Kristy on the floor."

"How did you enter the house?"

"Through the porch."

"The sliding glass door?"

"Yes."

"What did you do then?"

"I was scared. I knelt down and touched her. I shook her a little, but she was dead."

"Where did you touch her?"

"On her shoulder."

"Which shoulder?"

"I don't know, I think it was this one." Billy grasped his right shoulder.

"Did you touch any other part of her body?"

"No, I don't remember. I only remember touching her shoulder."

"And you're sure it was her right shoulder?"

"I told you, I think it was her right shoulder."

"Did you see anyone else? Did you see anything suspicious?"

"No, nothing."

"Did you go straight to the Janson house after you called Kristy?"

"Yes, but it's a long walk."

"How long did it take you?"

"I don't know. I took my time."

"How did you get the blood on your shirt and pants?"

Billy squirmed in his chair. "I don't know, it must have been when I touched Kristy."

"So you touched only her right shoulder?"

"Yes, sir."

"How did you know she was dead?"

"I don't know. She wasn't moving. She looked dead. I shook her and she looked dead."

"You knelt down beside her?" Bell asked.

Billy nodded.

"How did you kneel?"

"What do you mean?" Billy asked.

"Did you squat? Kneel on both knees? On your left knee? On your right? How did you kneel?"

"I don't know. I don't remember. I guess I squatted."

"Like how? Show me."

Billy got up and sat on his haunches next to the chair. "Like this."

"So your knees never touched the ground?"

"No."

"Then how did you get the blood on your clothing?"

Billy looked down at the spatters at the bottom of his T-shirt. "I told you I don't—"

"Wait a minute here," Ed Keenan burst in. The father stood up and walked behind his son. "What the hell is going on? You're acting like he did it. What the hell are you doing?''

"No, no, Mr. Keenan, not at all. We just have to know his movements precisely so we can rule out his footsteps and such. It's very important we get every detail.'' Bell paused for a moment. He went to the window and drew the shade down, obscuring the view of the jail wall. "I'm sorry if it's sounding so serious. We just have to get it straight.'' Bell took a seat behind the D.A.'s desk and leaned back in the chair. Maybe he had gone too far.

"Can we continue?'' Bell asked.

Ed Keenan paused, then nodded yes.

"Okay, Billy, let's move on. You saw that Kristy was dead, then what?''

"Well, I was scared and I ran.''

"Which way did you run?''

"I ran out of the house.''

"Through the sliding door?''

"Yes, sir.''

"And then?''

"Then I started running home down the path.''

"The same path you came up?''

"Yes.''

"And that's when you found Sherry.''

"Yes.''

"How come you didn't see her when you first came down to the house?''

"I don't know, I must have ran by her. The trail isn't really a trail. I must have missed her by a couple of feet.''

"So you found Sherry. Did you touch her also?''

"No, I just ran. I was real scared.''

"You didn't kneel down and touch her, too.''

"No, I barely got near her. I saw she was dead and I ran home.''

"And that's it. You went to the house, saw Kristy, started running, and saw Sherry.''

"Yes, sir.''

A brisk knock on the door interrupted the conversation. "Mike," a deputy said. "Phone call."

Bell excused himself and stepped into a nearby office.

It was Jim Harrington. "Mike, how's it going?"

"The kid's got a pretty good story," Bell said. "How about you?"

"No knife. We found some blood on the ceiling and we're casting the footprints going back and forth between the bodies."

Bell stopped and listened to Harrington's words. "What do you mean back and forth between the bodies?" Bell asked.

"The killer visited the bodies more than once," Harrington said.

"But that's not what the kid said."

"That's what we found."

Bell hung up and searched out Vic Reichman. He told Reichman about the sprays of blood on Billy's clothing, Harrington's findings, and the discrepancy between the evidence and Billy's story.

"Vic, we need to keep the kid tonight," Bell said. "We can't take the chance of losing his shirt and pants. That's all we got."

"Stall them a little," Reichman said. "Let me do some research and see how to handle this."

Bell walked back into the office where Billy and Ed Keenan waited. He closed the door behind him. He walked to the window and opened the shade again. The jail wall stared back.

"Okay, Billy, we're almost done now. Let's walk through this one more time."

Billy eased up a bit and retold his tale.

Then Bell turned to Billy's father. There was no easy way to say this. "You know, Ed, we have to keep Billy's clothing. Because of the bloodstains."

Ed pondered the request. "What do you suggest?"

"We could give him a jail uniform. It's not very flattering but it's clothing."

Ed thought for a moment. "No, I don't want my son in jail clothing. We'll give you the clothing tomorrow."

"No, sorry, we'll need the clothing tonight." Bell had no intention of letting the boy destroy the only solid evidence they had. "I'll tell you what. Why don't we follow you out there, Billy can change at home, and you can give us the clothing tonight."

Mr. Keenan paused. "Okay," he said.

"One more thing, Billy," Bell said, turning to the boy. "We're going to have to stop at the hospital and get a doctor to scrape under your fingernails."

Billy looked up. "What?"

"Well, sometimes blood from the victims can collect under fingernails. It's fairly routine."

A pall came over Billy. He looked at his father, longingly. Bell watched Billy from the corner of his eye. The fear in the boy's face was obvious.

Slowly at first, but soon with abandon, Billy began picking at his fingernails with his teeth, furiously trying to clean out the debris.

Bell had hoped for this reaction. The boy wasn't so confident after all.

Bell leaned back in his chair.

"Now, one more time," Bell said, "tell me how you got the blood on your shirt."

6

Assistant District Attorney Vic Reichman sat in the law library of the courthouse just a few offices away from where Mike Bell was interviewing the thirteen-year-old suspect and his father. Reichman scanned the leather-bound tomes of Colorado's criminal statutes lining the library walls. He pulled from a shelf the thick volume that contained Colorado's Children's Code.

Juvenile delinquency was not new in La Plata County. Remote as it was, or perhaps because it was remote, the county had had its share of juvenile vandalism, burglary, assault, drunkenness, and even a few suicides. Every few years the subject of juvenile delinquency was raised at school board meetings. Lately, even "the specter of satanism" had been mentioned. And at every meeting, "boredom" and "lack of a youth recreation center" were cited as the reasons. "Get your children to participate in church or home activities," parents were told. And as for satanism: "There simply was no evidence of it. Just the work of pranksters." But juvenile murder was a new frontier for the county and for Reichman.

Like everyone who had viewed the grisly murders that day, Reichman was deeply disturbed by the scene. On his return from Bayfield, his wife had brought him some dinner and a change of clothes. He hated the con-stricting suits required during court sessions and much preferred working in open-neck pullovers and polyester pants.

Though he had been raised in Denver, Reichman possessed those East Coast qualities that silently aggravate Westerners to no end. A wiry-haired angular man with a sculpted brown beard, close-set eyes, and a Semitic nose, Reichman had a reputation for being frank to a fault.

He spoke with machine gun precision and rarely cloaked his intentions behind diplomatic euphemisms. In court, he hit hard, ferreting out inconsistencies in testimony and slicing witnesses' logic to pieces. He succeeded in making witnesses appear unqualified or doubtful, but failed in endearing jurors to him. They resented his approach and often empathized with the defendants. Several defense attorneys had attributed jury trial wins not so much to the case they had presented but to Reichman's personality and the jury's reaction.

Nevertheless, few questioned Reichman's knowledge of the law or his acumen, which bordered on brilliance. He was sharp, pragmatic, and dogged, and some of the lawmen working the Janson case were glad it was Reichman's assignment and not his boss's, the more polite and politically savvy District Attorney, Mike Wallace.

In the cramped library quarters, Reichman took a seat under the glare of the fluorescent lights and began reading the Children's Code:

. . . "Violent juvenile offender" means a child thirteen years of age or older at the time the act complained of was committed.

Reichman stepped out and asked a deputy for Billy's date of birth. He knew the boy was in his early teens.

The deputy returned. "May 7, 1969," he said.

Reichman made the quick calculation in his head. This was April 25, 1983. The boy's birthday was May 7. That meant he was thirteen, almost fourteen, years old. Reichman paused and counted on his fingers once more. Billy was twelve days away from turning fourteen. So far so good.

Reichman read a case law citation he found in the same section:

> The intent of the children's code is to restrict the institution of felony charges in a criminal proceeding against a juvenile under 18 years of age.

That would be difficult in this case. If the boy committed the murders, either in the first or second degree, it was an outright felony. Reichman could not in good conscience bring anything but felony charges against Billy.

In fact, Reichman's preliminary strategy was to get the case moved quickly out of juvenile court and into district court, where adult charges and penalties applied. He searched out the section that dealt with moving a juvenile case up:

> When a petition alleges a child fourteen years of age or older to be a delinquent child . . . by virtue of having committed an act which would constitute a felony committed by an adult . . .

Reichman did a double take. If he was reading the statute correctly, then the operative phrase here was "fourteen or older." And since Billy was thirteen, he could not, under any circumstances—including the heinous nature of the crime—be transferred to district court. Instead, the case would have to remain under juvenile jurisdiction, where criminal statutes did not apply.

Reichman skipped ahead to the section labeled "Disposition," a euphemism used in juvenile proceedings that meant sentencing. The case citation was fairly specific in this regard:

There is a very fundamental difference between a criminal proceeding and a delinquency proceeding, and the clear legislative intent is that the handling of juvenile delinquents should be oriented towards rehabilitation and reformation, and not punishment as such, even though the actions of the child if committed by an adult would justify a criminal proceeding.

But what did it mean in terms of sentencing? Reichman found the answer in section 19-1-114:

A commitment of a child to the department of institutions . . . shall be for a . . . period not to exceed two years, except that the committing court may renew the commitment for an additional period not to exceed two years.

Reichman froze in his chair. Did this mean that even if he could prove that thirteen-year-old Billy Keenan was the murderer, the boy would be labeled nothing more than a juvenile delinquent and put away for two years, perhaps four?

If so, Billy would walk before he was eighteen.

Reichman checked the statutes again and called a juvenile expert in Denver to see if he was missing a key provision or was not aware of some esoteric interpretation that would allow him to prosecute Billy to the fullest.

No, the expert said, Reichman was correct.

Had Billy committed the murder two weeks hence, when he was fourteen, he could have been tried as an adult and quite possibly sentenced to life imprisonment.

By twelve days, Billy Keenan saved himself ten, twenty, perhaps forty years in a state penitentiary. And by twelve days, Reichman missed the biggest conviction of his career.

There was more. Reichman was vaguely familiar with

the juvenile process, but now he paid attention to every detail.

> There is no constitutional requirement that pro-
> ceedings in juvenile cases shall be conducted ac-
> cording to the criminal law, or that proceedings
> need take any particular form, so long as the
> essentials of due process and fair treatment are
> accorded.

No formal proceedings, no code of conduct—this meant that Reichman could not necessarily depend on the strict protocols of grand jury and preliminary hearings that he had mastered through the years. True, he could also benefit from the provision, but so could the defense. It was a wild card that he would prefer to do without.

Mike Bell came knocking. Reichman looked up from the law book.

"It's time to go, Vic," Bell said.

"What did you tell the Keenans?" Reichman asked.

"They want to go home so Billy doesn't have to change into prison greens. I told them that was all right."

"Okay, let's go," Reichman said.

Bell escorted the boy and his family to the parking lot, never letting Billy out of sight. After some discussion, it was decided that the Keenan family would drive together in one car, followed in another by Reichman, Al Bell, Mike Bell, and Jim Harrington, who had returned to the sheriff's office from the scene late in the evening.

It was pitch-black now, nearing 11:00. The air was frigid and thin. The car seats were cold and hard and the lawmen could see their breath as they huffed to keep warm while the car's heater kicked in.

The first stop was Community Hospital just a few minutes away, where a doctor scraped underneath Billy's fingernails and placed the grit in a plastic bag.

Though Billy showed signs of uneasiness, he cooperated throughout the quick procedure. His fingernails showed evidence of bite marks.

As the car warmed up during the long trip to the Keenans', the investigators began discussing options.

"Okay, we get his clothes and then what?" Reichman asked.

"We can't leave the kid at home tonight," Bell said. "I don't think he's safe and I don't think his family is safe."

"What do you mean?"

"I mean, I think the kid is capable of killing again." Bell retold Billy's story and recounted the inconsistencies.

"We can't arrest him for inconsistencies," Reichman retorted.

"We can't leave him at home," Bell said. "What if he slips out and runs away? What if he wants to do in a neighbor like he did those girls? Or his family?"

Reichman nodded silently. He knew that this was to be one of the most difficult decisions he would ever make: arrest Billy wrongly and say good-bye to any thoughts of running for district attorney; don't arrest him and others might be hurt or killed.

And what of the boy's safety? It was entirely possible that Joe Janson would find out that Billy was the "suspect in custody." Then nobody in the world could stop the father from finding Billy and taking what many would believe was justified revenge.

That would be quite a complication: Juvenile kills neighbor's girls; neighbor kills juvenile. The county would have a war on its hands.

If only there was more evidence. If only a knife had been found, with prints, Billy's prints.

"We have probable cause," Bell continued.

"But we can't prove the case beyond a reasonable doubt. Can we?"

Bell couldn't answer.

The men were nearing Wallace Gulch. Only minutes

remained before they would arrive at the Keenan home. A decision had to be made quickly.

"Okay," Reichman said, "we'll take him tonight." He paused just long enough to reflect on the gravity of his decision. "Now, what are the logistics?"

The men decided there was no need to flood the home with officers. Harrington and Reichman would wait in the car, Mike and Al Bell would follow the family into the house.

"Are you sure you want to do this, Vic?" Harrington asked. "It's your call."

"No, I'm not sure. But I don't see a choice."

As they turned the corner into the driveway, they saw that the Keenans had already arrived. Phyllis Keenan was on the landing when she turned and saw the police car pulling up.

"Why don't you leave us alone?" she screamed from the porch, even before the officer's car came to a halt. Her arm flailed in the air as she pointed skyward.

"Why don't you leave Billy alone? What have we done?" Her voice wavered with emotion as she beseeched the officers to go away.

"For God's sake, leave us alone!"

She stopped, broke down crying, then walked inside and wept some more. The men followed her inside.

Billy's grandparents sat around the dining room table. The entire Keenan clan stared solemnly at Mike and Al Bell as if they were angels of death. The grandfather passed a comment but Mike couldn't make out what was said.

Billy showed the men to his room. He changed and surrendered the clothing he had worn during the day. Al Bell asked if Billy had any knives. He did, and he gave up willingly his entire collection of four knives.

Ed Keenan joined the officers in his son's bedroom. He was becoming impatient for the men to leave.

"We need to talk to Billy one more time," Al Bell said.

Ed Keenan sighed, then nodded his assent.

The men asked Billy the same questions they had asked him earlier in the evening. They asked him to draw a diagram and explain once more his route. They told Billy the end was near and they needed just a few more details.

Billy was getting cocky now, talking freely, almost jovially. The policemen would leave soon and his life would return to normal. Billy would still have to tell his father about today's encounter at school with Mr. Winter. How long ago that was. But first the policemen must leave.

Billy retold his story, bored from repeating it so many times.

"Did you ever run near the sewage pond?" Mike Bell asked.

"No, I told you, I went from their house to mine by the trail."

"You're lying," Mike Bell said firmly.

His changed tone of voice startled Billy.

"What?" Billy said.

"You're not telling the truth. You're lying about your route, you lied about touching the bodies, you lied about everything."

It was the first time all day that the officers had confronted Billy like this. They had believed his story all along, concurred with his innocence. They had said his story was sound.

"I don't know what you're talking about," Billy said, unsure of this latest turn of events.

"*You* killed Kristy," Mike Bell said, standing up. "*You* killed Sherry." His voice intensified. "You killed them and now you're lying."

Billy was dumbfounded.

"We know you killed them. We have proof. You killed Kristy and Sherry."

"I didn't do it."

As they mounted their surprise attack, the men watched Billy closely for signs of breaking. Startle the boy, overwhelm him, make him feel ashamed, hopeless, a liar, and see how quickly he breaks down. Now was the time to strike for a confession. The charade was over.

"No." Billy shook his head. "I didn't kill them. I didn't do anything."

"Billy," Mike Bell said, "knock it off, damn it. We know you're lying. You lied about how you found them. You lied about the blood on your pants. You lied about being in the house just once. You've been lying all day, and it's making me sick."

Billy and his father sat in shock. Billy shook his head no and murmured faint objections. Ed Keenan looked at the officers with puzzlement.

"What's going on?" the father demanded. "What's going on?" The officers ignored Ed and intensified their verbal assault.

"You killed those girls," Bell continued, pointing his finger at the boy, crowding his space, raising his voice another notch. "You killed those girls. We know you killed those girls."

Billy shook his head no.

"You went there to the Janson house. You found a knife. You killed Kristy. You stabbed her over and over. You murdered her. Isn't that right, Billy?"

"No," Billy said. "No."

"Then you chased Sherry down and murdered her on the trail. You caught her and stabbed her until she hit the ground. And then you stabbed her some more. Then you went back and stabbed Kristy some more. It's all over, Billy. It's all over."

Billy sat silent.

"You're a liar and you're a killer, and you didn't fool us for a minute. You told the lady in the ambulance which girl was killed first. How did you know?"

"What lady?" Billy looked up at the men, searching for pity, looking for a sign that this was all a joke.

"You knew who died first because you did it. Damn it, Billy, just admit it. We've got the proof. You lied and now you're caught. It's over, boy. Admit it."

Billy lowered his shoulders, his body deflated of air.

"I need to talk to my dad," he whispered.

Al Bell looked over to see if Mike Bell agreed. Bell nodded.

"Sure," Al Bell said.

The two officers walked from the room and shut the door behind them, leaving Billy and his father alone.

Grandpa Keenan shouted down the hallway, "What's going on?"

Bell and Bell didn't respond.

The officers stationed themselves directly outside the thin bedroom door, fearing Billy would attempt an escape, with or without his father's approval.

The father and son began talking. Bell and Bell looked at each other incredulously as they listened. The door was so thin the men were able to overhear most of the conversation.

"Now tell me, Billy, did you kill those girls?" Ed said, questioning his son's innocence perhaps for the first time of the day.

The two policemen moved closer to the door. They could not hear Billy's response clearly, only his muffled voice.

Then the policemen heard Ed Keenan speak again, this time more softly.

"Oh, no," the father cried. His words carried the weight of his horror and shock, and though the police officers had not heard Billy's answer, the father's response echoed the message clearly.

"Why did you do it?" Ed asked after a moment of loaded silence.

Again the police officers could hear only a muffled response from Billy.

Then they heard a shuffle in the room.

Was Billy escaping? They couldn't break in. Not yet. Not when they had a chance of overhearing a killer confess. Not when they were this close.

"Now you stay here with me, Billy," they heard the father say. The shuffling stopped.

Billy spoke again, and again the men couldn't make out his words, only his sobs. They heard Ed Keenan say to his boy, "No, no, they won't kill you."

Then there was only silence.

The two officers could wait no longer. They burst through the bedroom door, hustled past the father, grabbed Billy, and slapped him with handcuffs.

Billy was too startled to object, and by the time Ed thought to protest the officers were hustling Billy down the hallway, past the grandparents, and toward the front door.

But Phyllis blocked their exit.

"What are you doing?" she cried. "Where are you taking my baby? I won't let you take my baby. Not my baby! My baby!"

Ed tried to calm his wife. "It's okay, honey, I'll explain later. Let the men leave. Let them take Billy."

"No," she cried. "You can't take my baby!"

Bell tightly held on to Billy's arm.

"Let them go," Ed commanded.

Mike moved Phyllis back.

"My baby, don't take my baby!"

Grandpa Keenan turned to his wife. "Get the gun," Mike Bell heard him say. "They're not taking Billy. Get the gun!"

The lawmen quickened their pace and moved for the front door.

"Let's go! Let's go! Let's go!" Bell shouted to Harrington and Reichman waiting outside. Harrington fired up the car.

Phyllis continued her wailing. "Bring back my baby!"

Grandma Keenan disappeared.

A shootout? Lord no, Mike Bell thought as he ran the distance from the porch to the car.

"Let's get out of here!" Al Bell shouted.

Bell and Bell pushed Billy into the back seat of the waiting sedan. They watched behind for Grandpa Keenan and a rifle.

Harrington floored the car and the men sped into the night. As they tore off for Durango, they looked back at the Keenan house but never saw Grandpa Keenan or a gun.

Instead, they saw Phyllis standing on the front porch, weeping and shouting Billy's name.

Twenty minutes earlier she had pleaded for the lawmen to leave her family alone. Now she begged them to return with her baby boy. She screamed into the night until the lawmen could hear her no more.

The ride back was silent. At the jail, Billy was given a set of prison greens to wear. The jail had no holding cell for juveniles, and the young suspect was placed near the control station in a cell reserved for women prisoners.

The on-duty guard watched Billy through the bars. The boy sat on his cot, emotionless, sometimes pacing, sometimes lying down. He didn't look like a killer. Just a boy, a very unaffected boy.

Deputy Vic England was left with the formality of filling in the booking sheet. He answered the questionnaire with printed letters.

Name: William Peter Keenan
Date of Birth: 7 May 69
Age: 13
Height: Five feet, six inches
Weight: 122 pounds
Place of Birth: Los Angeles, Calif.
Marks, scars, physical oddities: None
Clothing: Worn Wrangler jean coat, tan and brown
    belt, brown boots, T-shirt, blue Levis
Time of Report: 4/26/83, 0235 hours
Bond: None

England slid the completed sheet to the young man. With a slight backward slant, Billy Keenan certified with his signature that the report was correct.

On another line, with a second signature, Billy

agreed not to hold the "sheriff or jailer responsible for clothing, money, or other valuables."

Billy didn't have much to worry about. In the space alloted for itemization of other property, England penned a single entry: "black comb."

The booking form allowed three lines for the officer to record charges against the arrested party. On the advice of Vic Reichman, England left the top two lines blank and filled in just the third line. He looked at the boy-man sitting before him and with a slight hesitancy, neatly printed out the charge: "One Count Juvenile Delinquency."

PART 2

A Question of Innocence

To Kristy,
A good friend
even when
she makes weird faces

—Billy's inscription in Kristy's last yearbook

7

The morning-after press conference in Sheriff Al
Brown's office began approximately at 9:00 A.M. The
small room could not accommodate the herd of reporters, and many were forced to listen from the hallway.

Reporters from the Denver newspapers and television stations and correspondents from the national news
organizations, still harried from the early-bird flight into
town, trickled in while the press conference was in session. One local radio station carried the press conference live, including seven minutes of dead air as Sheriff
Brown waited before reading his prepared text.

The sheriff's desk was crowded with microphones and
tape recorders. Temporary lighting tripods obscured the
view of many, and people tripped over power cords.
The air was stale and the cacophony of voices bounced
off the cinder block walls.

The room quieted when Brown cleared his throat. He
adjusted his eyeglasses and began reading.

"My heart goes out in sympathy to the parents of
Sherry Janson, eight years old, and Kristy Janson, thirteen years old, who attended school in the Bayfield
school district and who were murdered yesterday between one-thirty P.M. and three-thirty P.M. in their home
approximately fifteen miles east of Durango. We have
a thirteen-year-old male juvenile in custody. We will be
seeking homicide complaints against the juvenile from
the district attorney's office."

Brown told the members of the media that the deaths appeared to have been the result of stab wounds. He described the scene as "real bad," and said it "was quite apparent the murder weapon was a knife."

Brown said the boy was being held "based on the physical evidence" and that the boy had been "in our presence, not necessarily in custody, but in our presence, since around three-thirty or three forty-five yesterday."

"Is he the only suspect?" a reporter asked.

"He is the only suspect at this time," Brown said.

"What's his name?" a reporter asked.

"Because he is a juvenile, I can't release his name at this time, but we will be seeking homicide complaints against him."

"Were the girls stabbed repeatedly, mutilated?"

"I can't say."

"Was there evidence of sexual molestation?"

"None whatsoever, none from outside appearances."

"What was the boy's motive?"

"I can't say."

"Did you find the murder weapon?"

"All I can say is that we have enough physical evidence to feel confident in holding the juvenile, and officers are on the scene combing the area for more evidence."

After several more questions, Vic Reichman stepped before the microphones. His rapid diction prompted several reporters to throw up their hands in surrender as they scrambled to take notes. Reichman took it upon himself to explain the arcane machinations of the Children's Code.

"We will be filing a petition with the juvenile court alleging that a person is a delinquent child. That is the allegation against him. We then have to explain to the court what the underlying reason is for that allegation, what makes him a delinquent. We then turn to the adult criminal code, find the crime that the district attorney believes is the appropriate one, and allege that as the delinquent act.

"The whole idea is to treat the children differently," Reichman continued after a brief pause. "The whole idea created by the legislature is to protect the best interest of the child. The notion of punishment, by and large, is not what's intended."

Reichman did not answer questions about possible sentencing, saying only the issue was "under review."

The reporters grumbled at the lack of information, especially Brown's refusal to divulge the boy's name.

But the media were given a reprieve.

Shortly after the news conference broke up, as if it were the second act in an unfolding play, Billy Keenan, flanked by two deputies, was led into the courtroom upstairs. The suspect was bound by handcuffs but wore the street clothes he had changed into at his home late the previous night.

During the short hearing before District Court Judge James D. Childress, Billy stood silently and motionless, his chin to his chest in a real or contrived show of contrition. His parents sat dutifully in the first row of benches behind him.

The lone item on the agenda was a motion for postponement submitted by Billy's lawyers, Dave West and Denny Ehlers, who had been hastily summoned in the early morning hours by Ed Keenan.

The judge instructed the attorneys in the case to refrain from mentioning the boy's name. During the short proceeding, however, while the press gawked at Billy, someone unwittingly called out the name "Billy Keenan."

"Billy what?" a reporter asked a colleague nearby.

"Billy Keenan," said the second journalist, spelling out the last name as it seemed it should be spelled. Reporters scribbled the name in their notebooks. It was that easy. The mysterious identity of the boy-killer was a secret no more.

Billy's name was news to all except Barry Smith, city

editor of the *Durango Herald*. Ed Keenan worked at the *Herald*, and the news had already spread among staffers that Billy was the suspect. The slip only confirmed what Smith had already known.

From that point on, the hearing was strikingly brief. The defense was granted the postponement until later that afternoon. Billy was led away back to the women's cell. His parents huddled with their lawyers. And the reporters were left to decide if they should print the boy's name.

Smith looked at his watch. It was just after 10:30 A.M. Deadline was two hours away.

Smith raced back to the office and held a brief meeting with the *Herald* management. They called their attorney, Russell Yates, the only attorney in town specializing in libel and media affairs.

Yates also had as clients the town's two major radio stations. He had been busy all morning discussing options with them. The stations had the same dilemma as the *Herald* but without the limitations of a deadline. Programming could be interrupted at any moment with the news of the suspect's name. It would make for great breaking news coverage, but the cost of a lawsuit could tumble the stations, already on fragile financial ground. The stations decided to wait and see what the *Herald* would do. Once the name was published—however fresh the ink—it was then public knowledge, and the stations were freed from litigation.

Like most states, Colorado had laws designed to protect the identity of juveniles. The Colorado legislature, however, was in the midst of liberalizing its stance on this issue and had recently repealed a key provision that had made it a misdemeanor to disclose a juvenile's name or place of residence, or reproduce a juvenile's picture. Other statutes on the books prohibited disclosure but made no mention of criminal penalties. Lawmakers had failed to draft new legislation in the time between the legislative repeal and Billy's arrest. As it stood, the law was precariously obscure and the high courts had yet to clarify the issue. Yates advised his clients accordingly.

The *Durango Herald* took its chances, and when the paper hit the stands at 2:30 P.M., Billy's name, the names of his parents, and the Keenans' address were stated plainly in the front-page story, which ran under a 72-point banner headline that read: BOY, 13, HELD FOR KILLING TWO GIRLS.

The story was accompanied by recent yearbook pictures of Kristy and Sherry and a photograph of the Janson driveway, the closest the press would ever get to the scene.

The Denver television stations led their news broadcasts with the story, complete with Billy's name. The *Denver Post* and *Rocky Mountain News* followed suit the next day, as did many major dailies. Billy was a brief star, and his debut turned the spotlight once again onto a system that had little clue of how to handle kids who kill.

Even though many neighbors had gotten wind of the slayings the night before, the majority were finding out this morning via radio or friends. The school board had decided to hold classes, since many students would be coming to school not knowing the circumstances. "School's probably the safest place as any," High School Principal Jon Miller told reporters.

Miller described the mood at the Bayfield elementary and middle schools as solemn. "I tell you, it's really quiet here today," Miller said. "I think everybody's in a state of shock . . . I don't think people believed this could happen in Bayfield. They're saying what happened last night is one of the reasons why they moved out here. They moved here to get away from that sort of thing . . ."

When it became obvious teachers were having difficulty conducting classes, school officials decided to hold an impromptu mid-morning assembly for the two schools involved.

"It is true," Principal Miller told the teachers and

students huddled at the assembly. "Kristy and Sherry Janson were murdered yesterday afternoon."

The children listened quietly to Miller, as if he were announcing the assassination of the President of the United States. He told the children that they should pray for Kristy and Sherry and their parents.

He made no mention of Billy.

The younger children held hands or slung arms around each other's shoulders as they sat cross-legged on the floor in front. Teachers dabbed their eyes. From the sea of murmurs, the name of Billy surfaced again and again.

A state patrolman was asked to address the children to provide assurance. "We have a suspect in custody and there is nothing to worry about," the patrolman said. His crisp uniform with its badges and stripes helped comfort the children and teachers alike.

During the assembly and in interviews with reporters, teachers characterized Kristy and Sherry as "bright" and "nice" students who "were always voted the most popular kids in their class."

"Sherry was vivacious," an aide said. "If you had wanted a perfect little doll, Sherry would have been it."

"Kristy was a straight-A honor student," said Jon Keirns, the last teacher to see Kristy alive. "She was just effervescent. She had everything going for her. It's a total waste of human life, a total deprivation of human potential. The only other time I cried was when my dad died." These were the type of quotes the media loved.

In Joleen Stephenson's third grade class, Sherry's desk was removed from the room before class began, as if the absence of the girl's belongings would help her young classmates forget she had existed or had been murdered.

For the little ones, Sherry's murder was sad and confusing. At their young age, Sherry, no doubt, was to be missed. But they still had trouble comprehending the finality of death.

However, for the classmates of Kristy and Billy—the small band of thirty-one thirteen-year-olds going through the traumas of puberty together—the deaths were stupefying. These teenagers knew Billy and Kristy better than anyone. Kristy and Billy had entered the class during the second grade, within months of each other. In the cubicles of the mind, the two belonged together.

Five years of sharing teachers and classes had since passed. Five years of playground monkeying and over-due school reports, church Sundays and thank-God-it's-Fridays, fleeting romances and forever friendships, budding breasts and changing voices.

Now one of their own had murdered one of their own. It was a personal tragedy, and collective guilt intermingled with the initial shock. Many in the group felt they had missed the signs, ignored the evidence, failed Kristy, and in doing so colluded with Billy.

They also felt guilty because they couldn't find much to differentiate themselves from Billy. He was a mischief maker, true. But they were just as mischievous at times. People were referring to Billy as some kind of monster. If they were like Billy, weren't they monsters, too?

And since many of them still cared for Billy, weren't they callous and unfeeling, now that all the talk was about Sherry and Kristy and their parents? No one could instantly hate Billy. Their feelings for him had evolved from years of putting up with him, teasing him, fighting with him, but ultimately accepting him.

Worst of all, the thirty-one were compelled to deal with all these feelings under the hideous glare of television cameras and parental questioning.

Denver television crews sneaked into the school building to shoot video footage of the halls where a juvenile killer walked. When school officials discovered the trespassing, they ordered all reporters off school grounds. Reporters obliged, then accosted children as they left school. ''Did you know Billy? What was he like? Did he do bizarre things? Was Kristy his girl-friend? How does it feel?''

As the children walked home on the first day, video crews preceded them, walking backward, zooming in and out. Despite directives from school authorities to ''by all means, avoid the press,'' the students reluctantly spoke and the badgering persisted.

While the schoolchildren listened to hastily prepared eulogies in the school auditorium and the media reported on the ''all-American'' victims, investigators continued sifting for evidence around the Janson home. The murder scene had lost the overwhelming sense of eeriness that pervaded the night before. The sun shined brightly, validating the consensus that the spirit of the unknown had been vanquished. Men were in control again.

Investigators from the Colorado Bureau of Investigation had arrived in the morning and had talked over the specifics of the scene with local investigators. Blood samples were shipped to the CBI lab in Montrose. The bodies of the girls were unceremoniously bagged and shipped to Albuquerque for autopsies, much to the relief of the deputies in charge of guarding them. Still more photographs were taken, and after the footprints had been analyzed sufficiently, the colored ribbon that ran alongside the path to Sherry's body was taken down. The press lurked outside the property but police let none of them onto the scene.

The pump truck was working at emptying the sludge from the sewage pond. Jim Harrington walked over. A deputy stood nearby in waders with a metal detector waiting to enter the pool. Another deputy monitored the sewage as it billowed from the hose.

When the pond finally was emptied, the deputy lowered himself in. He swept the metal detector from side to side in search of a half-buried knife. But the contraption never signaled with a beep. It sounded only when it came in contact with the aluminum ladder.

The deputy began again, slowing his sweeps, stopping at every rock and sliver of weed that shined in the sun and could possibly be a knife. Still nothing.

Again the deputy ran the detector across the bottom of the pond. Nothing again.

After several attempts, the men gave up and the pond slowly filled with sludge.

It was not the outcome Harrington had hoped for.

One hundred yards away, cleaning crews scrubbed the walls, floors, and ceilings of the Janson home. Police had talked to Joe Janson that morning, and arrangements were quickly made to bring in a professional cleaning crew. Joe had volunteered to come to the house and help with the investigation. Maybe he could spot something missing or clue investigators in to anything suspicious, unfamiliar as they were with the residence. Harrington wanted to make sure that Mr. Janson would not see bloodstains anywhere. The pain of the visit would be pain enough.

Like a film crew dismantling a set, deputies worked to remove the last vestiges of the dramatic scene. The smell of ammonia filled the air.

It was busy work, and it was late afternoon by the time Jim Harrington was able to break away to visit the Barkers. Ben and Cindy had called police earlier in the day to report a strange discovery on their property. Since the pond search came up empty, Harrington hoped this would be the break he needed.

The Barkers lived directly across the street from the Keenans. Like the other subdivision homes, the Barkers' place was large and partially hidden behind the trees.

Ben Barker greeted Harrington and led him to the side of the house, not far from the front screen door that Billy had knocked on the previous day to ask Cindy if he could "play with the boys."

Ben pointed out his find to Harrington. It was an old hunting knife plunged into the ground. Only its wooden handle protruded from the earth. Next to the knife lay a short section of lead pipe.

"Have you ever seen the knife before?" Harrington asked.

"No," said Ben. "Neither has Cindy."

"How long has it been here?"

"I don't know, but I think I would have seen it if it was here for a while," Ben said.

"And the pipe?"

"The pipe is mine. I keep it in the garage. It's a tool."

Harrington knelt down and scanned the ground looking for shoe prints. There were none.

Was this the murder weapon? The dogs hadn't followed a trail to the Barkers'. And why, after killing the girls, would Billy have run past his house to the Barkers' to plunge a knife in the ground? It made no sense at all.

After noting the positioning and placement of the six-inch blade, Harrington withdrew it from the earth with a handkerchief and zipped it into a plastic bag. Then he went inside to ask the Barkers some questions. Maybe they could tell him something about Billy.

Cindy told Harrington that she certainly was the one to ask. Besides being the Keenans' closest neighbor, she had also helped tutor Billy in math, and she was fairly friendly with Ed and Phyllis.

Cindy said she believed she was the last adult to see Billy before the attack. She explained that she had met Laura and Billy at the bus stop. She recounted the odd conversation she had had with Billy after she discovered him standing silently behind her screen door.

In the years past, Billy was constantly at her house, Cindy said. In fact, all the Keenans visited often because the Keenans didn't have a phone installed at their home when they first came to Bayfield.

In their rural area, eight households are attached to each party line. The ninth household had to start and pay for a new party line, which could cost thousands of dollars. The Keenans were that ninth house and they couldn't afford the outlay of cash needed for a new line.

So it was over to the Barkers whenever a call had to be made. And it was Ben and Cindy taking messages for the Keenans. The Keenans even had a key to the Barker home, which displeased Cindy to no end because she didn't trust Billy, she said. Three years passed before the Keenans got their own phone. The favor had become a grand imposition with no proper thanks at all. Cindy even had to ask Ben to go over and get their house key back. After that, the Keenans weren't as friendly, which was fine with Cindy.

Cindy also told Harrington that even though Billy and Laura were old enough to care for themselves, Ed and Phyllis disliked leaving the children home alone after school. Ed phoned the children each afternoon, but that didn't prevent a fair number of incidents from happening at the house, secluded as it was.

Such as the time someone shot the window out of Ed's truck, or the time some vandals used the windows of the Keenan home as target practice. Other neighborhood homes were spared similar trespasses, leading neighbors to believe that Billy was the perpetrator and doing a fine job of withholding the truth from his parents.

The neighbors' suspicions intensified during several weeks when persistent gunshots were heard early each afternoon, coming from the vicinity of the Keenan home. Billy denied being the culprit, but the gunshots stopped when Billy's father took a six-week break from work and stayed home all day. That was enough proof for neighbors.

Though Ben and Ed were friends, Ben told Harrington that Ed liked to "act macho." Ed would say things like "They're never going to get me off my mountain," or "I'd just as soon kill a trespasser as look at him."

Once, during hunting season in early November, Ben and Cindy were suddenly awakened by the sound of gunfire. The startled couple peeked through their window to see what was the commotion. They saw scores of elk and deer running across an open field. Ed and a friend were chasing the animals, shooting indiscriminately.

Of course, there was no hunting allowed in the subdivision, but there was Ed Keenan shooting up a storm. It was typical Ed, Ben told Harrington. Ed had No Trespassing signs all over his yard, yet here he was on someone else's property shooting with abandon.

Everything eventful always happened at the Keenans', Cindy recalled. But nothing perplexed the neighbors more than the mysterious case of the disappearing cats.

Many of the homes in the area kept pets, some rabbits and birds, but mostly dogs and cats. In the country, it's understood that cats tend to disappear and never return. It's their nature. But after the Keenans moved in, it seemed to several neighbors that too many cats were disappearing—even old neutered toms that had made it their business to stay well within their territories for years. Ben and Cindy were among those who had lost several cats.

One day one of the Barker cats came home with his eye nearly torn from its socket. Moments later, an excited Billy appeared at the Barkers' door and explained that the cat had just gotten into a fight with the Keenan cat. Billy had seen it, he swore. Cindy thought the wound seemed terribly severe for a cat fight.

"Are you sure there was a fight?" Cindy asked Billy later.

Billy shrugged and said, "Yes."

It didn't seem right, but Cindy had no reason to disbelieve Billy's explanation, in part because the Keenan pets were suffering similar misfortunes.

Such as the time in March, when Billy was experiencing his latest round of scholastic difficulties. He came running down to the Barker residence visibly upset. He found Ben working in the garden.

"Something got into our cats," Billy told Ben. "Something just ripped them all up, a bear or something."

The attack prompted Billy and his dad to pull out the guns and prowl the neighborhood for bears. The behavior was typical, Ben said. Ed and Billy never found a bear, of course, or came up with an explanation of how the cats got torn up or why everything always happened at their house.

It wasn't the first time the issue of the Keenan cats was the topic of conversation. One of the Keenan cats was often pregnant, at least according to Laura and Billy. But Cindy never heard of any kittens at the Keenan home, no news of births, no Laura or Billy running over with a count or description of newborn kittens all cuddly and cute.

"What happens to all the kittens?" Cindy once asked Billy.

"I don't know," he mumbled. "I guess she just loses them."

It wasn't much of an answer.

But then, Billy was not very fond of Cindy.

After Harrington left the Barkers, he met with school officials. He discovered that Billy's parents moved from California in part because of Billy's behavioral and scholastic problems.

But the move was not as rehabilitating as the family had hoped. In his first year in Bayfield, Billy failed the third grade. From the fourth through the sixth grades he placed near or in the bottom half of his class. Now, in the seventh grade, Billy was again in danger of being left back. His math scores were below failing, and his grades in other classes were poor.

Just one month earlier, right after the principal of Bayfield Middle School advised the Keenans that Billy was in danger of failing again, Harrington discovered that the boy's parents tested their son for learning disabilities or psychological impediments that could be causing his behavior.

During a series of tests and interviews, Billy told the psychologist that he found nothing at school particularly difficult, merely that he was bored and preferred to spend his time at more pleasurable activities. Billy said if it were up to him he would spend all his time raising rabbits, hunting, trapping small animals, collecting knives, or watching videos.

The psychologist agreed with Billy's self-diagnosis. In his report the psychologist wrote that Billy had no "particular weak areas either in overall intellectual function or in particular sensory or perceptual deficits." In fact, the youngster's IQ tested out fairly well. His verbal IQ was 100, and his performance IQ was 117. That gave him an overall score of 108, enough to place him "in the average to high-average intellectual range of functioning."

Instead, the psychologist suggested a cause closer to home. He wrote: "Billy is a boy with some degree of lack of self-confidence that seems to be restricted to the area of academic achievement in school . . . Possibly because of some fear of failure."

It was true that Billy excelled elsewhere. The neighbors respected his hunting and trapping skills. Each autumn, during deer or elk season, Billy and his paternal grandfather ventured into the high country in search of big game. This was the highlight of Billy's year and quite nearly all he talked about with neighbors.

Hunting, though, was not confined to a few short weeks of fall. Billy had placed small game traps throughout the subdivision and each day after school he checked the traps for rabbits and ground squirrels. When he captured one, Billy bludgeoned the animals unconscious before slitting their throats. Billy had made a belaying pin expressly for this purpose. Then, with one of his knives, Billy skinned and gutted his catch and saved the pelt.

Sometimes, he told neighbors, he let the animals go.

Unfortunately, Billy couldn't discover a way to apply this enthusiasm to his schoolwork, which prompted the psychologist to make his final suggestion: "Billy certainly seems to have a very strong adolescent identity with his father . . . this could be a very good stepping-stone into the academic area if his father would take some additional time to use his legitimacy to set up appropriate expectations.''

Ed and Phyllis followed up on the evaluator's advice by using hunting and fishing forays with Billy's grandfather as incentives for improved study habits and grades. Billy's performance improved briefly, but after the hunting excursions were over, his scores fell to failing levels once again. Regardless of how hard his parents tried, nothing seemed to get Billy motivated. Billy failed and Billy couldn't motivate himself to do better.

Maybe school just wasn't Billy's thing. Lord knows he wasn't the only boy with problems in Bayfield. He was a boy. And boys have trouble sometimes.

8

Within eight hours of Billy's arrest, Judge Childress wrestled with the first of the many dilemmas he would face in the Keenan case. The law required that a detention hearing be held within forty-eight hours of a juvenile's arrest. Should the judge wait the full two days or hold a hearing immediately?

The boy was being held in an adult jail, not a juvenile detention center, as the law required. That could be a sticky issue later, and Childress wanted no technicalities to snarl the case.

Furthermore, in the wake of the murder revelations, the community was rife with fear and uncertainty. Some feared Billy's release. Others doubted Billy's guilt and felt the murderer or murderers were loose and lurking. Waiting two days for answers could only increase the anxiety. Double homicide was uncharted territory, and Childress could not be sure how certain elements within the community would react. It was his responsibility to prevent a second tragedy.

The choice made itself clear. If the court hearing was held promptly it would serve as an appropriate show of law and order. So during the morning-after postponement hearing, Childress meant it when he told attorneys on both sides to be prepared with arguments by the afternoon, impossible as it seemed.

There was another reason to hold the hearing early. With the county crawling with reporters, Childress felt compelled to decide whether the hearings should remain open to the public and press. The statute, as in so many juvenile matters, was of little help: "The general public shall not be excluded unless it is in the best interests of the child." When was it ever not in the best interests of the child to exclude the general public? Once again the law offered precious little direction.

By mid-afternoon there were few people in La Plata County who had not heard of the events of the night before. The afternoon detention hearing, which began at 3:20, quickly became the hottest ticket in town. The media lined up first, then friends and supporters of both families, and finally the curious throngs interested in getting a peek at Billy.

They were to be disappointed, at least initially. Although Billy had appeared at the morning hearing, he was absent during the start of the afternoon hearing to "preserve his privacy," according to his attorneys. The agreement to refrain from using his name was still in effect, though many in the courtroom were reading the *Durango Herald*'s report of the boy's alleged crimes even as Judge Childress, robed in black, entered the courtroom.

Dave West and Denny Ehlers took their places at the defense table. The young lawyers looked nervous but determined. The two had reputations as among the best in the county. Their commitment to the Keenans was evident in their faces as they took the few minutes before the start of the hearing to review their strategy.

Behind them in the first row of spectators sat Ed and Phyllis Keenan. The couple sat tensely and spoke occasionally with their two new attorneys.

Assistant District Attorney Vic Reichman strode into the courtroom and took his familiar place behind the prosecutor's table. Russell Yates, the attorney for the local media, was also in attendance, and sat in the first row of benches behind Reichman.

"All rise."

"The court calls 83-JV-54," Childress said. "This

hearing is a hearing before a detention hearing. And the purpose of this hearing is to ascertain whether further proceedings will be open to the public.''

After a few technical matters, the defense opened with an objection to Yates's presence in the courtroom.

''I would submit to the court,'' Dave West told the judge, ''that this hearing does not involve competing issues of the Constitution. The basis of this hearing—at least the initial hearing—is strictly as to the best interest of the juvenile.''

Childress leaned forward and in his deliberate and measured voice spoke directly to West.

''The court *does* consider this to involve a conflict between two constitutional rights. This has gone to the United States Supreme Court in just this context, that is the competing rights . . . of the First Amendment and also the right of a juvenile to have a closed hearing . . . If I tell Mr. Yates to get out of the courtroom and take his clients with him, then certainly I am depriving them of a constitutional right.'' The judge cited several cases and, without saying it outright, overruled West's objection, at least temporarily.

The members of the press sighed in relief. They were in, and if the judge's tone was any indication, they had a good chance of hearing the entire proceeding.

Judge Childress again turned to West. ''Please call your first witness.''

''Dr. Christopher Berry.''

Berry was a forensic neuropsychologist from Durango who specialized in juvenile cases. Earlier in the morning, Berry had been contacted by West and Ehlers and asked to interview Billy to determine his emotional and psychological state. During the half-hour interview in Billy's jail cell, the attorneys prohibited Berry from asking Billy questions concerning his guilt or innocence.

''State your full name,'' West asked.

''George Christopher Berry.''

''Your occupation?''

"Psychologist."

"Have you had an opportunity to examine a juvenile that's in detention at this time?"

"Yes, I have. I talked to"— Berry stumbled over his words as he caught himself blurting out the boy's name—"for approximately a half hour."

"In examining the individual, were you able to determine whether or not a public hearing would be in his best interest health-wise?"

"Yes, I have."

"What is your conclusion?"

"I have absolutely no reservations in stating that a public hearing would be detrimental to his emotional stability at this time."

"Thank you. No further questions," West said as he returned to his seat.

Judge Childress turned to the Assistant District Attorney. "Mr. Reichman?"

Reichman rose and paced the floor before the witness stand.

"Doctor, you say that you have been with the juvenile for approximately a half an hour. Is that correct?"

"Yes."

"What occurred during that half hour?"

"We had what's normally known as a psychiatric interview. I talked to the juvenile in question, asked him questions regarding his emotional state at this time. And he responded."

"Have you conducted such interviews in the past?"

"Yes."

"In your expert professional opinion, how long . . . would you have preferred that the interview to have taken?"

"I suppose I would have preferred the interview to be possibly an hour long. However, I certainly feel that within this half hour the information that I gathered was adequate."

"Dr. Berry, would it not be a fair statement that it

would always be in the best interest of the child *not* to have a public hearing?'' Reichman asked.

''No.''

''You are aware then of situations where it would be in the child's best interests to have a public hearing?''

''Yes.''

''Under what circumstances?''

''When you can consider that the child was not in such emotional turmoil as to reinforce the seriousness of the incident, sometimes perhaps this would make an impact upon the child that would be, psychologically speaking, a benefit to the child.''

''Why do you not feel that is present in this situation?''

''I don't believe that this juvenile is stable enough to withstand that pressure and that more pressure would certainly cause some sort of psychological problems.''

''But, Doctor, you have stated that you have only spent a half an hour with this juvenile. Had you ever met him before?''

''No, sir.''

''Did you know his psychological makeup in the past then?''

''No, sir.''

''Did you interview anyone else to determine what his general psychosis had been up to this time?''

''No, sir. I think you're making an assumption that there was a psychosis before. I can't make that assumption.''

''How would you characterize his mental status?'' Reichman asked.

''Significantly emotionally disturbed.''

''He was able to communicate with you, was he not?''

''Somewhat.''

''Was he reserved?''

''I'd say withdrawn.''

''Withdrawn. That is not necessarily any form of psychosis . . . is it?''

''I didn't say it was.''

''It simply could be a reticence to speak, could it not?'' Reichman asked.

''I think in this situation, it would certainly have to be more than that because there were other indicators, emotional indicators.''

Berry moved around uneasily in the witness chair as he fended off the verbal attack, then he continued. ''I liken this situation to the dehumanizing aspect of brainwashing in the Vietnam War and what was known to have occurred with Patty Hearst. When a person is under stress such as in the jail: when the child is clothed in paper clothes, is physically uncomfortable, is not in familiar surroundings, has nobody familiar to talk to, is removed from any sort of aspect of environment which is familiar to him. And then further pressure is applied to the person, normal defenses are let down to the point that erratic behavior often occurs. That is what I see in this instance. Sometimes there can be a complete restructuring of the psyche in a situation like this, a complete change in personality.''

Reichman assumed one of his patented incredulous stares that bordered on the comic.

''Doctor, are you saying you have ascertained that from this half-an-hour interview?''

''Yes, sir.''

''Please continue.''

''I was pretty well finished.''

''Are you aware,'' Reichman asked, ''that we do not have an official juvenile detention facility in La Plata County?''

Berry nodded his head yes.

''You're also aware we do not have one within forty miles?''

''Yes, sir.''

''Are you not telling the court, then, that every single juvenile brought into this system in this jurisdiction will be in that stressful situation, and each and every lawyer who comes before this court would be able to say exactly the same thing?''

"No," Berry responded.

"Why not? Where is the distinction?"

"You're talking about the stress created by the situation. I'm talking about this particular individual's ability to handle that stress. That could be different for all juveniles."

"What signs of inability have you seen?" Reichman asked as he moved back to the prosecutor's table.

"The child appears to be extremely dependent. Obviously when a person is dependent, they feel insecure. I have seen these things in that child. There are gross motor tremors. Shaking, constant shaking. The child showed uncontrolled crying at the mention of his family.

"The child was in a fetal-like defensive position. This is commonly found in animals when they're scared and have no recourse of action, they curl up in a fetal position to escape from being hurt. This is a psychological mechanism also. This was apparent in that child. The child appears immature for his age, unable to deal with things that even another child of his own age would be able to deal with."

Berry paused for a moment. Except for the sound of reporters' pens scratching paper, the courtroom was hushed.

"I suppose," Berry continued, "I left out, perhaps, the most important part. The child made it very clear both in words and gestures that he was frightened to death of the proceedings—"

"Doctor," Reichman interrupted, "isn't that a common fear that anyone would have of the unknown?"

"I suppose most people are frightened of the unknown, yes."

"Are you saying as long as a person says, 'I don't know what's happening to me, I'm scared of what's going to happen,' that means they shouldn't be brought into the courtroom and subjected to that experience?"

"I'm not saying that," Berry replied.

"We are talking about a child of juvenile age. Most

children that age are by their own chronology dependent to a great extent, are they not?''

"Not to that extent, no. This is an extreme case."

"You have also picked up on this in just a half hour?"

"Yes, sir, Mr. Reichman. The child, within a five-minute period, made seven to ten references to his family. And their particular protection to him is what I see as uncommon in this type of case. A person should be able to deal with other issues."

"So in layman's terms, then, a child of this age that is dependent upon his parents is not acting appropriately?"

"That's right."

"You spoke of a fetal-like position. Are you telling the court he remained in that position for thirty minutes?"

"Yes, sir."

"Well, Doctor, if you have a child, you block out thirty minutes on a clock, he's lying in a fetal position—no sarcasm meant at all—it's difficult to speak to someone in such a position. I mean, it's uncommon?"

"This child was sitting in a fetal-like position," Berry said, stressing the word *sitting* in response to Reichman's wisecrack.

"If you might illustrate," Reichman asked.

Berry wrapped his arms around his knees and hunched his shoulders as best he could within the constraints of the witness box.

"Forgive me, Doctor. Again, just talking as a layman, but what I saw you doing was a person who doesn't want to look somebody in the eye."

"I would assume," Berry answered, "that there was some fear in looking me in the eye, but I particularly stressed the rounded shoulders. When a person draws their head in and moves their shoulders up around their head and neck, it's a natural defense to keep from being physically beaten. The stress is so much that it's similar to and perceived in his mind as a physical beating."

"In terms of the physical setting," Reichman asked.

"If you only had two choices—that child could be in this courtroom, or down in that cell—which would be more reassuring to him?"

"I assume he has been in the cell and feels more comfortable there," Berry replied.

"Having not experienced the courtroom?"

"Well, out of familiarity, yes."

"Wouldn't you agree, though, once brought up here: you can see outside, you can see the general public, the citizenry moving around. The sunshine would not be uncomfortable surroundings, would it, once he recognized where he was and what type of surroundings?"

"You're speaking of outer environmental-type influences. I would think that other psychological—inner psychological—influences would certainly overweigh those."

Reichman sensed he wasn't getting anywhere and changed his tack once more. "All right, Doctor . . . you have said you have seen throughout this interview a dependency towards his parents?"

"Correct."

"Wouldn't you agree that that is long-term in nature—has existed in the child for a long period of time?"

"I would assume, yes."

"That's not going to change no matter when we bring this child during the process into a courtroom, is it?"

"I would think that the newness of the experience would make that dependency more heightened."

"The other factors you spoke of, they would also diminish; for example, the fetal position. If the child felt more acclimated to the surrounding, he would not round the shoulders, would not fear the assault. True?"

"I would assume," Berry concurred, "that as the child becomes more familiar with the situation and gets over some of the initial reaction to the proceedings and so forth, that after time, if he were allowed to speak with his family and were put back in whatever more familiar surroundings that are possible in this situation, that the effect of that pressure could be subsided. I cannot predict that, but I would probably suspect that would occur.''

"You were a total stranger when you walked into the cell of this child, and yet he was able to converse with you, true?''

"In a very limited fashion," Berry answered. "His sentences were no more than four to five words at a time, and often he would break down crying after that.''

"One final matter, Doctor. Your choice: to have the parents in the courtroom or not?''

"Right now, he's very frightened of dealing with his father because he's afraid he has let him down. Actually having his father in the courtroom might make it more frightening for him. Ideally the child would have some time to spend with his family before any type of proceeding.''

Reichman returned to his chair and sat down. "Thank you, Doctor. I have no further questions, Your Honor.''

The judge turned to the defense table.

"Mr. West?''

"No redirect, Your Honor.''

"Dr. Berry, you may step down. Thank you.''

West rose and began his pacing before the bench.

"Your Honor, I would submit to the court that it is not a balancing test that we have to be confronted with here today. I would submit to the court that the statute, the way it is written, is a balancing test whether it's in the best interest of the child and not in the best interest of the child. We're not here weighing anything else. We submit to the court that the evidence is overwhelming and would not be in the child's best interest.''

The judge turned to the prosecutor. "Mr. Reichman?''

"Your Honor, I think Mr. West is correct but only up to a point. I think Dr. Berry has been candid with the court, and I think both parties can be well served. I would suggest . . . to delay the proceedings, allow the doctor to continue his observations and report back to the court to determine if at that point a public hearing could be held.''

"Thank you, Mr. Reichman," the judge said. "Mr. Yates, any comments?''

The attorney for the media rose and began with a scholarly discourse on the competing interests of the First Amendment right of access and the Sixth Amendment right of a fair trial.

Then Yates did something rarely seen. He argued against the interests of his own clients.

"We're not talking about the right of the child to a fair trial because of publicity, we're talking about the rights of the child to his emotional health. I don't know what the answer is, but as an officer of the court, I think I have to make arguments which are not always in my clients' best interest. In this case, I think there may be a difference that the court ought to really look to very seriously: the interest of the health of the child versus the fair trial.''

Yates sat down.

Judge Childress cleared his throat. "There is a child in the jail, and accordingly, the court must act either to release the child today, right now, or to order him held or moved to a better facility. I will ask you, Mr. Reichman, if a petition is going to be filed in this case?''

"It's contemplated, Your Honor, but we have not completed our investigation.''

The judge shuffled papers on his high bench. He chose one and held it up slightly for the attorneys to see. "I have before me a letter from Mr. Steve Now, the juvenile intake officer, indicating that the juvenile is suspected of—''

Dave West sprang to his feet and launched his hand into the air. "May it please the court," West said as he rounded his table and approached the bench. "I think that we would certainly like to have the court rule on the question of whether or not this is going to be an open proceeding. And certainly if we start talking about the allegations, I think the juvenile has a right to be here.''

"Mr. West," Judge Childress replied quickly, "I'm going to disagree with you in this regard. The court recognizes the fact that this juvenile is in no shape to come to court. Not only is he in no shape to come to court before an audience, the press, but he's not in any shape according to your witness to even confront his own father.''

"Well," West said, "we would like our objection noted for the record as a continuing one as to any statement made by the juvenile officer.''

"All right, thank you. The court at this time will enter the findings that the proceedings will continue to be public and that the defense has not proven that it is in the best interests of the child to exclude the public.''

West returned to his table, barely able to camouflage his astonishment at the judge's back-door ruling. "Could I just have a moment please. Can I have a five-minute recess, please, Judge?''

"Yes, you may. Court's in recess," Childress said with a pound of the gavel.

The crowd erupted in a burst of chatter.

West and Ehlers turned around and huddled with Mr. and Mrs. Keenan, speaking feverishly. Despite the convincing testimony from Dr. Berry, Childress had ruled against them. The public would stay.

When court would reconvene, the judge would rule on Billy's detainment and his bond. The Keenans hoped desperately for a bond that would allow them to free their son. Would the judge rule against them again? The defense attorneys decided their best chance for leniency was to have the boy present, to show the judge that he wasn't a wild and crazy delinquent, just a scared young boy.

When court returned to session, West approached the bench and told Judge Childress that he wanted a few minutes to bring Billy to the courtroom. Reichman had no objections.

Word got out that Billy was being escorted through the long public corridors outside the courtroom. Many in the crowd left their seats and scurried out to catch a glimpse of the accused as he walked through the hallway. They joined scores of people who hadn't been lucky enough to get a seat and now waited anxiously outside the courtroom.

Captain Boyd was in charge of escorting Billy through the flash of cameras and the crush of human curiosity. Billy had caused no problems in jail the night before, and the captain was worried not so much about Billy attempting an escape as about reprisals against the boy.

The memory of finding the girls just twenty-four hours earlier was still vivid in Boyd's mind. He shuddered to think he had made the mistake of leaving Billy unattended in his patrol Jeep with a loaded shotgun as he set out to discover the bodies.

Now Billy, with hands cuffed in front of him, floated through the crowds without acknowledging a soul. Billy was composed, oblivious to the proceedings surrounding him. Was it steel nerves or paralyzing fear? Boyd wasn't sure.

Boyd fell into line in front of the boy and forged a path through the crowds. The onlookers opened up a path to let Billy through, falling silent as he passed. His starry-eyed composure caught many spectators waiting for a monster off guard.

Then, with the stares of the entire room fixed upon him, Billy entered the courtroom and took a seat between his attorneys. He wore a red sleeved T-shirt and blue jeans. West smiled at Billy and tried to make him feel comfortable. The boy looked back briefly at his father, then turned and sat quietly.

After the delay, Reichman called Undersheriff Mike Bell to the stand. Bell had gotten little sleep since the night before. Yet he had little trouble explaining how investigators were led to believe Billy was the suspect and the implications of the evidence against him, particularly the bloodstains on his clothing and the footprints outside.

"What was the significance of the location of the footprints to you and to members of your department?" Reichman asked.

"Well, the primary significance was that Billy Keenan told us that he had gone to the house of the victims to return her dog. That he discovered the first victim deceased in the kitchen of the residence, ran outside and started to run and almost literally ran across the second victim laying in the scrub brush outside the residence and then continued on home. A single trip to the house and back and no other diversions, if you will. The physical evidence was to the contrary."

"Please explain why."

"The footprints indicated that, along with other evidence, the suspect had returned again to the house and very likely washed his hands in the sink. There were what appeared to be bloodstains and hair in the kitchen sink."

"Now as to the second deceased person . . . was there physical evidence to indicate what happened?"

"Physical evidence indicates that she was drug a short distance and then killed. The evidence would indicate that she was deceased almost as she hit the ground because there was no further movement once she was on the ground."

"Now, sir, you have talked about these footprints, which you say appear to be identical to shoes worn by Mr. Keenan. Where are they in relation to the prints or marks left by deceased person number two?"

"Her footprints and the footprints of Mr. Keenan appear to run parallel from the deck area where the sliding glass door is, directly out to the point where she was found deceased."

"Was the second victim visible from the residence?"

"No," Bell said. Reichman hoped this response would make it apparent to the judge that Billy did not simply discover Sherry's body, but chased her from the porch until he caught up with her and killed her some one hundred yards away.

"No further questions," Reichman said.

West's cross-examination was perfunctory. The defense hadn't had time to investigate the case, nor had the two attorneys had access to investigator reports, few as they were this early in the case. This was simply a detention hearing. There was no use damaging their client by stumbling upon incriminating facts that could harm arguments later.

The final witness called by Reichman was Steve Now, the juvenile intake officer for the county.

"Mr. Now," Reichman began, "the Rules of Juvenile Procedure specify that a person such as yourself can render an opinion as to whether or not release of the child into the community would be detrimental to his welfare or whether his being retained would be necessary for the protection of the community. Do you have an opinion?"

"Yes, I do. I feel that there is a real and present danger to the community if the child is released, that there would be other violent acts that could be committed upon the community. If the child were released, I believe that Billy would be in definite jeopardy by certain elements of this community or other communities that might want to do him harm."

"No further questions," Reichman said.

"Mr. West?" asked the judge.

West approached the witness stand.

"Steve, are you aware of any possible motive?"

"I asked that question myself, and I have never received an adequate answer."

"And who attempted to answer that? Who did you ask that question of?"

"Representatives of the law enforcement community."

"Thank you."

It was getting near 5:00 when Judge Childress asked

Bayfield was supposed to be a sanctuary for both of these families—a haven from the pressures and dangers of modern urban life. (Photo by author.)

Sherry Janson's last school picture. (Photo courtesy of the family.)

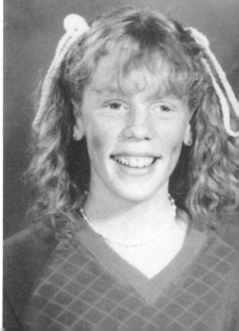

Kristy's school photo clearly shows the girl's zest for life. (Photo courtesy of the family.)

Sherry, Kristy, and their
constant companion, Tubby.
(Photo courtesy of
the family.)

Sherry and her butterfly
net, taken the day before
the murder.
(Photo courtesy of
the family.)

The Janson family at home six months before the girls were murdered. (Photo courtesy of the family.)

"Hill Hollow Ranch," the Jansons' secluded home on ten acres in the mountains of southwest Colorado. (Photo by author.)

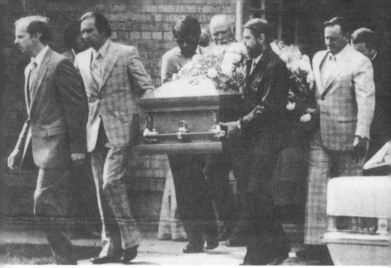

Despite a ban on photographers, a reporter snapped a shot of the two adult-sized coffins leaving the church. (Photo courtesy of · *The Durango Herald*.)

Vickie Janson with Joe behind her as the couple leaves the funeral service to bury their children. (Photo courtesy of *The Durango Herald*.)

Kristy and Sherry's final act of sharing—a plot in a cemetery overlooking Durango. (Photo by author.)

Kristy and Sherry Janson. (Photo courtesy of the family.)

for final arguments regarding detention. Dave West took a moment, then began.

"Briefly, Your Honor, the District Attorney, by his own statement, says that he does not know what charges will be brought. I would submit that the evidence that is being presented is circumstantial at best, questions of there being no motive, being no weapon that could be positively identified. The fact that footprints are found at your nearest neighbor's home would not be unreasonable whatsoever. We submit to the court that there is really no showing of Billy's involvement at all in this; quite to the contrary, his denial. And we would submit to the court that if you should determine that a bond be set, we ask that it be in the amount of ten thousand dollars."

Again the judge refused to respond specifically to West's request. Instead the judge said, "Well, the court at this time will continue the case to the sixth of May at nine forty-five A.M."

West looked at Ehlers in alarm. Did this mean no bond? West looked at his calender. "May it please the court," West began his plea, "today is the twenty-sixth and we would ask the court that we set it for the twenty-ninth. I don't see what problems they would have with getting the petition before the court in two days."

Then the judge dropped the second bombshell on the defense. "The reason I chose that date," Judge Childress replied, "is because the court intends to have Mr. Keenan transported forthwith to Pueblo to the juvenile facilities there. And we could do it so that he's transported today or tomorrow and then brought back Thursday night or Friday morning. But I thought that it made more sense to do that over a ten-day span than over a three-day span."

The juvenile facility at Pueblo was a six-hour drive away through the mountains. West couldn't have his client so far and prepare a case at the same time. And what of the boy's mental health? He would suffer tremendously from such isolation. West believed in his client's innocence and would not allow such an injustice to occur without a fight.

"Judge, first off, we would object to the juvenile being transferred to Pueblo. That certainly puts him out of our ability to have access and to do many things that we need to do in order to prepare him, assuming that a petition was filed."

At this point, Reichman interrupted. "For the record, Your Honor, the People would also like to note their objection to the transfer of the juvenile to Pueblo. I do not wish to find ourselves in a situation where the court has placed Mr. West in a posture of arguing effective assistance of counsel and I think that may very well be likely. I would join in his request that detention be had in La Plata County and in the jail."

West continued his objection. "Judge, I have a couple of other things for the record, if I may. First of all, to note our objection to the juvenile being held without bond, we'd ask that bond be set in the matter."

"The court finds that it is necessary," Childress declared, "to protect the community from further serious bodily harm. And furthermore, that it is necessary also to protect the accused juvenile from imminent bodily harm. Now the court does at this time refuse to set any bond."

West again rose in objection. "Judge, we would ask that any—I don't mean to interrupt if you're not done, but I do mean to interrupt if you're finished. If transportation to Pueblo is what the court is ordering, we would ask that that be delayed to tomorrow morning so that we could recall Chris Berry to what effect that would have on the juvenile, away from his attorneys, away from his parents. We think that would be extremely more effect—"

Childress cut off West in mid-sentence. "Your request is denied, and the Sheriff is ordered to transport Billy forthwith to Pueblo."

Phyllis Keenan began to understand what was happening. Her baby was going to be taken away again.

She edged up on her chair and began shaking her head in denial, whispering no, no, no, over and over again. Those in the courtroom were equally in shock. Few had expected the judge to release Billy, but nearly everyone, including Reichman, was surprised by the judge's demand that Billy be transported 250 miles away at this very instant.

"Judge," Reichman said, "I would advise the court that it is now after the hour of five o'clock. Unless there is a prior notice, they will not accept a juvenile."

Ed Keenan comforted his wife, who was growing ever more emotional. He put his arm around her shoulder as if to hold her back.

"I don't want to be unreasonable," Childress said, "and certainly I don't intend to deprive him of counsel, but counsel can see him in the nearest youth facility and this is not an uncommon problem. Children are transported from the Western Slope regularly to the Eastern Slope. Of course, they can talk to their counsel between now and the time that the Sheriff leaves for Pueblo, whenever that shall be, but I would like the Sheriff to transport the juvenile as soon as possible."

"Judge," West entreated one last time, "we would request that such transportation at least be delayed two hours after the conclusion of this hearing so that the parents can have an opportunity to see their son, which they haven't had."

"I have no objection, none whatsoever," Childress said.

West grappled for time. He made some final technical motions, all of which were denied by the judge. Childress struck his gavel and closed the hearing. The defense had lost every battle of the day.

Phyllis was crying openly now, nearly shouting at the judge as he rose to leave the courtroom. Billy turned and looked at his mother, silently imploring her to stop. The crowd once again burst into an uproar with a smattering of applause.

Billy was whisked through the hallway to the jail. He

was joined there by his parents for a brief and tearful meeting. Mrs. Keenan embraced her boy and wept. Deputies watched as Mr. Keenan gave the boy assurances that this was only temporary.

As it turned out, Billy was not transported that night. The youth detention facility in Pueblo would not accept the boy until the following day. The suspect spent a second night in the women's cell in the La Plata County jail dressed in a paper gown that hung on him like a clown suit.

At six the next morning, he was awakened, fed, and handcuffed once again. Then with two officers escorting him, Billy Keenan slid into the back seat of a patrol car heading east for the long, silent journey through the midst-shrouded mountains to a world a million miles away.

9

The second day after the murders passed much like the first day for Vickie Janson. Relatives crowded around her but she barely recognized them. They wrapped her in blankets when they thought she was cold and unbuttoned her blouse when she felt warm. If Vickie indicated even the slightest desire for food, they offered her trays of snacks and soft drinks. But she ate without tasting and her thirst could not be quenched.

The sleeping pills helped lessen the shaking, though Vickie knew that nothing short of unconsciousness would ease the pain. Yet even when she slept she never rested, and invariably she awoke to a nightmare greater than she could ever dream. She felt as if each minute compounded the agony and no clock could measure the passage of time.

The reverend spoke of God but his words took no form. Only Joe offered the slightest solace. Vickie had lost the will to live and endured only at the insistence of her loved ones.

For Joe, the pain was just as excruciating. He had always been his daughters' great protector. His gentle strength had made the world safe for Kristy and Sherry to explore, but Daddy hadn't been there to protect them at the end. It maddened Joe so that he felt his heart pounding inside him. His fists clenched and released unconsciously, and his nostrils flared when the thought of the girls' last moments entered his thoughts. Even

121

though he was now some twenty miles from his home, Joe gazed out the window as if sheer desire could transport him across the miles and return him through time to protect his children one final time.

His anguish was eclipsed, however, by two more powerful emotions. The first was concern for Vickie. It was obvious she was on the edge of breaking down. Had Vickie not been with him or, God forbid, had she perished also, Joe could never have summoned the courage to maintain his fortitude. But as long as Vickie's agony would last, that was how long Joe knew his strength must endure.

The second emotion was anger, a fierce, consuming, unremitting anger. There existed someone, some monster out there who had killed his girls, and nothing would prevent Joe from finding the killer if the police didn't. Joe possessed the cunning. He had the weapons. And the Lord knew the motivation was there. Over and over again, Joe replayed in his mind the satisfying scenarios of revenge: Joe training his rifle on the killer and firing away, unloading clip after clip in an intoxicating rush of exploding gunpowder. Or Joe strangling the killer with his bare hands, squeezing so hard he could feel the bones snapping. Either way, any way, it would be a relentless and redeeming act with no thought of penalty. The deed was worth any price.

Joe's pledge of vengeance was tempered by the Reverend Jerry Boles and other friends from the Presbyterian church.

"Come on, hit me, Joe," the reverend said. "Hit me if it will make you feel better."

It wouldn't, of course, and even in his pain Joe thought the request rather silly. But the pleas and rational arguments of friends and family convinced him that, at least for the moment, it was best to leave things to the authorities. Only for the moment, though, and should that moment pass, Joe would quietly prepare.

In the meantime, it was Joe's idea to contact investigators and offer his assistance. Did they need him to identify anyone? Reveal if anything was missing from his home? Mike Bell accepted, surprised by Joe's courageous offer coming so soon after the murders.

On late Tuesday afternoon—at the same time that Billy sat quietly in court listening to the allegations against him—Bob Shanks drove Joe along the back gravel roads toward his home.

The episode was brief, three minutes at most. The house was cold despite the beatings of the warm April sun. The smell of ammonia lingered.

The father walked through the hallway past the family photographs tacked on the wall and up the stairs to the bedrooms where the girls had slept. Kristy's bed was made. Sherry's bed was a mess. Just as they had left them.

Joe walked back downstairs to the living room where the girls had played. The furniture was in place. His collection of antique and replica guns was still hanging on the walls. The father walked into the kitchen where his older daughter's body had lain just hours before. There was no room for emotion.

Shanks pointed to a silverware drawer left open. "See anything missing in here?"

"Yes," Joe said. There was. A knife was missing, a Forgener-brand knife that Joe had recently purchased, special order. It was a large butcher knife, perhaps fourteen inches long, with a contoured black plastic handle. The knife's green sheath lay empty in the drawer.

Joe's swallow was audible.

"Anything else missing?"

Joe pained to look. Nothing else. But as he turned to leave he spotted a hatchet mounted on the living room wall near the fireplace. He walked closer to it. There was something odd about it.

Then he noticed its blade was covered with a thin layer of dried blood. Joe pointed out his discovery. Police had missed it.

The men looked at each other. Would the killer have been so perverse as to remove the hatchet from its mount, use it to kill two little girls, then neatly remount it? It seemed unlikely, but the murders were bizarre enough so that anything was possible.

Joe was hustled out of the house and into the waiting car. It had been a long three minutes.

As they drove, the father stared out the car window at the mountains and hills that looked so foreign now. He remembered when he and Vickie first saw this country, how enraptured they had been. He remembered asking Vickie and the girls if they wanted to move to Colorado. The girls were so excited. Yes, they said. Oh, yes.

Joe and Vickie had watched their children bloom here. Now the hills were gray and brown and inhospitable. Joe wasn't sure if he and Vickie could ever find the courage to reclaim this land.

The car turned into the driveway of the Shankses' home. A police guard waved them through.

Inside, Undersheriff Bell waited. Bell pulled Joe off to a corner.

"Joe," he said. "Joe, I have to tell you something." At first, Bell wasn't sure if he should tell Joe about Billy. But he was convinced by Joe's composure and his willingness to help with the investigation. Anyway, it wouldn't be long before Joe found out. Better he hear it from the police.

Bell minced no words. "We have a suspect. We think it was Billy. Billy Keenan, the boy next door."

Joe looked at Bell in utter disbelief.

Billy. How could it be? Joe had seen Billy's father the day of the murders. He had hugged the man, for God's sake. Billy's mother had comforted Vickie. They were neighbors. Billy had found the girls and called for help. The boy was screwy but never this. Not Billy.

Then again, it did make sense. Joe had seen firsthand Billy's fascination with knives. Joe remembered his distaste when Billy talked about the gory movies he liked. Joe had mopped up more than once after Billy's pranks.

Before yesterday, Joe would have never thought of Billy as possessing the capacity to kill. Today, strangely, Joe found himself not surprised that Billy was the only suspect. And he felt a twinge of remorse for not suspecting Billy earlier, when it counted.

Bell pulled from his briefcase a knife, the knife found on the Barker property.

"Have you ever seen this knife before, Joe? Does it belong to you?"

Joe handled the small knife, then handed it back to Bell.

"I've never seen it before. It's not ours."

Bell hesitated, then pulled out a Polaroid photo of a bowling club found near the sewage pond.

"Do you know anything about this?"

Joe looked at the photo under the light. "What is it?"

"It's a club of some sort. We found it floating in the sewage pond near your house."

"Never seen it." Joe didn't ask why he was being shown a photo of a club when his children had been stabbed. Bell didn't offer an explanation. He thanked Joe and left.

Joe found Vickie where he had left her, on the couch staring into space and time, oblivious to the chatter of brothers, sisters, mothers, and fathers.

"Everything is okay," Joe whispered to Vickie as he pressed her hands in his. "Everything is okay."

Joe didn't tell his wife right away that Billy was in custody. She wouldn't have comprehended. It wouldn't have mattered.

Sometime later in the week Vickie learned about Billy. It didn't surprise her; it just added to the pain. She thought of Phyllis and Ed, whom she liked. She thought of clumsy Billy in her kitchen, laughing with the girls. She thought of the four children trumpeting through the woods in whatever fantasy game they were playing that day. She thought of Billy the boy.

She prayed for him. She prayed for Ed and Phyllis and Laura, too. Vickie prayed for all the children.

Vickie might have been the last person in Bayfield to learn of Billy's complicity, but not everyone believed he was the culprit. Many who knew Billy from 4-H, school, or the neighborhood would not accept that he could possibly be guilty. They *knew* him, for God's sake. Billy was one of theirs and Bayfield did not produce killers.

Within twenty-four hours of the first press conference, the sheriff's office began receiving anonymous phone calls demanding Billy's release and blaming the force for not finding the real killers. Officers on the streets were derided as incompetent. ''If you can't do it yourself, damn it, get somebody in here who can.'' Other disbelievers contacted the Keenans and expressed condolences at their having to suffer from the sheriff's ineptitude. Why must two families suffer? Wasn't the Jansons' suffering enough? A defense fund was set up for the Keenans. The boy's two attorneys took the case largely based on a firm belief in Billy's innocence.

Billy quickly became the major topic of conversation in every bar, restaurant, and meeting place in Bayfield and Durango. He was described as an angel by some, as the devil by others. The rumors were rampant: His family had been forced to leave Southern California because he had done the same thing there. He mutilated animals. His father beat him. He was into devil worship. Billy's arrest was a setup by police because one of their own did it.

There were so many rumors that the *Herald* ran an article under the headline NEIGHBORS WANT END TO RUMORS. The article said that friends and neighbors of the tragedy-stricken Janson and Keenan families were upset by the number of rumors, half-truths and falsehoods being spread. ''Peggy and Roy Jenkins, speaking for friends who live in the area . . . appealed to local residents to use discretion when discussing the incident. 'People should stick to the facts,' Mrs. Jenkins said. 'The rumors are not necessary and they are not doing any good at this time.' ''

The lack of evidence as the days passed bolstered the arguments of those who believed that the police simply had screwed up. There were rumors that two transients with blood on their clothing had been seen the night of the murders in Pagosa Springs, forty miles to the east, and that the sheriff's office failed to follow up on the lead. And why couldn't police find a weapon? And how about a motive? As the days passed, the grumbling grew louder and the police were viewed with ever-mounting suspicion.

The ranks of those who reserved judgment dwindled as the community divided into two camps: those who saw Billy as victim and those who saw Billy as killer.

The first letter to the editor appeared within a week of the murders:

Having grown up in the Bayfield area, and having relatives living there, I have a vested interest in the tragedy of the Janson murders. I was absolutely shocked that two beautiful little girls were senselessly murdered and the police had arrested Billy Keenan for the killings.

But most of all, I was completely incensed when I read that Al Brown is confident that the right person is in custody. How can he be that confident? Does his conscience justify not even looking for further evidence? . . .

This whole thing sounds like a lynching mob to me. I understand that it indeed looks bad for Billy Keenan, but on the other hand there are a lot of positive aspects that speak very loudly and clearly for Billy. It seems within the realm of possibility that someone could have planned the murders to happen at the exact right time and then disappear. Murders are planned and executed every

minute of every day in the United States, sometimes for reasons only God knows.

I think about what I would've done if I had, at
the age of 13, found my friends murdered. I probably would have knelt down beside them and gotten blood on my pants. I might have even picked
them up and held them close to me for a minute.
I certainly would not have cold bloodedly washed
my hands in the sink and then automatically
turned on the hysterics . . .

Don't let this become a lynching mob . . . I hope
when this is all over Mr. Brown and all concerned
can rest their consciences in peace that every
possible angle was explored.

Within days, a response was printed in the same section by a Bayfielder:

You have accused Sheriff Al Brown of not having enough evidence to say he's confident that
he has the right person in custody. Where did you
get your information and evidence against the
sheriff to make your statements? How do you
know that he doesn't have any further evidence?

I don't remember reading how sheriff deputies
arrived at the scene of the murder, grabbed Billy
Keenan because he had blood on his clothing,
called Sheriff Al Brown and the case was closed.

How can the sheriff give every bit of information
on any evidence he has to the public? He has to
be careful and is responsible for every word he
gives on this case or any other case. And anytime
a minor is involved we are talking a whole new
set of rules . . . As bad as I feel myself for the
Keenan family, Billy Keenan is not the victim in
this tragedy.

Meanwhile, by order of Judge Childress, investigators and prosecutors remained silent about the slim case

they were preparing. "No comment" was repeated a thousand times by everyone involved. Despite the doubt registered by skeptics, Sheriff Brown was happy to abide by the judge's decision. He didn't have much to report, and since little hard evidence was surfacing, "No comment" suited his purposes just fine.

Investigators didn't tell the press that they had learned that Billy had a history of uncontrolled temper tantrums, and that on the day of the murders he had been told in school that he was in danger of failing again. They didn't let on that preliminary reports confirmed that Billy had had serious trouble in California. They also refrained from disclosing the discovery of the pipe and the knife plunged in the earth near the Barker home.

And when the preliminary autopsies arrived from Albuquerque, police didn't reveal the details to anyone.

They didn't talk to the press about the knife wounds, more numerous and far more malicious than originally believed. They didn't say that Kristy's face and throat had been slashed repeatedly and that she had been stabbed in the abdomen many times. They didn't mention that the assailant had attempted to gouge out Sherry's eyes and had stabbed her in the back and shoulder again and again. Police remained mum about the wicked brutality evident from the start and now documented with glaring objectivity in the autopsies. The murderer didn't just kill the girls, he used his knife to play with their bodies like a child plays with food.

The biggest secret revealed by the autopsies, however, was that in addition to being stabbed, the girls had been bludgeoned repeatedly. Kristy was hit from behind by a blow so severe that it shattered her skull and damaged her brain. She was beaten again on the head and face.

Sherry was also hit from behind with a terribly vicious blow and hit again repeatedly on the body and legs. Boyd and the others had apparently overlooked the contusions because of the severity of the knife wounds.

The discovery of the bludgeoning explained another mystery: the lack of blood surrounding the victims' bodies. If the police theory was correct, the girls were killed not by the knife wounds but by the blows to the head. There was no major loss of blood because the girls' hearts had ceased pumping by the time they were stabbed.

This theory brought a twinge of solace to the investigators. If it was true, at least the girls had been dead when the worst damage was done. It was entirely possible that Kristy, who had been cutting cheese at a kitchen counter, never saw or heard the intruder. He might have sneaked in and hit her before she turned around. There were no signs whatsoever of a struggle, nor signs of an attempt to flee on Kristy's part.

For little Sherry the scenario was different. The footprints indicated that she had been running on the trail with the intruder apparently chasing her. At the least, she'd had to endure the terror of the chase. Whether the first blow to her head knocked her unconscious was unknown. Based on the small amount of blood surrounding her body, it appeared she was dead before the cutting began.

The revelation that a blunt instrument was involved had sent Harrington and Boyd back to the murder site to recover the handmade bowling pin that was seen floating on the sewage pond the night of the murders. The pin was dense and heavy and could easily have been the bludgeoning instrument.

Harrington was sure it was the weapon.

Boyd marked, tagged, and wrapped the pin carefully before sending it to the Colorado Bureau of Investigation for prints.

But still there was no knife.

The hunting knife found at the Barkers' house did not provide any fingerprints or bloodstains. Police believed it had been discovered too far from the murder scene to be taken seriously as the murder weapon. If Billy was indeed the killer, why would he have run with a bloody knife to the Barker home, plunged it into the ground there, then run home to call his father? It made no sense.

But Billy had visited the Barkers' that day, literally minutes before the girls were killed, or perhaps right afterward. He had asked to play with Cindy's boys, but Cindy had shooed him away. Cindy was Billy's math tutor and he had been told that day that he was failing math.

It was entirely possible that Billy set out that day to kill Cindy and her sons and not the Janson girls. Were the Barkers the primary targets and the Jansons the unfortunate victims of circumstance? The Barkers considered it a certainty. Police thought it a possibility. If so, was Billy planning other murders that day?

The knife on the Barker property posed intriguing questions, but investigators had more pressing worries. They had a murder to solve.

Even though the bowling pin was now suspect, investigators didn't think to drain the pond a second time until six days later, eight full days after the murder.

Deputy Dave Allmon had been in charge of draining the pond the first time. During the week following the failed attempt, Allmon couldn't shake the feeling that the weapon was in the pond and, despite a valiant effort the first time, they simply had missed it. He asked Jim Harrington to let him have another go at it. Harrington agreed.

On May 3, Allmon and several others returned to the Janson home with an aluminum ladder, a pump truck, a pair of hip waders, and a metal detector.

The pond smelled as putrid as it had the first day. Allmon fired up the pump truck and sucked out the muck until there was just four or five inches of smelly sludge at the bottom. Then Allmon laid the ladder across the pond and crawled out onto the ladder, lowering the metal detector down into the emptied lagoon. Again it beeped only when it came near the aluminum ladder.

Nothing. Allmon then put on the hip waders and slunk down into the muck to push the pump's hose farther down.

An hour passed. It wasn't looking good. The pond was nearly empty and no knife.

But then, as Allmon turned to adjust the hose once more, he saw a black plastic handle protruding from the mud about a foot below the original water line. The handle was grimy and half hidden by dead weeds.

Allmon asked for a camera. He took pictures of the object undisturbed. Then, with the entourage looking from above, Allmon began withdrawing the object from its earthen sheath.

He pulled slowly, revealing a flash of blade. He pulled some more, revealing still more blade. He pulled slowly until he unsheathed all fourteen inches of a butcher knife with a black contoured handle. It was an ominous-looking blade, pointy at the tip and fat at the base. Allmon looked at the brand marking. It was a Forgener. It matched exactly the description of the butcher knife that Joe had told police was missing.

If Allmon was right, this was the knife that had eluded them all these days.

Allmon had failed to find the knife the first day because he had expected to find it settled on the bottom of the pond. He had looked past it, and every time he had brought the metal detector near it, the detector's alarm sounded due to the proximity of the ladder.

Allmon prepared the knife tansport to Montrose. He doubted it would yield fingerprints since it had been submerged in a sewage lagoon for over a week. Nevertheless, another mystery seemed solved. All the pieces were beginning to fit together. Harrington would be happy.

As he prepared to leave, Allmon looked back over the rise to the house. He visualized all too clearly the bodies as he remembered them from the first day. Like many of the other officers who went on "the tour," he was having terrible nightmares in which the images of the girls appeared more real, more disfigured than they had that first afternoon. The images followed him in his dreams, causing him several times to wake in a sweat.

Allmon packed up the truck and headed for home. For the second time in a week, he washed off the grime and the stink of the sewage pond. He took a long, hot shower, but the cleansing did little to rid him of the awful vision.

10

For reasons long forgotten, road crews bypassed the town of Bayfield when they laid down U.S. Highway 160, the modest artery that cuts through Colorado just above the New Mexico border. To passing motorists the town appears little more than a glorified truck stop, and few motorists make the effort to wind down the business route that leads to the tree-covered depression cradling the small downtown.

There's little reason to stop. Except for a few stores, schools, and churches, Bayfield is merely an adjunct to Durango. With its sparse population of just less than nine hundred souls, it's an odd mix of old-fashioned farm town and bedroom community for those who commute to Durango. In appearance, at least, Bayfield resembles any of the thousands of small hamlets that dot the sprawling mountains and plains of America's West.

To most Coloradans, however, even the little city of Durango is considered "out there." La Plata County is accessible only via two of the most rugged passes in Colorado. When the winter snows descend in mid-season fury, it's not uncommon for the southwest corner of the state to remain inaccessible by automobile for a day or more.

For most Bayfielders, that's just fine. They are an independent lot, skeptical of big-city people and ideas.

Even Durango, with its college professors and liberal city council members, is viewed with some skepticism.

Bayfield is also Christian territory, one of the last outposts of the Baptist Bible Belt that gives way to Utah's Mormon country. The area is largely populated with folk who believe in the Word and hard work, and who disapprove of anyone or any life-style that doesn't.

The town's three-block-long main drag, Mill Street, is a wide and bucolic thoroughfare that ends almost as soon as it begins. Many of the storefronts are vacant or boarded up with plywood. A few four-wheel-drive pickup trucks and several large, dusty American cars with fifteen-inch tires are usually the only cars in town. It takes just one quick glance to understand that Bayfield's downtown is drying up.

Bayfield's enterprising grocer saw the demise coming, and in the late 1970s, he vacated his old storefront on Mill Street and built a shiny corrugated-metal-and-concrete structure near the highway within easy view of the travelers speeding between Denver and Los Angeles.

Once other retailers saw the grocer's success, they let their in-town leases expire and also built new shops by the highway. If the highway wouldn't come to Bayfield, Bayfield would come to the highway. It didn't take long for the Pine River Bank to move. And once the town bank moves, the soul of the town moves.

Several old-timers grumbled that the businesses should remain in ''historic'' downtown Bayfield, that the town was losing character. But no one dared pass an ordinance. You can't stop a man from making a living.

Behind the new shops by the highway, new houses sprang up, all cut from the same square pattern. This was the new Bayfield.

Yet despite its modest success, the heart of the community remained outside the city limits, spread out among the ranches that stretched east toward the national forest and south along the lush Pine River all the way to Ignacio and the Southern Ute Indian reservation. Bayfield was built on grain and horses and pinto beans and all else that was tied to the land. This was its heart and soul.

It was on one of these ranches on the Wednesday or Thursday after the Janson murders that four or five men gathered quietly. No one formally arranged the meeting, but each knew why they gathered.

They talked of the seasons and the horses, of the wives and children, of the local politicians and their follies. They shared cigarettes and chews of tobacco. Then the talk turned to the true reason for the assembly.

It was Billy.

It was Billy and the unforgivable deed he had done. It was Billy and the punishment he deserved. If the courts had their way, the boy would get nothing more than a slap on the wrist. He'd be out by the time he was eighteen. The Jansons would suffer a lifetime.

The men reasoned that a thirteen-year-old boy knew right from wrong. He wasn't a child. The boy needed to be punished like a man. If the lawyers and politicians in Denver didn't have the guts to do it, there was no choice. They would have to.

There was more reason. He had to be done away with for the safety of the town. It wasn't a matter of mercy or justice. It was a matter of life or death. A man has the right to protect his family. No judge or jury can take it away. It's God given. Billy was a wild dog, and you can't let a wild dog run free.

Then the talk turned to how. Rifle and scope from long distance was agreed upon. The boy would be coming back for a court hearing sometime. You just got to position yourself right and take good aim.

It was clean. One shot. No prosecutor could assemble a jury of twelve men and women from the county to convict you. Besides, police wouldn't pursue it too hard.

Word was sent to Joe Janson that these deputies of the unwritten law were on his side and prepared to do what was necessary. It was up to Joe. He just had to say the word.

Though he was tempted, Joe never said the word. And the men never met again. But when the conspirators saw each other in the feed store or the bank, they discussed the matter in murmured tones, hiding behind their mustaches and cowboy hats.

Soon a new pact emerged, agreed upon as informally as the first. If Billy Keenan ever set foot in La Plata County a free man, he was a dead man. It was that simple and it was forever.

For Joe, even with his anger, such talk was all too soon. He had yet to bury his children, and his waking hours were a confusing mix of the hardships of reality and the mysteries of the eternal. Talk of what should be done with the dogs was intermingled with tales of angels and the face of heaven. Questions about which cemetery the girls should be buried in were followed by speculation over the destination of their souls. Did they suffer at the end? Are they with Jesus? Why did Billy do it? Would he suffer eternal damnation?

As the days passed, the mood at the Shanks home shifted from shock to grief. The house was crowded with a cushion of humanity for Joe and Vickie.

Sympathy was abundant. Local grocers donated hams, cases of soda pop, sandwiches, salads, paper plates, and plastic silverware. Baskets of fruits and cakes came from neighbors. Calls were intercepted from concerned citizens across the nation who had heard the story on national newscasts. Hundreds of letters of condolences arrived from around the state and country.

A letter came from Senator Gary Hart expressing "sincere condolences on the death of your daughters." Governor Richard Lamm wrote: "For whatever it is worth, I will bring this matter to the Legislature next January and we will see if we can't make the punishment better fit the crime." U.S. Congressman Ray Kogovsek arranged to fly a flag at half-staff atop the Capitol

Building in Washington, D.C., on the day of the funeral. The flag was later presented to the Jansons.

Even the White House sent a personally signed message of condolence:

Dear Mr. and Mrs. Janson:

Nancy and I send our heartfelt sympathy on the tragic deaths of your daughters. I join all who condemn such senseless acts of violence.

While words are inadequate in the face of your great loss, as parents we share a measure of your sorrow.

May God give you peace and strength. With our deepest condolences.

Sincerely,
Ronald Reagan

The days passed and the letters kept arriving and finally it was time to lower the bodies into the ground. April was giving way to May, and each day of the week dawned warmer and more beautiful than the previous. It was weather like this that made locals forget the long winter and return to calling the land "God's country."

Friday was the most spectacular day of them all, with a sweet morning breeze and skies as blue as turquoise.

Joe and Vickie's families had made all the funeral arrangements. They were happy to have plans to work on, anything to focus their energies. Everything was to be done in Durango. Services at the cemetery were to be for the family only. The church services would be opened to everyone since the public had to mourn, too.

Durango's only funeral parlor offered its services for free. The local floral shop chipped in with sprays of pink roses and white carnations to top the coffins and to decorate the church and graves. Scores of flower arrangements arrived from strangers.

The funeral service was held at the First Presbyterian

Church, the tallest structure on Durango's prestigious Third Avenue, a grand boulevard of towering oak and maple trees and large Victorian houses set back from the road. The oldest churches in town were here. The First Presbyterian was one of the more stately churches, with a towering belfry, stained-glass windows, and a long and tall sanctuary, which created a holy-sounding echo that served the pastor well during sermons.

Shortly after ten in the morning, yellow buses from the Bayfield schools began unloading children in front of the church. The school district had suspended classes for the funeral and hundreds of students from first-graders to seniors dressed in their Sunday best to attend services. The townspeople came in droves. Some Durango businesspeople shut their stores on Main Avenue, two blocks away, and walked the short distance to the church. In keeping with the pioneering spirit of the land, neighbors temporarily set aside personal animosities to confront with solidarity the face of tragedy. Acquaintances from the outlying areas drove in, and Durango had a veritable traffic jam on its hands. Officers tried to move traffic but to no avail. Third Avenue was a stagnant river of cars. Other officers were posted as sentries on the lookout for network cameras.

The media, of course, showed up in full force, and police had contingency plans devised should things get out of hand. Joe had requested no pictures whatsoever and police intended on enforcing that request. Even members of the local media who wished to attend services as private citizens were barred.

Throughout the day, only one photographer, from the *Durango Herald,* succeeded in slipping through the police barricades. He hid behind a tree a good distance from the church and with a high-powered lens snapped a shot of the coffins being carried out and another of the grieving family. The townsfolk cried foul when they saw the pictures splashed on the front page of the afternoon edition, but few copies were left unsold by day's end.

The crowds that couldn't fit in the sanctuary were seated in the church's recreation hall and listened to the sermon on loudspeakers. Latecomers could get no farther than the church foyer and soon even that space filled, spilling crowds onto the sidewalk outside.

Joe and Vickie were escorted through a side door to a pew in the front near their daughters' caskets. Joe wore a black tie and jacket and Vickie wore a black dress and a leopardskin coat.

Earlier in the morning, Vickie had been given her dose of pills just as she was ready to prepare herself for the funeral. The pills knocked her out and her mother and a friend were left with the task of attiring Vickie as she lay groggily on the bed. As if they were dressing a rag doll, they held up her arms to slip on her dress, fitted her shoes, and applied dabs of blush, hoping the color would bring Vickie back to life.

In church, mourners strained to get a view of the grieving parents. But Joe and Vickie were well insulated by the relatives surrounding them. The two huddled together and spoke quietly as they awaited the final good-bye. Sunlight streamed in through the stained-glass windows. Mourners, still in the habit of dressing warmly for winter, stripped off layers of clothing and fanned themselves with whatever they could find. Their chatter echoed in the rafters high above.

When the woeful organ stopped, the crowd grew quiet. The Reverend Boles ascended to the altar to pray. He cleared his throat and looked solemnly onto the throngs of mourners before him.

"We gather today," he began, "to honor two lives and pay our respects. To give thanks for the love that was given and the love that has been shared and to give thanks for that eternal quality of love which remains, the lives of Kristy and Sherry. And let us seek now God's comfort for us as we read from the book of Psalms . . ."

In the audience sat Rick Salano, one of Kristy and Billy's teachers, listening more to his internal conflict than to the preacher's words. Like many of the teachers, Salano harbored a sense of guilt for not picking up the signs that Billy surely must have flashed, if indeed he was the killer.

Salano recalled two incidents concerning Billy that he could consider out of the ordinary at all. The first was minor. It happened sometime during the beginning of the school year. Class was in session. Billy got mad about something, really mad. He turned blood red and stood up, the whole class looking at him. Then, with all his might, he threw a rubber eraser across the room and hit the windows on the other side. Nothing broke and the act itself was harmless, but Salano and the class were startled by Billy's sheer fury. When Billy realized what he had done, he sat back down, a little embarrassed, as if the outbreak was not his conscious doing but an aberration that surfaced through a channel even Billy was not aware of.

The second incident was more striking. Billy was in trouble again, for what Salano couldn't remember, and Salano had escorted him to the assistant principal's office. As usual, Mr. Winter chewed out Billy. This time, however, he also threatened to call Billy's father to come and take his boy home.

When Billy heard that, he began pleading. "No, don't call my father. Please don't call my father." Billy grew animated and begged with such drama that Salano thought it almost degrading. "I'll be good, I promise, if you don't call my father. Please. Please."

Mr. Winter put the call through. And when Billy heard that his father was on his way, he tucked into a fetal position on the chair and began sobbing and rocking gently. Billy stayed like that until his father arrived.

Salano thought that the boy's overreaction was odd, but when you teach the seventh grade you see a lot of odd behavior, and at the time Salano passed off the behavior as yet another unexplainable vagary of puberty.

Now, as Salano listened to the words of God, he felt

guilty for missing something. Had he been too busy to see the problem? Would a more experienced teacher have gathered the clues? Was he an unwitting conspirator in the death of Kristy and her little sister?

The minister continued. "Would that I could now wipe away the tears and remove the sorrow of these moments, remove the loss and the pain that we all feel at this time. That I could answer all the questions and cause all those answers to make it all make sense. But I cannot. It is at times like these that every minister and every Christian is painfully aware that we are human and there is that which we cannot explain or satisfy for ourselves, much less for others."

Standing on the side of the crowd in a crisp uniform, Nick Boyd looked out over the sea of mourners. He also had thoughts on his mind. He raced through the vision of the slain girls and of Billy and his sister watching from the parked Jeep in the Janson driveway. Finally, his mind settled on his first daughter, and the painful memory of her funeral after she died mysteriously in her crib. It was for Nick the most crushing moment of his life, and though he and his wife were blessed with a second daughter, the haunting specter of their first child lingered.

The officer turned his attention again to the pulpit. "A reading from Paul's letter to the Romans," the minister continued. " 'I consider that the sufferings of this present time are not worth comparing to the glory that shall be revealed in us. For all of God's creation eagerly awaits the moment of the revealing of the children of God. For the creation has been subjected to meaninglessness not by its own choosing. But in that moment and in that time, all of God's creation, sons and daughters from his own hand will be set free from their bondage to decay to obtain glorious liberties as children of God.' "

In the church recreation hall, listening to the minister's words over the cheap loudspeaker, sat the friends and schoolmates of Kristy, Sherry, and Billy. The younger children mostly looked around and fidgeted, understanding that it was important to remain quiet and respectful. The older children asked each other questions, recalled Kristy and Billy, and spoke of the mystery of it all. They couldn't make much sense of it.

The minister continued. "Our focus at the time of these events is most important. For we are all filled with questions. Too often the questions cause us to find meaning in the meaningless, to make sense out of the senselessness of these events. Questions of why and how and what are questions that newspapers, and news media, and legal systems are led to ask. And we, because of human nature, ask as well. But we must look beyond such, for they can only lead us to senseless answers and to a meaningless life of tragedy, and that none of us can live with."

As soon as the minister finished his talk, the organist hastily began playing, as if the mourners couldn't bear a breath of silence. The music signaled the pallbearers to approach the pulpit. They lifted the adult-size coffins and began the long journey down the aisle to the waiting hearses. The arrangements of roses and carnations tottered on top of the large caskets.

Joe was escorted down the aisle clutching Vickie, followed by Joe's mother and Vickie's mother and father and eight of her nine brothers and sisters.

Joe didn't notice him right away, but in the back of the church, among the many mourners, Ed Keenan stood with his head bowed as the procession passed.

Joe wouldn't see Ed until later, when Joe was in the limousine on the short drive through town on the route to the cemetery. Joe spotted Ed among the hundreds of well-wishers who lined Main Avenue with their hands over their hearts.

As soon as he saw Ed, Joe ordered the limousine driver to stop. Joe rolled down the window. He motioned to Ed to come nearer. Ed did.

Joe leaned out the window slightly and whispered.

"I forgive him, Ed. We forgive him."

Their eyes met for only a brief moment. Ed said nothing.

Joe rolled up the window and the procession continued.

As if they were viewing a presidential motorcade, the citizens strained to look inside the mysterious limousine for an ever-so-brief glimpse. The procession continued through town and made a right onto Ninth Avenue and up the winding road to Kristy and Sherry's final resting place.

Durango's Greemount Cemetery is located on a gentle rolling mesa on the western edge of town overlooking the city. It is the resting place of the founding fathers and mothers of the county. The grave markers tell of pioneers, soldiers, and families who died during wars, calamities, and terrible winters. There are many children buried there.

Throughout the older sections of the cemetery, old leaning piñon trees shade the tombstones. But at the extreme south end of the cemetery, two holes had been prepared for the county's latest departed. The plots had been purchased by Vickie's parents, who bought four plots in all. The middle two plots were to be used today for Kristy and Sherry. Joe and Vickie would one day occupy the outer two.

Clouds rolled in from the south as the procession proceeded slowly to the site. Winds whipped the piñon trees in marked contrast to the gorgeous, still weather of the morning. The sky darkened quickly with shifting shades of gray. As Joe and Vickie stepped from the limousine, they were greeted by a sharp gust of wind.

Only twenty or thirty people were present for the short graveside ceremony. Among these were Assistant D.A. Vic Reichman and Undersheriff Mike Bell, attending out of respect as much as to safeguard the proceedings.

The group huddled in a big square around the two coffins ready to be lowered. The preacher said his words.

Then, just as the coffins were being lowered into the ground, the skies turned ominously dark and a bluster of wind stormed into the cemetery, spraying cold rain on the mourners. It was an eerie, stinging rain, like little spikes. It was unrelenting.

Only after the bodies had been lowered and the families hurried to the shelter of the waiting limousines did the rain retreat. The skies remained the color of ash for the remainder of the afternoon.

And like the rain, the participants scattered.

Joe and Vickie returned to the Shanks home, where they would stay for the next month. Ed Keenan went home to his wife and daughter. Reichman and Bell returned to their offices to prepare their case against the thirteen-year-old suspect. The children of Bayfield boarded the buses for the solemn trip home.

La Plata County went back to business as usual that Friday afternoon. Yet most people realized that life would never be the same. They understood that they could never again tell their relatives living in the cities that "it couldn't happen here." They knew the funeral that day had been a rite of passage into a new era, even if Billy hadn't yet been proven guilty. The girls were dead and the time had arrived to lock your doors at night and investigate your children's doings. It would be an era of mistrust and apprehension.

The people were sad because they had always feared this happening. They had moved away from Southern California, Denver and Dallas to distance themselves from crime and murder. Now the big cities had stalked them and found them and it would never be the same.

They also were sad for the Jansons and Keenans because of the tribulations ahead for each, so different yet each so cruel. The Jansons were left to deal with the utter finality of death, the Keenans to face the endless torture of guilt. People wondered which was worse, to have your children killed or to raise a killer. No one knew. No one wanted to find out.

What they did know was that the lives of everyone

in this little paradise had changed forever. And that the two small graves at the south end of the cemetery would serve as perpetual witness to this terrible loss of innocence.

11

Billy didn't do it. He was innocent, he swore it, and this was all a bad dream. And why was he locked up here in a juvenile detention facility so far from home? And what had he done wrong? And when could he go home? Please, when could he go home? He pleaded with his lawyers. It was all a big mistake and just get him out of here.

The detention center, on the grounds of the state hospital in the aging steel town of Pueblo, was no place for a thirteen-year-old adolescent from the outlands. It smelled of too many bodies and echoed with catcalls. It was populated with big black teenage drug pushers from Denver's housing projects, car thieves from Colorado Springs, and Hispanic junkies from Pueblo with gold teeth and homemade tattoos on their hands, arms, or faces. Billy's cellmates included petty thieves, rapists, burglars, muggers, and prostitutes, all under the age of eighteen. Some were serving their fifth or sixth detention, others were children whom the courts had labeled "unmanageable," and still others were kids whom society had deposited there because there was no place else for them. This was the holding tank for the state's abandoned, unwanted, and criminal juveniles, and each had a story that had led him or her to this frightful place.

To the staff, Billy seemed like an all-American golden boy. The lanky kid in T-shirt and sneakers with a puzzled look frozen onto his innocent face seemed so lost here that it was hard for many to believe Billy could be guilty. Whenever he spoke with anyone in a position of authority, he swore up and down he didn't do it, there was some mix-up, and please get him out of here.

While Billy waited desperately for a reprieve, his mother waited for justice. According to friends, she didn't for a moment believe her baby could do such a thing, regardless of the evidence the police were amassing. Her son was the victim of a grave injustice and she knew better than anyone. She was his mother.

Phyllis had always been protective of her son and now she pleaded for his release.

Dave West and Denny Ehlers pursued the case with enthusiasm. They believed in Billy's innocence. They visited with him in the corridors and meeting rooms of the detention center. They listened to his pleading and they were convinced. It seemed impossible that he could have done it. If this wasn't a confused, scared kid, then it was the best acting job the attorneys had ever seen.

Billy's denial wasn't the only thing that convinced the attorneys. West and Ehlers felt that the evidence against their client was circumstantial at best and that the methods used during the investigation had been equally suspect.

On the night of the murders, police had misled Billy and his father into thinking the boy was being interviewed as a witness, when in fact he was their prime and only suspect. That was a clear violation of the boy's civil rights. Fate had played a cruel joke on Billy, who would spend his fourteenth birthday behind bars if nothing was done.

More important, the real killer was out there somewhere and police were not attempting to find him or at least follow up other leads. Their negligence was endangering the community. In good conscience, the defense could not let such malfeasance pass unchallenged.

Their first line of defense was to hire private investigators to challenge police assertions about the evidence. Too many stories had leaked out about how police had botched up the investigation. Deputies, for instance, had trampled all over the murder scene, yet police claimed they were able to isolate Billy's footprints.

Babe, the best tracking dog in the county, had led officers on a wild-goose chase, and though Rotten had apparently picked up Billy's scent, so what? Billy admittedly had been at the Jansons' before running back home. There was nothing incriminating about a scent leading to the Keenan home.

Mike Bell had mentioned in an offhand remark that, based on preliminary examination of the girls' wounds, police were searching for a knife with a small blade, perhaps four or five inches long. But now that police had unearthed a fourteen-inch knife from the sewage pond, they assured the press that the murder weapon was in hand, even though it was ten inches longer than the knife they had hoped to discover.

Billy's inconsistencies during the interrogation on the night of the murders were easily ascribed to the shock of discovering the bodies. As for the spray of blood, well, that could be damaging, but the damage would hinge on the testimony of an expert, and experts could always be contradicted.

All in all, the attorneys felt that the investigation had been conducted with negligence and the assumption of Billy's culpability was unfounded. The case was not only winnable, but a day in court would demonstrate the follies of the police and the district attorney's office, and lead quite probably to someone's dismissal.

The defense's second line of attack was to challenge the rulings of Judge Childress. West and Ehlers were unhappy with Childress's findings and even more distressed with the summary fashion in which they appeared to have been made. The judge had denied bond, ordered the boy transported 250 miles away, and kept the court hearings open to a hostile public and press.

Not one week passed after the first hearing before West and Ehlers filed an appeal with the Colorado Supreme Court. Their client was not to be denied.

The defense's third tactic was to petition Childress once again during an upcoming advisement hearing, scheduled for May 4. Maybe the judge would reverse himself and at least set bond for their client.

In the week following the murders, investigators were also hard at work pouring over the evidence. Using phone records, statements, the coroner's reports, and other evidence, they attempted to re-create the murders minute by minute.

Sometime after visiting the Barker home, investigators speculated, Billy returned home and called his mother to say he was returning Tubby to the Jansons. Police had no reason to discount the possibility that the dog had indeed wandered down to the Keenan house. As he walked the trail between the two houses, Billy carried with him the homemade club that he often used to kill the small game he caught in his traps.

He entered the Janson house through the sliding glass door, walked through the living room and into the kitchen, where Kristy was cutting cheese. Since Kristy knew Billy, there was no need for her to fear, though it was possible that Billy surprised her.

Whether they exchanged words or argued was unknown. Regardless, at some point Kristy turned her back on Billy. Billy seized the moment and struck Kristy on back of the head with his club. The blow was severe enough to kill her instantly.

After bludgeoning Kristy, Billy reached into the knife drawer and chose the butcher knife that Joe later identified as missing. For whatever reason, he chose not to use the knife sitting on the counter near the sliced cheese. Nor did he use the hatchet that Joe had discovered with blood on it. The CBI lab determined that the blood came from an animal, apparently the residue from a deer that Joe had cut up after a hunting trip.

At this point, Billy either began stabbing Kristy or

possibly was distracted by Sherry, watching in horror from the porch behind the sliding glass door. If Sherry was watching, Billy left Kristy's side and dashed out the sliding door in pursuit.

The eight-year-old ran away from the house, away from the home of the closest neighbor and into the woods. With her butterfly net in hand, Sherry was able to elude Billy for a distance of over one hundred yards.

But Billy was too big and too fast. And in the small clearing out of sight from the house, he caught up with her and smashed her skull with his club. The force of the blow sent Sherry tumbling onto the fallen pine needles and sent her butterfly net to the ground near her. How much time passed at this juncture, police could not speculate, but presumably Sherry was dead when Billy began plunging the knife into her small body.

When satisfied, the boy returned to Kristy's body in the kitchen. It was possible that he had not stabbed Kristy earlier, but began now, after Sherry was killed.

When he finished, he washed his hands in the sink, grabbed the knife, and ran toward home. He detoured slightly to stop at the sewage pond, where he plunged the knife into the earth a foot below the water level. Then he continued on his way until he reached home.

Somewhere on his way home, however, if police speculated correctly, Billy was thrown a curve so wild that it forced him into a panic. This twist of fate quite possibly drove Billy to his fatal mistake and ended up as the police's lucky break.

By a stroke of good fortune, Captain Nick Boyd was patrolling the subdivision, oblivious to the nightmare unfolding just a few houses away.

But Billy didn't know that. Billy rarely, if ever, saw police cars on the loop. Now, though, to his utter horror, at precisely the moment he was fleeing the scene of his greatest transgression, his eyes fell upon Nick Boyd's ominous-looking patrol Jeep driving slowly along the dusty road.

What did it mean? Certainly it could not be a coincidence. Police *never* came up here. It must mean that the police knew what was going on. Somebody must have heard the screams. Somebody must have called the police.

Somebody must have seen.

The encounter panicked Billy. If investigators theorized correctly, Billy had had no intention of calling his father after killing the girls. But when he saw the patrol Jeep, and when he feared Boyd or someone else had recognized him near the Jansons', he had to do something.

He calculated quickly. Only suspects hide things. What better way to prove his innocence than to alert the authorities himself?

So Billy called his father and recounted his tale. He sobbed hysterically, pleaded for help, and acted like any child would.

The phone call to his dad, police concluded, was the beginning of a first-class con job that continued throughout the murder-night interrogations and persisted still.

Billy had killed those girls in cold blood. There was no question in the minds of the investigators. If he denied it now then he was a liar in addition to a murderer. And if his attorneys believed him then they were the latest victims of a very proficient thirteen-year-old con man.

But how did police know that Billy saw Boyd? Perhaps the boy called his father out of sheer panic once he realized what he had done. Perhaps a wave of remorse overtook him. Perhaps he wanted to confess but couldn't bring himself to readily admit the crime and the call was the first step in that direction.

Those possibilities were discounted when police listened carefully to the dispatch tape of Ed Keenan's frantic call to police.

At one point in the conversation, Ed paused very

briefly to listen to an instruction from Billy, who was holding on another line.

"All right now. All right," Ed said to Billy. Then Ed turned his attention again to the dispatcher. "There's one of your officers over there in the area," he said.

That was the incriminating line.

How could Ed Keenan, sitting in an office in Durango, know that a deputy was patrolling near his home nearly twenty miles away? Like Billy, Ed knew that police rarely made the effort to patrol the subdivision. Ed could have known only if Billy had told him so.

The significance of Billy's chance sighting of Boyd was not lost on the officers. If Billy had not panicked and called, Boyd would never have picked up Billy and his sister on his way to the murder scene. The marshal's wife would never have heard Billy intimate the sequence of the murders, leading her to suspect him. And Harrington never would have interviewed the boy in the back of the ambulance and spotted the spatters of blood. The entire chain of events that led police to suspect Billy never would have occurred.

It could have been days, conceivably, before a deputy would have been dispatched to interview Billy and his family. By then, the bloodstained shirt and jeans could easily have been washed and stored away in the teenager's chest of drawers. "No, I didn't see or hear anything," Billy might have told the officer, who would have tipped his hat and gone on his way still thinking an elusive motorcycle gang had committed the killings.

Boyd's presence in the area resulted in one final blessing. If Billy had not seen Boyd and called police, Vickie would have discovered the girls.

It would have been dark. Joe was not expected home until later. Vickie would have made the panic-stricken calls to police and Joe. She would have been forced to wait a half hour for help to arrive, all the while staring at the body of Kristy in the kitchen.

Sherry's body was lying in the woods a good distance away from the house. Until police had arrived and dogs searched the area, Joe and Vickie would have had to entertain the notion that anything could have happened to Sherry, that she had been kidnapped, molested, lost to mystery forever.

Police sincerely believed that if Boyd had not been patrolling, the killings of the Janson girls might still be a mystery.

Moreover, many officers swore that if Billy hadn't been caught, he would have committed more murders that evening in the obscure little subdivision up Wallace Gulch.

Vic Reichman was fully aware of the sequence of events the day of the slayings. He, too, spent the week following the murders preparing his strategy. Reichman had no recourse but to petition for a charge of juvenile delinquency as prescribed by law. Based on the investigation, however, he took the opportunity to elaborate.

Reichman's petition alleged one count of first-degree murder and one count of second-degree murder. The second-degree charge was for the killing of Kristy. It was entirely possible that Billy killed her in a fit of rage, which would preclude the element of premeditation, a necessary component for a charge of murder in the first degree.

In Sherry's case, however, based on the deductions of the investigators, Billy must have thought about killing her. He must have planned it, even if it were for only the few seconds he saw her at the porch door and chased her into the woods. For that brief premeditation, Reichman added the first-degree murder charge.

Reichman knew all too well, however, that the murder charges were merely polemic. Regardless of his assertions, Billy could only be charged with juvenile delinquency, a crime that carried a term of two years confinement with the possibility of two additional years. No more. The nature of the crimes had no bearing on the outcome. If found responsible, Billy would be free by his eighteenth birthday, and if he kept clear from trouble, his criminal record would remain sealed for his entire adult life. No one would have the privilege of considering his past.

On May 4, the date of the second hearing, a La Plata County sheriff's deputy took the long ride over Wolf Creek Pass and through the great basin of south-central Colorado to pick up Billy in Pueblo. From the back seat of the patrol car, the handcuffed boy quietly watched the scenery passing by him.

Billy was in appreciably better spirits for this hearing than he had been for the first. He dressed in a white-and-yellow football jersey and brown corduroy pants. His thin brown hair was combed neatly, though his limp bangs still hung slightly over his eyes. A few spectators chuckled when Billy and West stood up at the same time because Billy was taller than his attorney. As he awaited the judge's entrance, Billy smiled and waved to his parents. He acted as if it were a relief to be back in La Plata County, despite the fact that he was about to be charged with the killing of Kristy and Sherry Janson. Anything was better than Pueblo.

His parents also were in better control of their emotions. They took their usual seats directly behind the defense table and listened calmly. Whenever Billy turned to look at them, they nodded and smiled as if to say, "We're on your side. Everything is going to be okay. We love you, son."

The hearing contained none of the theatrics of the first hearing. The defense and prosecution parlayed in legal phrases, citing procedures, statutes, and case law.

Defense attorney West again motioned for bond, which again was flatly denied by Childress. West made a second motion to exclude the press and public from any further proceedings. The motion was again denied by Childress. This time West and Ehlers were not surprised.

The spectators were slightly disappointed that their long wait for seats wasn't rewarded by a better show. The only drama of the day was provided by two dozen friends of the Keenans who waited outside the courthouse hearing room to show their support. They waved as the Keenans walked by and shouted words of encouragement. The men shook Ed Keenan's hand. The women clustered around Phyllis. They told the Keenans that now was the time to buckle down and persevere until Billy was freed and this nightmare ended.

The judge concluded the hearing by setting up a date three weeks hence for a preliminary hearing. West and Reichman would have to wait until then to do battle, and the press would have to wait to learn the lurid details of the murders.

Billy waved one last time before following a deputy escort through the back door of the courtroom and down the corridor, where a patrol car waited to whisk him back to the detention facility. His guest appearance was brief and uneventful.

The scenery was the same as on the ride out, the wild curves and steep grades of Wolf Creek Pass, the monotonous plains near Alamosa, the bluffs near Walsenburg.

It was late at night before Billy was delivered back to his teenage purgatory in Pueblo, and it was early morning the next day before the deputy arrived back in Durango, weary but happy to be home.

12

Late spring arrived like a welcome relative in La Plata County. The Pine River in Bayfield and El Rio de las Animas Perdidas in Durango overflowed with the melted snows of the San Juan Mountains. For a few weeks, the water had run turbid with the soil and residue that had filled the high-country gullies during the fall and winter. Now, with June nearing, the rivers turned clear again and rushed with a fury that would last just a few weeks.

The adulation due spring, however, was tempered by the fresh memory of the slayings. The initial shock had subsided and townspeople and rural folk alike tried to settle down to life as normal. But one month after the killings, they found their anger lingering. They were angry at the police for not wrapping up the case sooner or more definitively. Angry at the media for covering the event with naked eyes. Angry at being compelled to share in the Jansons' pain. Angry at La Plata County's isolation, which provided no escape from thinking, talking, and hearing about the murders. Angry at life for its capacity to change so capriciously. And angry at Billy, not only for letting his hostility lead to such a bitter end but also for putting a black mark on the county and everyone who lived within it. They were guilty by association, and that angered people the most.

Several callers anonymously phoned the sheriff's office to threaten Billy's life, but police paid little attention. Any serious killer would never be as cavalier as to call police beforehand.

Nevertheless, security on the morning of the preliminary hearing was tight. A deputy stood guard at the hearing room entrance and passed a hand-held metal detector over the bodies of those who lined up hoping to snatch one of the few seats in the gallery. A second deputy inspected purses and briefcases. The procedures were repeated after each recess.

No cameras were allowed in the courtroom, and deputies placed sheets of paper over the windows of the rear doors of the hearing room to prevent video crews or photographers from angling their lenses into the courtroom from the hallway. More deputies were stationed at strategic points throughout the courthouse watching for anything suspicious. Many of the deputies were scheduled to testify at the hearing and would have to be relieved of duty sometime during the day. The manpower crunch was further aggravated by the absence of an officer assigned to pick up Billy from Pueblo, a duty that had become routine by now.

Even though it had been just one month, for the public it seemed like a long time had passed since that April evening when they first heard the terrifying news of the murders. Everyone welcomed the preliminary hearing. There was an unspoken need, if not for closure then at least for revelation, and today's hearing would bring to light the first new information about the killings since the morning-after news conference and the few details that had been leaked to the press in the ensuing days.

Nor was the drama of the occasion lost on the public, who jammed into the courtroom and spilled out onto the courthouse lawn. The anticipation had run high throughout the week preceding. As the crowd shuffled into the courtroom, the predominantly somber mood was offset by an odd spirit of festivity. This was an event, and custom had it that all events were to be approached festively. It was a difficult custom to break, even for an occasion as serious as this. Furthermore, the preliminary hearing meant that the regional and national press would descend once again on town. As much as the public professed disdain for the media, they were fascinated with the attention.

As with the other hearings, the Jansons were not in attendance. Several of their friends made it a point to attend each hearing, but the particulars of the proceedings were not brought back to Joe and Vickie. Nor did the parents read the newspaper accounts of the murders or the hearings. They had little use for an itemized account of the killings of their daughters. Their focus was inward and heavenward, searching for the larger meaning.

When the silver-haired judge entered the courtroom through his chamber door, the spectators silenced their chatter. The prosecutor and defense attorneys took their places in the courtroom, as did the Keenans. Phyllis Keenan sat down dutifully, clutching the strap of her purse cradled in her lap. Ed looked tired and pale. Billy was dressed in the same yellow-and-white T-shirt he had worn at the second hearing several weeks before.

It had not been a good week for the defense. The Colorado Supreme Court had declined to hear their motions seeking the closure of all hearings to the press and public. The high court in Denver had also denied the motion dealing with bond and advisement of rights. West and Ehlers would make the motion again today but they had little hope that Judge Childress would reverse his rulings now.

"The court calls 83-JV-54," Childress said as he opened the court folder before him.

Reichman's first witness was Captain Nick Boyd.

The officer took his oath, and in his low, brooding voice told the judge how by coincidence he was just a few miles from County Road 503 when the dispatcher radioed with three beeps followed by the message that two little girls were apparently molested and not moving at a residence nearby.

"So what did you do, Captain?" Reichman asked Boyd.

"I drove into the Keenan driveway using red lights and sirens so that people would know I was there."

"Did that cause any response from the residence?"

"When I drove into the driveway, there was a young girl that a neighbor found to be Laura Keenan, age eleven, standing in the front door or behind the front door looking through the glass, and she was obviously upset. She was crying. She had tears. She was nervous and flaying about with her hands."

"Were you able to gain entry?"

"Yes."

"What happened once you got inside? What were you able to observe?"

"I stepped inside and saw a teenage boy later found to be Billy Keenan standing in the edge of the front room near the dining-kitchen area holding a phone extended from the cradle to his hand, speaking on the phone."

"What did you then do, Captain?"

"I went up to Billy Keenan and began speaking with him, asked him what was the problem. He was continuing to speak with somebody on the phone and told them that the police were there. And to get his attention I took the phone out of his hand and hung it up. And I asked him face-to-face what the problem was, what was going on."

"Did you receive a response from Mr. Billy Keenan?"

"Yes, I did."

"That was, Captain?"

"He said they were dead, or they are dead, and that they are cut, and that they were up on the hill."

"Did you explore it further then with Billy Keenan?"

"Yes."

"What did you learn from him?"

"I asked him what he meant that they were dead, and he said that they were cut like with a knife, and that they were bleeding, and that they were not moving or talking or anything of that nature, and appeared dead.''

"What did you then do with that information, Captain Boyd?''

"I led Billy Keenan and his sister to my patrol car, put them in the car, and told them to show me where they were.''

"Whose direction are you following?''

"Billy Keenan's.''

"Where does he lead you?''

"He led me back from his house to the Joe and Vickie Janson house, and at the entrance to the driveway that said 'Jansons, Happy Hollow' or 'Hill Hollow Ridge.' He said they were down there, indicating down the driveway. I drove the patrol car down the driveway to near the end, and again continued to ask Billy where they were, and he said, 'Kristy's out there in the house.' I stopped the car, left the two Keenan children in my patrol car, ran to the front door of the Janson house . . . walked into the house, and found a female later found to be Kristy Janson lying on her back in the kitchen on the floor. And in walking up to her and kneeling beside her, found her to appear to be dead. There was no sign of life. There were numerous injuries, and I could get no reaction from shaking her, and in feeling her skin, her skin was cold to the touch.''

"What did you do next, Captain?''

"I quickly looked around the house, did not find or hear anyone else, see anything disturbed, and I went back down the hallway to the front door and . . . yelled over to my patrol car, where Billy Keenan was still sitting in the front seat, and asked where the other one was, and he pointed and yelled: 'She is over there,' indicating off to the east-southeast past the Janson house and among the trees. It's a wooded lot. I walked south and then east, and after walking about a hundred yards or seventy-five yards, I saw a figure lying on the ground and walked up to near that figure within a couple of feet, and found it later to be Sherry Janson who was lying facedown. She also appeared to be dead, had numerous wounds to her and dried blood on her skin, and there was no sight of movement.''

Reichman paused momentarily. There was a hush in the room, not only because Boyd's voice was low and nearly monotonous, but because the spectators hung on each word. Boyd finished his testimony with an account of the first few minutes after the other officers arrived.

Defense Attorney West cross-examined Boyd, but did not attempt to refute his findings. No one would dispute that the girls were found dead and that Billy led police to the bodies. Furthermore, this was a preliminary hearing; the defense did not have to prove or disprove anything. The prosecutor was the one who had to show that there was probable cause to hold a trial. The more the defense prodded and questioned, the more probable cause could surface.

The next witness was Undersheriff Mike Bell, who was sitting at the prosecutor's table until he was called to the witness stand. He explained to the judge how he took Billy back to the station for questioning, how he read the boy his rights and obtained permission from Mr. Keenan before questioning Billy. He described how he also received permission to take fingernail scrapings and how he retrieved the clothing and knives from Billy's room.

Before Dave West began his cross-examination, he rose and looked one last time at the yellow legal pad at his table. He approached the witness stand and paused another moment, then he began to interrogate the interrogator.

''Weren't you aware that Billy wanted to see his father?'' West was asking about the first hour after the murders.

''No, sir, I was not aware.''

''Or that his father wanted to see Billy?''

''Subsequently, when I talked to Mr. Keenan up on the road just prior to leaving with Billy, I didn't ask him if he wanted to see him. I assumed that he did and that's why he was there. I just told him how we were going to transport them and that we would be interviewing them in their presence and that he would be able to talk to them when we got to the sheriff's office.''

"What time did you get to the sheriff's office?''

"It would have been probably in the general vicinity of six o'clock.''

"From that point until two-thirty the next morning was Billy at any time free to leave?''

"No, he was not.''

"During your observation of Billy on the evening of the twenty-fifth, or let's start with the afternoon, did he appear to be tired?''

Bell understood clearly the tack that West was trying to take. The defense attorney was attempting to show that the boy was coerced into making incriminating statements.

"Later,'' Bell responded, "in the evening of the twenty-fifth or early in the morning of the twenty-sixth, yes, sir, he appeared to be tired. So did I. We were all tired.''

"Did he appear to be scared?''

Reichman saw the strategy as well, and hurried to interrupt the line of questioning. "Objection, Your Honor. This is neither a minitrial nor is this a suppression hearing . . . I fail to see the relevance of this testimony.''

Judge Childress looked at the defense attorney. "Mr. West?''

"Judge,'' West said, "I think it's relevant to the hearing . . . It would seem to me that his general demeanor is a factor for the court's consideration.''

"I will allow limited examination,'' the judge said.

"I will limit it to two questions, if I could.''

"Thank you.''

West turned again to Bell. "Was he scared?''

"I don't know, Mr. West, if I would describe it as scared. At various times through the evening, keeping in mind that he was in my presence from about five-thirty until two-thirty in the morning, during that entire six- or seven-hour time frame, he displayed a number of emotions. I don't know that I could say that that was one of them. He was upset at various times through the eight-hour time frame.''

"Did he have any food during that time, any meal?''

"Not a meal that I know of. He had a couple of Cokes. I don't know that he was given any food.''

"Did you tell both Billy and his father that he was simply a witness until about one o'clock in the morning?''

"Can I explain that rather than just give you a yes-or-no answer?'' Bell asked.

"Sure.''

"When I put Billy in my car and drove him back to the office, we had no discussion whatsoever about the incident. We talked about where he had lived before and just general conversation. I told him that we were going to talk to him about what he had discovered. I asked him which parent he would be more comfortable with when we did the interview and he said his father . . . I told Mr. Keenan, then Billy subsequently, that we were going to advise him of his Miranda rights because at this point in time we didn't know what we had and that if it turned out that he had any knowledge whatsoever beyond that of a witness, it would be necessary for that Miranda advisement.''

"Did you tell Mr. Keenan that he was a witness, nothing more?''

"Yes. But in all fairness, I also stated I had to explain to him the reason for the Miranda advisement.''

"Did that change at one o'clock in the morning, when he became a natural suspect?''

"Did what change?''

"From mere witness in your mind to suspect?''

"Yes it changed, and that was a little before one o'clock in the morning.''

"Isn't it really more accurate that you had him as a

suspect the minute you found out that there was blood on his clothing, in your own mind?''

''In my own mind he was purely a witness who discovered it until I was advised by Harrington that there was possibly blood on his clothes. Then I entertained the possibility that he could possibly be a suspect.''

West moved to behind the defense table and looked down again at the yellow pad. ''Mike, there have been to my count approximately seven knives that you have gathered and had examined. Is this correct?''

''I would count six, but approximately, yes.''

''In a previous conversation that we had, and I'm not sure I have got it right, but did you indicate to me that the autopsy reflected that there was one wound on one of the two victims that would indicate that the size of the knife was approximately four inches long.''

''Again, if I could explain how that conversation came to pass.''

''Right.''

''Third-hand hearsay that I received that originated from Albuquerque as the autopsy was being conducted . . . then I relayed it to you.''

''But there was more to it than that?''

''There was more to it than that, keeping in mind that I was getting it third- or fourth-hand hearsay.''

''I understand.''

''That preliminary indications in the bodies indicated that the shank of the knife—the imprint of the shank of the knife in one of the girls could be seen on the body, indicating possibly that the blade could have been no more than four inches.''

''That's more than a possibility, isn't it? It's a probability?''

''At that time I got it, the autopsy was still in progress. At that time there was nothing absolutely conclusive. Again that's what I was told third- or fourth-hand.''

''So your initial theory in putting this case together

was that the weapon involved was a four-inch-long knife?''

Bell shifted in his seat. ''Well, I'm not certain that I would agree. That was our initial theory. We had a lot of theories at that point in time.''

''You have just testified that you had a lot of theories. Could you go over those and the order that you had them?''

Reichman stood up again, this time with a look of impatience on his face. ''Objection, Your Honor. I fail to see the relevance of that in a preliminary hearing.''

West turned to Childress. ''Judge, we have certainly no question concerning the deaths, the unfortunate deaths. The real question that this court is going to have to wrestle with is whether or not Billy is the gentleman involved. I think it's crucial to this hearing, probably every hearing, but especially this hearing, in establishing what theories show that it's Billy and what theories show that it's not Billy.''

''Objection sustained.''

''Thank you, Your Honor,'' Reichman said as he sat down.

West turned again to the witness box. ''In your investigation, did you suspect that one of the weapons that Billy gave you was in fact used in this double homicide?''

''At the time I took the weapons, I had not the slightest idea which weapon was used. I just wanted to get my hands on every possibility.''

''Was there also a knife found on the ground of the Barker residence?''

''Subsequently, yes.''

''Did you at any time suspect that that was involved?''

''Yes.''

''And for what period of time did you suspect that?''

''Well, it's hard to give you a certain number of hours or a certain number of days. We were interested in that knife because we knew from talking to Mrs. Barker that it didn't belong there. We knew Billy had been at the Barker residence.''

''In reviewing the case, are you aware of any positive identification of fingerprints of Billy Keenan on the Janson home or on any of these weapons?''

''No, I am not, but again, fingerprints in the Janson home of Mr. Keenan would not have been significant to me because he admitted being in the home.''

''Are there any positive results on the fingernail tests of Billy Keenan that would link him up to either of the Janson girls?''

''Again, hearsay, but I don't believe so.''

''From four o'clock in the afternoon until two-thirty in the morning, did Billy Keenan ever admit to you that he did this? Did he ever say, 'Yes, I did that,' to you?''

''In answer to that specific question, no.''

''As to those weapons, can you tell me whether or not there is a fingerprint match between Billy Keenan and the weapons?''

''Not that I know of,'' Bell said. ''Again, we didn't request fingerprints on some of those items because they were admittedly in the possession and owned by Billy Keenan.''

''And as to those items, did any of those have positive blood on them?''

''Not that I'm aware of.''

''So we don't have any independent evidence that any of the weapons were used in the killings?''

''Not that I am aware of.''

''Thank you, Mr. Bell.''

The crowd mumbled slightly as they filed out of the courtroom for a recess. Maybe the reason police had remained silent and aloof all these days was because they couldn't back up the arrest with evidence.

After the break, Reichman called to the stand Al Bell, the sergeant who had overseen the casting of footprints at the murder scene and then assisted Mike Bell in interviewing Billy that night. A balding man with pudgy cheeks, in his polyester suit Al Bell looked more like an insurance salesman than a police officer. At Reichman's prompting, Bell told the court about the footprints found near Sherry's body and how the imprint matched those on the shoes taken from Billy that night. The questioning harped on minute details of location, direction, spacing, frequency. The spectators grew a little bored with the focus, understanding that all this was important but not understanding exactly why.

"During the interview," Reichman asked Bell, "was there any time that there was a confrontation with Billy as to apparent discrepancies in his statement and the physical evidence you have just described?"

"That's correct."

"Would you please explain to the judge how you brought this subject up and what you stated to Mr. Keenan and then his responses, if any."

"Okay. We went to Billy Keenan's bedroom, where Mike Bell secured the evidence. At that point we asked Mr. Keenan, Edward Keenan, if we could talk to Billy again and he consented.

"I asked Billy Keenan to explain to me how he left the Janson residence. He did so, except in his explanation to me and my talking to him, we couldn't quite seem to agree on where he left, so we asked him to make a diagram on how he left the house."

"Indicating in essence what?"

"He stated when he went down the fence line, he observed Sherry Janson's body, went through a hole in the fence and went home."

"So he's near or at the sludge pond, he says, when he sees the body of Sherry Janson. Is that correct?"

"He's down the fence line when he sees the body."

"Based on your observation of the scene, did you concur with that or did you question him further?"

"No, I questioned him further."

"Why, Sergeant?"

"Two reasons. One is he was very adamant that he only left the residence once. We have two sets of prints leaving the residence, one at a very fast running gallop, if you will, towards the sludge pond, and one at a walk towards the body. The second reason is while I was at the residence, I walked down the fence line. I observed the hole in the fence line. At that point, I could not observe the Janson body.''

''Did you know where it was at that time?''

''Yes.''

''How tall are you?''

''Six foot.''

''You were not able at that height to observe the body of Sherry Janson?''

''I was not.''

''So with those two questions in your mind, what did you do?''

''I asked Billy Keenan basically when was the last time prior to Monday that he was at the Janson residence and he stated it was the week prior.''

''The reason for asking that question?''

''Because of the two sets of prints and the freshness of the prints, I wanted to clarify the fact that he had not been to the residence earlier in the day.''

''Please continue.''

''After we had the story exactly down, he was telling me the way he left and observed the body, and I then explained to him the evidence that we had found at the scene.''

''In essence, what you just explained to the court?''

''Yes.''

''Where did you go, from this point in your interview?''

''To a statement that Billy Keenan had made in the rescue squad while he was there prior, before Mike Bell transported him in to the sheriff's office. That statement was to a Susan Naholnik, who is the wife of Marshal Naholnik in Bayfield.''

''Why did you want to bring that up in this interview?''

''Basically because the statement was an impromptu statement on Billy Keenan's part on the fact that Kristy

Janson had been killed first and then Sherry Janson had seen whoever—I don't remember the exact words—and they killed her second.''

"So why did you want to bring this up?"

"The way everything appeared at the crime scene, that is how it appeared it happened, and in my mind I was wondering how Billy Keenan could have it in his mind the exact way it appeared at the crime scene. I asked him about making the statement, and he flat denied the fact that he had made the statement.''

"What happened then?"

"At that point Undersheriff Mike Bell talked to Billy, explaining again the problems to him.''

"Problems? What do you mean?"

"The discrepancies in his story compared to the evidence at the scene of the crime.''

"Any change in Billy Keenan's explanation?"

"Billy at this time stopped talking, he stopped denying. Basically, he put his head in his hands.''

"What happened then, Sergeant?"

"He asked if he could talk to his dad.''

"Was there a response from either of you law enforcement officers?''

"At that time, his dad asked us if we would step outside of the room and we did.''

"Was there a door to that bedroom?''

"Yes, there was.''

"What did you gentlemen do with it?''

"The door was closed.''

"Where did you two law enforcement officers go?''

"We stayed right by the door.''

"What happened at that point?''

"At that point there was a conversation between the father, Edward, and the son, Billy, in the bedroom.''

"Were you attempting to overhear or eavesdrop on this conversation?''

"I wasn't attempting to, no.''

"How was it you were able to hear it?''

"Basically I was not able to hear what Billy Keenan

was saying. His voice was low and mumbled. I could only hear the father.''

"Why is it you were able to hear Mr. Keenan?''

"The voice was louder.''

"What were you able to hear?''

The crowd in the courtroom leaned forward collectively, as if they were eavesdropping on the conversation as well.

"Basically the first thing I heard was Mr. Keenan, Edward Keenan, saying something to the effect, 'Now tell me, did you kill those girls?' ''

"Could you hear a response?''

"There was a response from Billy, but again it was a mumbling, low tone, and I could not hear what was said back.''

"When this mumbling, low tone ceased, was there any response from Mr. Keenan?''

"The response from Mr. Keenan was a very emotional 'Oh, no.' ''

"Then what?''

"Then another statement I heard from Mr. Keenan.''

"Which was?''

"To the point of, 'Why did you do it?' ''

"And what's the tone of his voice at this point?''

"Very emotional.''

"What's the volume?''

"Basically the volume rose a little bit, but not tremendously. The emotion increased but not the tone of the voice.''

"Was there a response from Billy Keenan?''

"There was, and it was very emotional. You could tell the emotion was there. But I could not understand the words that were being said.''

"And then, Sergeant?''

"Then there was, not a scuffle, a shuffle, more of a shuffle-type noise in the room. And Mr. Edward Keenan, I heard him say, 'Now you stay in here with me.' ''

"Then what?''

"Then I heard again Mr. Keenan say, 'No, they won't kill you.' "

The crowd noise rose and there was a flurry of activity in the back among the media. Bell finished his testimony by explaining how Billy was arrested and brought back to the station in Durango.

Defense Attorney Denny Ehlers stood up for the cross-examination. Bell's testimony was, by far, the most damning evidence presented. But did it constitute probable cause?

He pounded Bell with questions about Billy's state of mind during the conversation and alleged confession.

"Did you know that Billy Keenan had been without sleep for approximately twenty hours when you spoke to him at one-thirty on April twenty-sixth?"

"I did not have that knowledge," Bell responded.

"Did you know how long he had gone without food?"

"No."

It didn't matter how Bell responded to Ehlers's questions. No one in the courtroom cared if Billy had drunk only Cokes. The damage had been done and the story of Billy's closed-door confession was on its way to the front page of every newspaper covering the event. Still, Billy showed no emotion from his seat between his attorneys. His mother squirmed and his father hung his head briefly.

After lunch, among other witnesses, Reichman asked the tall cowboy-investigator, Jim Harrington, to testify. Harrington explained how he found the "bowling pin-type club" believed to be the bludgeoning instrument and how Allmon found the long butcher knife in the sewage pond near the Janson home. His testimony was matter-of-fact and not very controversial. After a few cursory questions by the cross-examiner, the defense asked Harrington to step down.

Then Reichman called to the stand Special Agent Gary Koverman of the Colorado Bureau of Investigation. Koverman had conducted the blood and fingerprint tests on the knives and on the clothing that belonged to Billy.

The agent began by explaining in detail the methodology used in isolating and identifying blood samples. Koverman said the blood found on Billy's shirt and pants was not Billy's.

"Were you able," Reichman asked, "to carry your test any further to establish whether the blood on the pant leg was either that of Kristy or Sherry Janson?"

"Yes, I did find one characteristic enzyme called haptoglobin. It's not necessarily an enzyme, it's a serum. This particular serum protein that I found on the trousers was found to be Type 1. Sherry Janson is Type 1, Billy Keenan is Type 2, and Kristy Janson is Type 2-1. All the way down, the two Janson girls matched in almost every group. Being siblings, that would not be uncommon. But in the haptoglobin, it was certainly easy to tell, one being 2-1, the other being 1. The blood on the trousers of Billy Keenan was Type 1. I could eliminate him. I could also eliminate Kristy Janson since she is Type 2-1."

"So everything to that point would say that the blood on the pants was consistent with whom?"

"With Sherry Janson," Koverman said.

Reichman knew he was presenting the most damaging evidence of the afternoon. Billy, in his talks with police, adamantly denied touching or even kneeling next to Sherry's body, and yet here was evidence indicating that not only did he have Sherry's blood on his clothing but it had splattered on.

"Let's talk about the front of the shirt. From visual observation, what, if anything, did you find of significance to a serologist on the front of that shirt?"

"I counted approximately nine different spatters that I found to be blood. The spatters were somewhat unique in size in that they were not of the normal drop size. A normal drop size of blood has a particular volume which is much larger than the ones I saw. These were much smaller, and it would be consistent with, I would say, an abnormal velocity of travel.''

"You're talking about velocity, sir. How are you suggesting that the substance, human blood, got onto that shirt, then?''

"From medium-velocity or high-velocity impact.''

"Elaborate on what you mean.''

"A medium-velocity impact would be something associated with possibly an instrument—something fast, something that would be capable of hurling blood faster than the normal acceleration of gravity. In other words, we had what you would find if you took a puddle and smacked it. You certainly would get these small spatters, and this is the type of thing we saw. It was something other than you would get from, say, a normal drop of blood just falling on an individual or being cast at a normal acceleration-of-gravity velocity.''

"Would that be consistent with the use of a sharp knife?''

"Well, it could. It probably would be more consistent with maybe a club or something or some type of a wielding instrument that someone could wield faster than the acceleration of gravity.''

"Let's return to the back portion of the shirt, the one you said has the decal of the lion on it. Was there something there that you were referring to earlier?''

"Yes, there was. I found a stain. Again it was Type 1, which matches that of Sherry Janson.''

Reichman was hoping the judge was listening carefully. Here was evidence that blood matching Sherry's was found on Billy's shirt, front and back, and on his trousers. Maybe the defense could argue that Billy had stepped in a puddle of blood unknowingly and splattered some blood on himself. But, with blood on both sides of his body, such an argument would be very difficult to defend.

Now Reichman moved on to the size of the knife used, hoping to dispel the myth that a four-inch knife had been the murder weapon. Koverman testified that by examining Kristy's clothing he had "no scientific way of knowing" what the length of the instrument was, but the wounds suggested a long knife was used.

Dave West took over the cross-examination duties once again.

"Well, first of all, let's start with the fingernail-scraping tests. Why would we even be worried about that?"

"Well, I would look at fingernail scrapings primarily looking for blood. You might find hair fragments or fiber fragments, but certainly I think you might want to look to see if there would be blood that would indicate whether or not an individual may have interacted in a course of violence and scratching or something of this nature."

"In your field certainly any type of violent crime would probably involve such a test, would it not?"

"It's standard operating procedure in sexual assaults; just about generally any type of violent crime, we do get some type of fingernail scrapings."

"And to your knowledge, you had no positive results concerning Billy Keenan's tests?"

"I did not find any significant blood or hair fibers."

"Vice versa: Did you find anything concerning the victims that would identify Billy Keenan?"

"I did find blood under the fingernail scrapings of the victims. The blood could not be grouped to be matched to anyone but I did find the presence of blood."

"So you couldn't match Billy Keenan to that blood?"

"I could not."

"Another comparable test in forensic violent confrontation–type situations is hair tests?"

"Yes."

"It that because hair falls out during these kinds of incidents or even no incident?"

"Yeah, you would generally expect to find hair. Sometimes it's pulled in a violent confrontation and sometimes it's just casually exchanged, and we certainly look for hair evidence in violent crimes or sexual assaults or cases like this.''

''In this situation did you do that kind of test?''

''Yes, I did.''

''Did you find any of Billy Keenan's hair on either of the victims?''

''No, I did not.''

''Vice versa?''

''And vice versa, I did not find any of the victims' hair on the suspect.''

''Did you find any foreign hair on Kristy that was not related to Kristy or Billy Keenan?''

''I did on her sock. I found a hair. I recall I found quite a bit of animal hair. I did find a dark hair on one of the socks that was submitted to me that did not match that of Billy Keenan, and it certainly was not of the victims.''

''So you weren't able to identify that hair as coming from any person?''

''That's correct.''

''Did you also receive some hair from the kitchen sink?''

''Yes, I did.''

''Wouldn't you assume, or could you reach the conclusion, that the assailant may have touched that hair?''

''Could I make an assumption that the assailant touched the hair in the sink?'' Koverman asked for clarification.

''Yes.''

''I doubt it.''

''How do you think it got there?''

''I have no idea how it got there. I think that was the victim's own sink, was it not?''

''Right.''

''I wouldn't want to conjecture where or how hair would get into a sink, especially a victim's own head hair getting into their own sink.''

At the prompting of West, Koverman testified that he could find no fingerprints or blood samples on the knives and club he tested, either. Finally the questioning turned again to the velocity of the blood.

"You testified in response to Mr. Reichman's question that a possibility concerning velocity would be if a person smacked a puddle of water—blood in this situation—a puddle of blood?"

"Yes."

"And they would act the same—the water and the blood would have the same characteristics under those circumstances?"

"Yes. If one would smack or compress a puddle, one could produce—subjected to a severe amount of compression—one could produce blood splattering that could be consistent with the size on the shirt."

"Then you couldn't reach any reasonable certainty that Billy Keenan was the assailant?"

"I couldn't say that he was an assailant," Koverman said. "He could have been a bystander."

The special agent took the two quick steps off the witness stand and another investigator, Cliff Cox, climbed aboard. He carried with him a huge chart detailing minute by minute the alleged movements and whereabouts of all the players in the children's drama. Reichman was well aware of the effectiveness of visual aids.

The investigator had the chart divided into three columns. The first column detailed events that police were certain happened, "times that we have documented proof of, such as telephone toll records." The second column included events believed to have happened based on statements made by those involved. The final column expressed projected times, such as the time the girls were killed.

"Please begin at the earliest hour on the chart," Reichman asked, "and explain to the judge what the statements revealed."

"Okay. At one-fifteen P.M. the Keenan children departed the school bus at their regular school stop. When they got off of the bus, they conversed with Cindy Barker for approximately five minutes. Then at approximately one-twenty P.M. the Keenan children, while en route from the bus stop to their residence, stopped in a wooded area and checked a trap of Billy's to see if he had caught any game during the day.

"At approximately one twenty-five they arrived at the residence. The children indicated that at approximately one-thirty P.M. they called their father. It was Billy that initiated the phone call. The purpose for that phone call was to make him aware that they had arrived home safely and to discuss their homework assignments for the day. At one thirty-five, or from the period of one thirty-five to approximately one-fifty P.M., by the statements of Laura Keenan, they had a snack or a light lunch."

"Who are 'they'?"

"Laura and Billy."

"Please continue."

"For a period of from approximately one-fifty P.M. to approximately two-forty P.M. the Keenan children were outside playing in the yard. During this period of time, Laura Keenan made the statement that Billy had started and was driving his father's tractor. Also during this time period, Laura Keenan went into the house and turned on the television and watched the middle portion of a TV program on Farmington channel 12, 'The Sale of the Century.' At approximately two-fifty Billy Keenan returned to the house, coming through the back door of the residence. Laura had to turn off the TV and go unlock the back door to allow Billy access through the back door into the house.

"From that point, Billy went to the kitchen sink and was washing his hands when it was noted that the Janson dog, that the small black dog belonging to them, was in their backyard barking at their dog. Laura then went outside to resume play, leaving Billy in the house. At approximately three P.M. Billy came out of the house and had told Laura—this again is by Laura's statement—that he had just called the Janson girls, or specifically Kristy, to tell her information that her dog was in their house or at the Keenan residence.''

Reichman interrupted the officer. "Now this is approximately what time Billy Keenan says he's calling the Janson residence?''

"The phone call would have been placed between two-fifty and three P.M.''

"How were you able to determine that?''

"By the statements of Laura Keenan, primarily.''

"Principally what did she tell you to help in setting down that time?''

"Her fixing of the time was determined by the TV program that she was watching.''

"Which was?''

" 'The Sale of the Century.' ''

"Were you able during your investigation to do anything to confirm that time and the showing of that program?''

"Yes. We got a copy of channel 12, Farmington's TV log for that day, which indicated that in fact from two-thirty to three that date that 'The Turn of the Century'—I'm sorry—the 'Sale of the Century' program was televised.''

"Would there be any way to confirm the telephone call between the Keenan and Janson residences?''

"No, there's no toll log. It's a local call.''

"Please continue.''

"As Billy was starting on the trail with the Janson dog following . . . Laura then went back into the house and turned the TV back on. This would have been right at three o'clock.''

"Was she able to indicate what she was watching?''

"She saw the beginning of 'The Richard Simmons Show.' ''

"Were you able to do anything to confirm whether or not such a show was aired, and if so, what time?''

"Yes. By the same viewing log or schedule for channel 12, 'The Richard Simmons Show' came on at three o'clock and terminated at three-thirty. According to

Laura Keenan's statements, just a few minutes prior to the end of the Richard Pryor—I'm sorry—Richard Simmons program, Billy came running down the hill or came, you know, running to the house—the front door of the house, crying and shouting that Kristy was dead. He ran into the front door of the house, fell onto the floor just inside the front door, and continued to cry and scream for approximately three to five minutes. Then he told Laura that he had to call his dad. She went to the kitchen and handed him the telephone, and he placed the first phone call to his father. He was unable to get through to his father the first time, so he hung up. And approximately five minutes later, again by Laura Keenan's statement, he made his second phone call, at which time he was put in touch with his father. And he remained on the telephone until the deputy sheriff arrived, took the telephone from Billy's hand, and hung it up.''

''Thank you very much,'' Reichman said.

West and Ehlers declined to cross-examine Cox.

The final witness of the day was Sue Naholnik, the Bayfield marshal's wife, who recounted the conversation she had had with the Keenan children in the back of the ambulance.

''We were sitting there,'' Naholnik testified, ''and we hadn't said anything for a while, and Laura said that it was hard to believe that the two girls were dead because she had just—they were on the bus that afternoon and were laughing and talking and it was hard to believe that they were dead.''

''What was said next and by whom?'' Reichman asked.

''Billy said that—you want it verbatim?''

''Yes, ma'am, as you remember it.''

''He said that Kristy was in the kitchen, Kristy got it first. And then he mentioned a girl's name. I don't recall that he called her by Sherry, but it was a girl's name, and he says something to the effect that she walked in or came in or something, and then he said they got her out on the trail . . . I asked him what he meant by *trail*, and he said that it was trails leading back and forth between the two houses that the kids all played on. He said he knew all of them real well because he used to build tepees on them.''

"Thank you. At this point did you have any background information to know what Billy was talking about?''

"No, I didn't. All I knew was that there was possibly two girls that were dead.''

"Do you of your own knowledge know what prompted Billy to make that statement to you?''

"No, I don't.''

"Then what happened?''

"I believe next Laura said that he had just talked to Kristy like ten minutes before he found them. And I said, 'What do you mean he had just talked to her?' She said that Billy said that he had called Kristy because he had their dog and was going to take their dog back to her, and he called. Kristy said sure, come on over, bring the dog back.''

"Please continue.''

"I think there was a time lapse. I got out of the truck at that time and did tell one of the officers there that there was like a ten-minute time that he had talked to the girls and they were fine and ten minutes that they were, you know, dead. And then I got back in the vehicle, and I think the next conversation we had was a little bit later, and we were talking about California.''

"How did that subject come up?''

"I was just trying to make conversation with them. They hadn't said anything for a while. I asked them where they were from and had they lived here long. They said that they were from California before they moved here. And I said, 'Well, it's someplace I would like to go. I've never been there.' And I believe it was Billy that stated that it was real hot there. And I said, 'Well, you can always go down to the beach and, you know, cool off there.' And Laura said that they weren't allowed to go to the beach. She said that her mother had grounded them from going to the beach, and I said, 'Why was that?' And she said because when they were littler, Billy used to tear her dolls up all the time, and one particular time he got hold of a doll and tried to tear the smile off its face and so her mother grounded them.''

''Was there any response from Billy at this point?''

''Yes. He said, 'Well, that was when I was real little, and I was about five.' And Laura said, 'No, because I would have only been about two then, and I know I was old enough to remember it.' ''

The crowd listened intently. Many of the rumors they had heard appeared to be true.

''I have no further questions, Your Honor.''

''Thank you. Mr. Ehlers?''

''Thank you, Your Honor.'' Ehlers approached the witness stand. ''Mrs. Naholnik, how old are you?''

''Twenty-seven.''

''What education have you had?''

''High school education.''

''Do you know if your husband is cross-deputized by the La Plata County Sheriff's Department?''

''I believe he is. I'm not sure.''

''Are you?''

''No, I'm not.''

''Have you gone out on emergency calls with your husband before?''

''I've gone on a couple of fires, but I don't recall going on any emergency-type calls.''

''How long were you in the van with the children?''

''I don't have a watch, so I just have to guess probably an hour and a half or two hours.''

''During that time after you asked them some questions, during these conversations, you would get out and report those answers to law enforcement personnel. Is that correct?''

''No. I just did that one time.''

''Just one time?''

"Uh-huh."

"Why wouldn't you let Billy Keenan see his father?"

"I didn't stop him. Nobody stopped him from seeing his father that I know of. When his father arrived, he was way down at the back of the road and there were a lot of cars in between us, and his father just never came up there."

"Were you in charge of the son in the van? Would you say you were in charge of Billy inside of the van?"

"No, I wouldn't say I was in charge of him."

"What was your functioning?"

"Just to sit there and basically see if they needed anything."

"Didn't he tell you he needed to see his father?"

"Yes. And I asked one of the officers if, you know, he could see his father. He said as soon as his father could get up there he would let them see him."

"Did they?"

"Not to my knowledge they didn't."

"Does it strike you as strange that for an hour and a half to two hours during an investigation of a homicide, that the major witness or what may be a suspect is left in your custody and you continue to have conversations and follow up on their statements asking questions?"

Before Naholnik could answer, Reichman jumped from his seat.

"Objection, Your Honor. Irrelevant, speculative, and calls for a conclusion which has no importance to this hearing."

The judge sustained the objection.

Ehlers continued with a few more questions, but Naholnik was off the hook. She stepped down. Reichman announced he had no further witnesses. The crowd let out a collective sigh. It had been a long afternoon.

Things looked grim for Billy. After a short recess the judge quickly announced that he found probable cause to bind Billy over for trial, or in this case, an adjudicatory hearing.

"How does your client respond to the petition?" he asked the defense attorneys.

They were swift with their answer.

"Not guilty, Your Honor."

Childress set a trial date for July 11. When he sounded the gavel ending the hearing, the crowd burst into spontaneous uproar and the media again went scurrying. Phyllis Keenan broke down crying. Billy was allowed to converse with his parents across the low wall that separated the gallery from the lawyers' arena.

As the courtroom was clearing out, West and Ehlers huddled for a minute. With a trial date six weeks away, their motions denied by the supreme court, and the evidence mounting, it was obvious their defense strategy was not working. Yet Billy still professed his innocence.

Perhaps they would have to take measures, drastic measures, to find out from Billy himself what happened, what really happened between 3:00 and 3:35 on April 25 after Billy meandered down the path through the woods for the simple task of returning Tubby the dog.

13

On June 8, two weeks after the hearing, Billy, his parents, and his lawyers waited anxiously for the psychiatrist to arrive. Dr. John Nagel was driving down to Pueblo at the request of West and Ehlers to hypnotize Billy.

The lawyers had contacted Nagel because Billy never wavered from his declaration of innocence. Even when confronted with the mounting evidence, Billy professed his innocence. West and Ehlers had believed him from the start, but now the preponderance of evidence had left too many questions unanswered. The biggest one was what was going on in Billy's mind.

Perhaps when Billy pleaded innocent, he truly believed it. Perhaps he had buried the event deep within his subconscious. It was not unheard of, and Nagel was retained to help the attorneys discover the truth, whatever it was, wherever it lay hidden in their client's soul.

The sessions with Billy were conducted in a private room at the detention center in Pueblo. Though Billy's parents were present at the facility, they did not witness the majority of the six-hour interview. Nevertheless, the encounter was designed from the outset to be the moment of reckoning for Billy and his family.

Billy was kept completely conscious during the first phase of the interview. To break the ice, Nagel began by asking the boy about his hobbies, his family, his likes and dislikes.

Billy told the doctor that hunting was the most important thing in his life. He boasted that he shot a .22-caliber rifle in target practice when he was just two or three years old. He said he received his first knife at the age of six or seven and owned his first "real" gun at nine years old. He enjoyed raising rabbits, he said, and liked watching television and videos, especially gory movies like *Halloween* and *The Shining*. His favorite television program was "The A Team."

When Nagel asked Billy about his family life, Billy shrugged. He said he didn't have many problems at home or with his family. He was on good terms with his sister, though he admitted to liking to "tease and scare her." If he had any problems, it was at school, where he had trouble concentrating and often "blocked schoolwork out of my mind."

Billy said he had been feeling a lot of pressure in school since January. On the day he found the girls, the principal had told him that he was going to be held back unless his grades improved drastically. Billy said he felt frustrated because no one understood him, and that his father would be really upset if he flunked. It would be tough to face his father.

Billy started to squirm in his seat as he spoke.

He talked about leaving his last class of the day, shop class, at about 12:15 in the afternoon. He got on the school bus home with Laura, Kristy, and Sherry and the others. After about an hour's bus ride, Kristy and Sherry were let off at their home and Billy and Laura at theirs. Billy said he went into the house, called his father at work, and then fixed himself a bowl of cereal and nachos.

After lunch, Billy went into his yard and noticed that the Janson girls' "fuzzy black dog" was running loose. He called Kristy to let her know. Then he called his mother for permission to return the dog. Billy said he visited Cindy before taking off for the Janson house. When he arrived, Kristy was in the kitchen and Sherry was catching butterflies in the backyard.

Now Billy was having difficulty speaking. Billy blurted out amidst tears that he hit Sherry and Kristy.

Nagel stopped the interview. He suggested to Billy it might be easier for him to speak if he were put under hypnosis. Billy agreed.

Within ten minutes, Billy was "visibly less agitated and gave good evidence of a trance." Nagel recorded what happened next in his psychiatric evaluation of Billy, which was later entered into court records:

He is brought back to the point where he had left off in his narrative description of what had happened with Sherry as they were playing in the Janson backyard "trying to catch butterflies." In his description, he had hit Sherry in the back "with my stick" and as Billy became afraid she might tell her sister or her father about his having hit her, he struck her some more with his stick about the head and neck until she fell to the ground. Then Billy says that he turned and was about to run home when he realized that Kristy would find her sister and tell her father, so Billy took his stick into the house and found Kristy in the kitchen working at the counter. He talked about hitting her with the stick about her head and neck until she fell to the floor, and then as he found a long butcher knife on the counter he "threw it" at her and "stuck her in the stomach" as she was lying on the floor.

As Billy recounted his story, he simulated the bludgeoning and stabbing motions. He acted as if he were at the Janson house and the girls were before him and he was killing them now. He reenacted the murders blow by blow with intense fury, his face contorting grotesquely as he described the stabbing and hitting motions he had used the day of the murders.

Then as Billy was leaving the house to go home, he found Sherry crying in the backyard "so I had to cut her with my knife" until she didn't cry anymore. He describes running home in a state of anxiety, fear and panic. He says "I threw my stick and a knife into the pond."

He talks about his sister recognizing his anxiety and distress but he denies having told her anything about what had happened. He went into the house and "I called my father to tell him what I had seen."

When Billy finished confessing, Nagel gave him the suggestion of amnesia "for as much of the events as he needed or wished to have."

Once out of the trance, Billy seemed "comfortable and relaxed" and "demonstrated good time distortion indicating deep trance had been achieved."

His attorneys, who remained in the room during the entire session, were awestruck by the drama that had unfolded before them.

After taking a break, the psychiatrist, Billy, and the observers closed the door behind them and continued the interview. Nagel again hypnotized Billy and asked him to scan his past history beginning with his childhood.

Billy achieved the trance more quickly than the first time. Nagel asked him about his earliest recollections as a child.

Billy described watching TV in the family home in Los Angeles. Billy remembered helping his mother bake chocolate chip cookies in the kitchen and working alongside his father's workbench in the garage. He spoke of his parents' discipline. He said he remembered his mother "yelling at me and she spanked me once with her hand." He recalled his father "yelling at me and spanking me sometimes with a belt." Billy said he felt hurt inside when his father was critical of his school performance.

He talked again about Mr. Winter, whom Billy said was

"mean and unfair." Billy feared repeating a year in school. He admitted feeling specially frightened and worried about his dad's reaction to his failing.

Billy denied any particular conflict with friends. He said he was friendly with Kristy some years back, but that ended after she "started telling her dad things about me that weren't true, like I had thrown a dead skunk down the well."

Then Billy became visibly more agitated as he described his relationship with Sherry, whom he described as "a real mean brat who said mean things to me and my sister." He also said that he feared Mr. Janson, who had confronted him when he was alone and had terrified him.

Dr. Nagel brought Billy out of his trance and suggested amnesia before awakening him for the last time.

The hypnosis session was over.

The group walked downstairs, where Ed and Phyllis waited. With Billy in their presence, West explained to the boy's parents what had happened upstairs, that Billy had indeed killed the girls and, for the moment at least, was not denying it.

Ed and Phyllis remained composed until Billy left the room. Then Phyllis broke down "into convulsions of grief and despair," Nagel reported. The psychiatrist found her too distraught to continue the meeting. He pulled her aside to calm her down.

She told Nagel that she didn't know how Billy could have done such a thing. Then Phyllis broke down again and said, "Now that this has happened, Billy will be cheated out of his childhood." Nagel got her to acknowledge that she and her husband both worked from an early age and in a sense had been cheated out of their own childhoods, too.

Phyllis said that Billy was just like his father in that he held "everything in until he exploded." That was the reason, Phyllis explained, that Ed had had his heart attack.

After Phyllis calmed down, she and the psychiatrist

rejoined the group. The family talked about the fact that they did not share feelings with one another very well and that family members needed to pull together to help one another and to help Billy.

Nagel suggested a therapist in Durango for the Keenans and made arrangements for the family to see a psychiatrist in Pueblo on a short-term basis. Nagel wrote in his evaluation that the parents "left with an air of resolve and determination to get themselves, Billy and their family through this difficult time."

Then, in his report, Nagel turned his attention to Billy once more for an evaluation of the boy's mental status.

Billy . . . seems to be of average intelligence. He presents his story fairly coherently and well. He denies any sleep or appetite disturbance since he has been in the hospital. He is alert and well oriented. His memory and concentration remain fairly well intact . . . there is no evidence of schizophrenic thought disorder. He denies suicidal or homicidal ideas. He seems cooperative and he responds to verbal support. He may have some capacity for insight. His judgment remains quite immature.

Mental disorders, like car parts, are itemized and cataloged. The "bible" of the mental health field is the Diagnostic and Statistical Manual of Mental Disorders, referred to by professionals simply as the DSM.

Nagel used this reference to explain in psychiatric jargon the possible "whys" of Billy's actions.

Under the heading "Provisional Diagnoses," Nagel wrote that Billy suffered from "Adjustment reaction of adolescence with undersocialized aggressive behavior."

The DSM describes undersocialized adolescents as juveniles who fail "to establish a normal degree of affection, empathy, or bond with others" and who "rarely show appropriate feelings of guilt or remorse." The term is broad and commonly used to describe any child who "lacks concern for the feelings, wishes, and well-being of others, and extends himself only when there is an obvious and immediate advantage."

Undersocialized juveniles "typically blame others for their difficulties and feel unfairly treated and mistrustful of others." Their self-esteem is usually low, though they may act "tough." They become easily frustrated and irritable, have frequent temper tantrums, and engage in "provocative recklessness." They fare poorly in school despite what may be average or above-average intelligence. If the juvenile's behavior continues into adulthood he usually ends up in jail labeled as "antisocial."

An undersocialized juvenile can earn an additional label of "aggressive" if he engages in repeated aggression in which the rights of others are violated by either physical violence or thefts outside the home involving confrontation with a victim. The physical violence may take the form of rape, mugging, assault, or, in rare cases such as Billy's, homicide.

As for the cause of this undersocialized aggressive behavior, the DSM suggests, among other reasons, "parental rejection" and "inconsistent management with harsh discipline."

But there was more to Billy's fit of rage. Billy didn't remember killing the girls. Only under hypnosis did he recall those critical thirty-five minutes. To explain the amnesia, Nagel suggested that Billy might also suffer from an "acute hysterical reaction related to atypical dissociative disorder."

Atypical dissociative disorder affects many victims of brainwashing and terrorist or cult indoctrination. The DSM describes it as "a sudden, temporary alteration in conscious functioning" for a period of time lasting for a few hours to several weeks. At the moment of disassociation, the sufferer experiences the world around him completely differently. Objects may change in size or shape. He loses his sense of reality. Others may be perceived as dead or mechanical. The world does not exist as it did before. All meaning is lost because the objects that give meaning to reality have lost their inherent value. The sufferer has temporarily severed his associations with his environment.

The disorder also produces a mental state known as "depersonalization," where the patient's sense of self changes dramatically or is lost altogether. More than two thirds of all young adults experience mild cases of depersonalization, though they don't necessarily experience any impairment. In moderate and severe cases, the sufferer feels estranged or mechanical. He feels as if he is living in a dream or has been anesthetized. There is a feeling of not being in control of one's actions or of perceiving oneself from a distance.

Dr. Nagel also suggested Billy might have suffered from brief reactive psychosis, "a sudden onset of a psychotic disorder of at least a few hours but no more than two weeks duration." Such reactions usually follow major stress in the patient's life, such as the loss of a loved one, the psychological trauma of combat, or any experience that could cause significant distress. In Billy's case the precipitating event may have been his fear of failing and fear of telling his father.

Once the stress comes, the sufferer loses the ability to make normal associations, becomes disoriented, loses recent memory, suffers from delusions or hallucinations, and acts with poor judgment. In most situations, brief reactive psychosis lasts only a day or two, then fades away gradually.

In nonscientific terms, Nagel was saying that Billy had personality problems aggravated by a stressful situation. He reacted violently after temporarily losing himself to another world. The girls were the unfortunate victims of his ensuing rage. Nagel wrote in his report:

I believe that Billy's capacity for dissociation has made it possible for him to put the events of that day out of his mind leaving him amnesic for most of what happened. He is able to recall only vaguely the violence and he has not realized fully the devastating consequences of his actions. It appears that Billy was responsible for the deaths of Kristy and Sherry Janson on April 25. From Billy's description, he acted impulsively and violently toward the Janson girls as he found himself in a state of fear, panic and desperation in relation to the threat that the girls' father might find out about his stick.

Despite the brutality of the killings and the seriousness of the diagnosis, the doctor's provisional prognosis for the boy was good:

The primary goal of this young man's treatment should be to help him come to a clear knowledge and understanding of what it is that he did. An important goal of therapy will be to try to reverse the traumatic effects of what he's been through and help him integrate important split off aspects of himself . . . Billy will need an environment that offers support, structure, safety and protection. Also he will need an empathically available therapist who can help him reconstruct the events of his life that predisposed him to this kind of acting out behavior and the events of that day which have been largely forgotten.

With therapy, appropriate assertiveness and more mature coping, protection from impulsive behavior and inhibition and control of violent aggressive impulses can be learned. In a secure holding environment and with psychotherapy, there is every possibility and hope for Billy to mature and develop into a better integrated, socially responsible individual.

The sessions were over. Nagel packed up and headed back north. The Keenans stayed in Pueblo to be near their son. The attorneys drove back to Durango. It was a long, silent ride.

When police got hold of the psychiatric evaluation a few days later, they found that it raised disturbing questions about their investigation.

Based on the evidence they had gathered, including Billy's footprints and his verbal slipup in the back of the ambulance, investigators had concluded that Kristy was killed first and Sherry, watching in horror from the sliding glass door, was killed last. Now, under hypnosis, Billy had told the psychiatrist that he had assaulted Sherry first, *then* Kristy after he realized that "Kristy would find her sister and tell her father."

If this was indeed the sequence, then police had it all wrong.

Furthermore, investigators believed that after killing Kristy, Billy had left the kitchen, dropped the club and knife in the sewage pond, then ran home. But under hypnosis, Billy suggested that after stabbing Kristy he returned to stab Sherry in the woods, *then* threw the knife in the pond. Again, if his testimony under hypnosis was accurate, Billy must have backtracked to the pond after killing Sherry. That couldn't be, according to investigators; the pond was not located between the house and the clearing where Sherry was killed, and police had no evidence—no footprints or dog tracking—of Billy's taking this route.

The police version could only make sense if Billy had used two knives: the butcher knife, which he deposited in the pond, to kill Kristy; and a second knife, the whereabouts of which were unknown, to kill Sherry.

If Billy was telling the truth—and police were told that it was impossible to lie under hypnosis—then all their theories were proven wrong.

Police, however, entertained one other notion to explain the discrepancies between Billy's confession under hypnosis and their own reconstruction. Perhaps

Billy had not fallen under a hypnotic trance as his lawyers and the psychiatrist were led to believe. Perhaps, for any number of reasons, Billy had decided it was in his best interest to lie, to feign mental illness with hopes that punishment could be averted, or to circumvent his father's disappointment in him. Perhaps his performance, animated as it was, had been yet another subterfuge orchestrated by a master deceiver. If so, what a splendid job he had done.

Intriguing as the thought was, the investigators never would get the chance to find out.

14

During the days after the hypnotic revelations, Billy's attorneys engaged in a series of closed-door meetings with Assistant District Attorney Reichman. Then, quietly, they asked the judge to cancel two preparatory hearings that had been scheduled in anticipation of the trial. Instead, they requested a disposition hearing be scheduled as soon as possible.

Judge Childress agreed, and Billy was escorted one final time from Pueblo to Durango on June 21, nearly two months after the murders of Kristy and Sherry.

At the request of the defense, Childress also reversed his ruling and agreed to ban the press and public from the hearing. He accepted a compromise suggested by Reichman to videotape the proceedings and show the tape to interested parties immediately afterward. This way Billy would be spared any embarrassment, while the press and public would not be denied their right to attend. It was also agreed that the $400 cost of the videotaping would be shared by the defense and the district attorney's office.

The public was aware that a disposition was in the making. Many feared, as the newspapers reported, that Billy could be placed on probation, in a foster home, or worse, returned to the custody of his parents. Neighbors, friends, and teachers who believed in Billy's guilt were by now well enough acquainted with the Children's Code to know that there was no mandatory sentence for the crime of juvenile delinquency. Billy would probably spend some time behind bars, but this satisfied few.

In marked contrast with the previous proceedings when every seat was taken, the courtroom was empty for the disposition. Only the video technician, lawyers, judge, Billy, and his parents occupied the room that day. Their voices bounced off the cinder block walls and wooden benches and echoed through the hollow space, amplifying their words. The room was cool despite the midday warmth.

Billy sat between his parents at the defense table with his head bowed in apparent contrition. He looked as if he had reconciled himself to accept a licking.

After the attorneys settled some preliminary matters, Dave West rose to address the judge. "At this time, we are prepared to admit both allegations of the petition, Your Honor."

Judge Childress turned to the boy.

Billy rose.

"Billy Keenan," the judge began with measured words, "do you understand what's happening this afternoon?"

Bowing his head even farther, in a sheepish voice Billy answered, "Yes, sir."

"And Mr. and Mrs. Keenan, do you also understand what is happening this afternoon?" The parents rose.

Ed Keenan answered for himself and his wife. "Yes, sir."

"Mr. West has just indicated that it is your desire, Billy, to admit the two allegations. Do you admit or deny these two allegations."

"Admit, sir."

"Both of the allegations?"

"Yes, sir."

"And Mr. and Mrs. Keenan, have you talked to your son sufficiently concerning the admission of these two formal allegations?"

"Yes, sir," the couple answered in unison.

"And do you support him in his admission of these allegations."

"Absolutely," Ed said in a low, sad voice.

"Billy, do you understand the first count of the petition, that on the twenty-fifth day of April, 1983, within the county of La Plata, that you feloniously, after deliberation, intended the death and did cause the death of Sherry Lee Janson?"

"Yes, sir."

"And do you understand that the People, the state of Colorado, would have to prove that you caused the death of Sherry Lee Janson and that you did this after deliberation, after thinking about it? It doesn't have to be very much thought, but it has to be some deliberation. And that you caused this death intentionally? Do you understand that they would have to prove that?"

"Yes, sir."

"Do you still wish to admit that you deliberately, intentionally caused the death?"

"Yes, sir." Billy clasped his hands in front of him.

"In the count," the judge continued, "on the same day in this county, it's alleged that you feloniously caused the death of Kristine Janson, but without deliberation. Do you understand that that's the second count?"

"Yes, sir." Billy's reply was barely audible.

"Similarly, the state of Colorado would have to prove that you caused the death. They would have to prove that you did this knowingly, that it was something you voluntarily did, even though you did not deliberate this act."

"Yes, sir." Billy choked on his reply, as if the reprimand had reached unbearable proportions and he would succumb any moment now.

"Billy, you have the right to a jury trial. Do you understand that?"

"Yes, sir."

"Do you want a trial of any kind?"

"No, sir."

"And Mr. and Mrs. Keenan, do you understand that your son still has this right to a jury trial?"

Ed Keenan nodded. "Yes, sir."

"Do you think he should have a trial of any kind in the case?"

"No, sir," Ed whispered.

"Billy, your admission must be voluntary. Is it voluntary?"

"Yes, sir."

"It is your free will that you are admitting these allegations?"

"Yes, sir."

"Has anyone coerced you into doing this?"

"No, sir."

"Mr. and Mrs. Keenan, do you conclude that this is Billy's voluntary admission?"

"Yes, sir," Ed said. "Absolutely."

"All right, thank you. Mr. West, what is the factual basis for the plea?"

West explained to the judge that during the hypnosis session with Dr. Nagel, Billy had admitted to hitting Sherry with his club and then to hitting and stabbing Kristy in the kitchen before returning outside to stab Sherry to death. Both murders were committed "in a state of panic and fear."

The judge turned to Billy once more. "Billy, is this what happened?"

"Yes, sir."

The judge paused. "Now the court will proceed with the sentencing, or commitment in this case. Is there anything more that you wish to say in that regard, Mr. West?"

"Your Honor, I think everyone in this room would like more than anything that the clock could be turned back. There are a lot of feelings toward the Jansons, toward the Keenan family. To quantify the loss to the Jansons is impossible. I would ask the court to consider a recommendation of treatment that is appropriate. I think that Billy needs some help. His parents, Billy, all acknowledge that.''

"Mr. Reichman, any comment?"

"Your Honor, I think it is clear that the court only has one course of conduct and that would be a commitment to the Department of Institutions for a period of two years. I would urge two matters upon the court. In the strongest words that the court can, I would ask that you recommend that a very firm treatment plan with psychotherapy be set forth and the court be apprised of what that plan is.''

"All right, thank you," Childress said.

The judge paused again. "At this time the court commits Billy Keenan to the Department of Institutions for the maximum period provided by the state statute, a two-year commitment, which may be extended for an additional period of two years on the petition from the Department of Institutions." The judge looked at the participants before him. "Anything else?"

Reichman asked that the gag order on the law enforcement officials be lifted. Childress obliged. Other minor matters were settled.

Then, without ceremony, the silver-haired judge set down the gavel on the case of Billy Keenan.

West and Reichman shook hands. Billy hugged his parents, then was led away by a deputy. With a "No comment" the Keenans slipped past the media, which waited outside the courtroom eagerly awaiting the news.

The video technician rushed to rewind the tape. When the room cleared, the media were let in. The blinds were drawn and the reporters quieted as they watched the video of the ten-minute hearing on the monitor. Afterward, Reichman and Captain Nick Boyd came into the courtroom to answer questions.

"How about the contradiction between the police theory and Billy's confession under hypnosis?" a reporter asked.

"We're not satisfied with the admission," Boyd said. "Billy is still playing denial games. The physical evidence doesn't match up." Boyd added that the sheriff's office would be filing a report soon presenting evidence that Billy's story was untrue.

Reichman interrupted to say that the investigation of the murders was one of the most professional jobs he had ever seen. Furthermore, he wanted to commend the investigators for withstanding the abuse of those members of the public who questioned their competence.

"Why did you accept his plea?" another reporter asked Reichman.

"What are the chances of getting twelve good and honest people to say a thirteen-year-old kid could do this?" Reichman said. "I would have loved to have tried Billy as an adult but the law didn't allow it because the boy was twelve days shy of his fourteenth birthday."

"What about a motive?"

Reichman said no motive was ever presented in court and he would not care to speculate.

His reply slightly disappointed reporters, who had hoped to jot down or capture on tape a reason for the insanity. They would have liked so much to answer that question succinctly, to write in their stories: "Reichman said that Billy Keenan killed Kristy and Sherry Janson because . . ." They knew that their audience liked pat answers. But they wouldn't get one. Not today.

Boyd finished up the press conference with a bit of home-grown philosophy. He said that he understood why certain segments of the community wanted to deny Keenan's complicity. "Like the Jansons and the Keenans, people moved to southwest Colorado to get away from crime. It changes one's life-style to believe that such a crime could be committed by such a young boy. It's one of those cases where you feel helpless."

Once the news of the disposition hit the streets, the reaction was as divided as ever. Many people were not ready to accept Billy's confession. They still believed that the police had erred and now the boy was being railroaded into a confession by his attorneys, his parents, whomever. He just couldn't have done such a thing. Not Billy. Not one of their own.

Others were angered by the meager sentence. Here was a ruthless murderer, an awful kid who needed to be punished, and all he was going to get was two years in a children's jail somewhere.

During the few days after the sentencing there was an uneasiness in town. In comparison with the knock-out punch of the news of the murders, the end was too ambiguous for pure celebration or anguish. People were mildly annoyed that the local drama had ended so flatly. They had been deprived of a grand finale despite all the time and energy they had spent following the events of the spring. There were no clear-cut winners or losers. It was one big, disappointing anticlimax.

Durangoans found it easier to put the case away. They had, in a sense, been voyeurs during the ordeal, since the murders happened in Bayfield, a town Durangoans looked slightly down upon.

The people in the tiny hamlet of Bayfield, however, were left to deal with the guilt and sadness. The dusty streets looked the same after the sentencing, but everyone knew things had changed. No one was sure, though, how the outcome would manifest itself in the days and months and years to come. It wouldn't go away. That was for sure.

The local paper remained the sounding board for the views of everyone. After the disposition, a series of letters to the editor appeared in the *Durango Herald* starting with this one:

To the Editor:

Thursday night headlines shout "Ex-mental patient suspect in 100 killings . . . !" All starting out with the stabbing of his mother 23 years before, how apropos this headline is.

Billy Keenan is, essentially, going to walk. Our so-called law is more concerned with the fact that he was a few days short of his 14th birthday than the fact that two bright beautiful girls were viciously and willfully destroyed.

I am sick of hearing about all the concern that he is so dependent on his parents, so concerned with his welfare, so concerned of trauma by an open court, etc., etc. Why shouldn't he suffer!? I ask all of those so concerned to look deep into their souls and ask "Would I be so concerned with this poor child's welfare if my own children had been butchered by him?" . . .

How many countless horror stories have we read and heard about so-called "rehabilitated" criminals going back out to kill again and again? The rights of vicious criminals are more important than those of decent citizens! When in God's holy name are we going to wake up and realize what's happening in this country? When do we get sick of hard criminals getting VIP treatment or starting lawsuits against legal institutions because they don't like the food or they don't have cable TV? How long are judges and lawyers going to be allowed to turn monsters loose on the streets using insanity as an excuse for destroying innocent people? Have we become so accustomed to atrocities that we don't see the ugliness and horror that is a Billy Keenan?

I strongly believe in the law of reasonable doubt, but when that doubt no longer exists what do we do, hope that we aren't next?

D. J. Murray
Durango

Several days later, a lengthy reply was printed from Ed and Phyllis Keenan. It was the only time the couple publicly responded to the case:

To the Editor:

While it was our intent to not respond to the various letters, pro or con, which have appeared in the paper, the letter from D. J. Murray requires response . . .

First, relative to the sentence, Billy was given the maximum sentence of two years. On completion of that two years the state can (and we have been assured they will) ask for an extension of two years. Following the second two years there is the possibility the state can cause an additional extension until he is 21 years old. He will not be free in less than two years. He will be in prison for a minimum of three years and a possible maximum time of seven years. What would you change the law to read? Life or Hanging? From a start at 13 years old, that seems like a case of overkill . . .

As to Ms. Murray's comments about insanity as an excuse, no one tried to use insanity or anything else as an "excuse" in the Jansen [sic] killings. We still do not know "why" it happened. We do know that it was not premeditated and that Billy was in an absolute state of hysteria during and following the killings. We do know that it was necessary for us to use a psychiatrist and hypnosis to find out "what" happened because the boy did not have conscious knowledge of the killings. We do know that killing people is totally inconsistent with the personality that anyone exposed to Billy has known. He is not a street thug who has lived a life wrapped around crime. We believe he can be changed with sufficient treatment to insure that he does not kill again under any circumstances. We have dedicated our efforts to insure this change before we allow his release.

Just for Ms. Murray's information, our attorneys

felt that we could have beaten the charges in court because of the poor handling by the law, lack of supportable evidence, and other things which are not worth repeating here. Instead, we (including Billy) entered a guilty plea to take the punishment due and to seek the help which is needed. I wonder, Ms. Murray, if you could have or would have done the same?

Ms. Murray asks "what miseries have the families of these people gone through?" Our hearts and eternal prayers go out to the Jansen family for their loss. We did not lose our children in death as the Jansens. But we did lose. We will relive the horror of that terrible day every day of our lives, our son is in prison for a long, long time, the joy in the young years of our family is also gone, our home was lost to pay for the honest investigation the law did not do and the legal representation we needed. I do not know if our lives can be set right any more than the Jansens. Yes, Ms. Murray, we are paying the price.

The last thought I wish to pass on to Ms. Murray is that there is a tremendous difference between the corrective actions needed to deal with a child who has committed a crime but is still young enough to be helped and a hardened adult criminal who cannot be changed. Be careful, Ms. Murray, the bed you are making could be slept in by your own children.

Ed and Phyllis Keenan

The Keenans' letter brought a response from Mike Bell, the officer in charge of the investigation:

To the Editor:

It's my turn now. I kept quiet during the initial investigation of the Janson homicides. The entire sheriff's staff kept turning the other cheek during the investigation, while everyone from the Keenans' family doctor to the neighbors of the Keenan family called and wrote letters telling us we had the wrong person in custody.

At the time, of course, we could say nothing, we could not disclose the evidence, for fear of causing some irreversible error should the case subsequently go to trial.

I spent about eight hours talking to Billy Keenan the evening of the homicides. I found him to be a very polished liar. Mr. and Mrs. Keenan retained the finest law firm in Durango and hired two additional private investigators in a desperate attempt to find some error in our investigation that would allow their son to go free. Their investigative efforts did nothing more than corroborate our initial findings. They even hired their own criminalist to double check the results of the CBI criminalist—the results never changed.

If you believe they let their son enter a guilty plea even though there was "poor handling by the law, lack of supportable evidence," you are not even remotely in touch with reality. This was a murder that destroyed an entire family.

If you want to direct your sympathy toward something constructive, ask your legislators to change the law so that people like Billy Keenan will never be released from custody. Mr. and Mrs. Janson don't get their girls back at 18 or 21—or ever.

For Joe and Vickie Janson, the news was disappointing but not a surprise. During the two months that had passed since the loss of their daughters, the couple had returned to consciousness. It had been a tormented stretch with spells of emotion that nearly swallowed them in suicide.

The couple left for Las Vegas on the day after the funeral. It was an unlikely destination, but Joe and

Vickie wanted to travel anonymously and remain anonymous. In Las Vegas the parents could hide their tears behind dark sunglasses and the countless flashing lights that illuminated little.

It was a sick time. The choice of destination was wrong. Joe knew it the moment the plane landed. The garishness of the lights, the cheap showgirls, the whirling slot machines, and the boredom on the faces of the petty losers alienated the couple at precisely the moment they needed reassurance that life was worth living. They looked for meaning in a place that disdained the meaningful. It made them feel disgusting and worthless.

The hotel room boxed them in and suicide seemed inevitable. It was only a matter of deciding upon the means of death and finding the strength to kill one another. Life had lost its reason. Even death had lost its reason. Joe and Vickie had lost the will to live and the will to die, and they were trapped in a purgatory between the two.

The first ray of light came from an odd source. It was late at night and Joe and Vickie returned to their room after spending the evening walking the streets, crying, getting lost. Vickie picked up the Bible looking for solace. Joe, for the first time during the week, turned on the television set.

An old James Arness movie was playing. A Western. Arness was lecturing a young settler who had just lost his family during an Indian raid. Arness told the settler that he wasn't the first person to lose his family, and damn it, he had better put his chin up and get moving because life didn't end, and there was no use wallowing in self-pity. You got to get on with your life.

Joe turned off the set. Odd as it seemed, the canned words coming from the flat screen of the television set had eased Joe's pain.

The couple left Las Vegas earlier than planned and came upon blessing number two in the form of the man seated next to them on the plane to Phoenix. Victor Teach was his name. Even his name was too unusual for coincidence. Without Teach's knowing what was happening in their lives, the conversation somehow turned to personal tragedy.

Teach spoke of a friend who had lost his family. In his grief, the friend threw himself in front of a train only to survive paralyzed for several more years before dying himself. "You've got to give it up to God," Teach said. "It's God's will when He takes away the ones you love and it's His will that you keep on living."

What a simple message. What a pure, complete answer, Vickie thought. She felt at that moment as if a giant weight was lifted from her heart and shoulders. For the first time she allowed herself to breathe a sigh of release.

The threesome disembarked in Phoenix, awaiting a plane to Albuquerque. They sat in the airport bar and talked for hours. Joe and Vickie told Teach their story. It was their first outpouring and it was cathartic.

They said good-bye to their friend somewhere amidst the airport bustle. Vickie got Teach's address in Texas and they corresponded once. Then Vickie wrote another letter, but it was returned stamped "No Forwarding Address." She had lost contact with her angel.

The following weeks were filled with meetings and preachers and counselors. Joe and Vickie turned to their church hoping to find solace. But they didn't find it. They felt all the answers were obscure, based on doctrine. They needed answers in black and white, not shades of gray.

They left the Presbyterian Church and turned to the evangelical Foursquare Gospel Church. It offered certainty. Things were clear. Well defined. There was Christ and his salvation and Satan and his evil. Joe and Vickie's survival was proof that Christ was savior. Billy Keenan was proof that Satan's tentacles could reach into every home, every heart. Christ was God, and Satan was the enemy, and Joe and Vickie thanked the Lord Jesus for showing them the difference.

The couple was on a business trip in Denver when

Vic Reichman called with the news that Billy had confessed and Judge Childress had sentenced him to the maximum penalty. Even though they knew beforehand that Billy could get only two years, the outcome angered them. Billy would only serve one year for each of their daughters lives. They called Governor Richard Lamm, who promised again to "address the juvenile code when the legislature met again in January."

If any good would come of the deaths of Kristy and Sherry, it would be a change in the law. Joe and Vickie swore it.

Back in Durango, arrangements were made to move Billy to the Closed Adolescent Treatment Center, the state's home for its most incorrigible teenagers.

Here is where the courts sent the juvenile killers, the torturers, the chronic rapists. Among juvenile workers, Pueblo's Youth Detention Center was considered a kindergarten when compared to the Closed Adolescent Treatment Center—or the CAT Center, as it was called. Pueblo was a mere holding tank. The CAT Center was a well-run brainwashing machine intent on radically altering the behavior of every twisted kid who entered its gates.

If Billy thought his two months at Pueblo were tough, he had a surprise coming.

PART 3

"Thy Will Be Done"

"I have seen the foolish taking root;
　　But suddenly I beheld his habitation cursed.
His children are far from safety,
　　And are crushed in the gate, with none to
deliver them."

—Job 5:3–4

"He shall gather the lambs with his arm
　　and carry them in his bosom . . ."

—Isaiah 40:11

15

Colorado's Closed Adolescent Treatment Center, home for the state's toughest teenagers, is located at the edge of a golf course in the upscale Denver suburb of Lakewood. It's only a few hundred yards from the well-maintained fairways kept ever green by a battalion of sprinklers. The two properties share a fence but the similarity ends there.

The CAT Center is a bunker of a building encircled by a ten-foot-high chain-link fence, which in turn is topped with a tangle of barbed wire. The doors are held shut with thick locks that buzz when disturbed. Inside there are a few meeting rooms used for daily therapy sessions, a living room, a library, staff quarters, bathrooms, and a dining room that doubles for any event out of the ordinary.

There is also the time-out room, reserved for inmates who get out of control. During violent outbursts, inmates are hauled there to vent their aggressions on themselves, the air, or the concrete walls. It's their choice. The room bears the marks where teenagers thrashed their heads, arms, legs, or entire bodies against the walls. A few inmates drew from a well of anger so deep that they smashed the door off its hinges.

The center holds no more than twenty-six juveniles. It is invariably full. Boys outnumber girls greatly, but gender has no privileges. Each inmate is assigned a private six-foot-by-six-foot room with concrete walls and floor. The only view is of the hallway through a tiny window of the room's steel door.

Upon arrival, inmates are provided a G.I. locker for personal belongings. For those just arriving, however, there are few belongings that are personal.

For recreation, inmates are sent outside to an enclosed concrete slab, which is used primarily for basketball. Its size limits play to half-court games. The lone hoop has no netting and the ball often gets knocked down during cross-court passes by the barbed wire overhead.

Of the thousands of juvenile delinquents the state deals with each year, only a handful end up here. They are the boys and girls no one wants or no one can deal with, the "isolated" cases that society prays are the exceptions. The juveniles brought here have failed or have run away from every other program available. Or, like Billy, they are guilty of crimes that make frontpage news.

These delinquents are often labeled by the courts as "chronic" or "incorrigible," too often self-fulfilling phrases. At the CAT Center they are referred to by a different term, Aversive Treatment Evaders. "Aversive" refers to how others react to these teenagers. Most people, even professionals, want to avoid them due to their habitual aggression and violent outbursts. "Treatment Evaders" describes the teenagers' uncanny ability to manipulate, disrupt, or sabotage any treatment program they encounter.

Though the label is used loosely, this class of violent delinquent is growing faster than any other—and getting younger all the time.

According to the FBI's Uniform Crime Reports, between 1983 and 1984, the rate of juvenile arrests for violent crime grew more than twice as fast as property crime arrests. The number of teenagers fifteen years old or younger arrested for murder jumped 11.5 percent. Forcible rape arrests in the same age bracket increased 26.8 percent, and arrests for aggravated assaults jumped 10.6 percent.

In 1983, Billy was one of 1,200 teenagers in the United States under the age of eighteen charged with criminal homicide, and one of 113 teenagers fifteen years old or younger charged with murder.

The specialists at the CAT Center knew very well that Billy and his crime were no anomaly.

Juvenile arrests for violent crime have increased steadily since the late sixties, with only a slight dip in the mid-seventies, due more to a nationwide change in the handling of juvenile cases than any slowdown of delinquent activity. The increase in crime even came at a time when the number of teenagers in the United States declined slightly.

The sad fact is that violent juvenile crime is becoming more frequent and the perpetrators are getting younger each year. Instead of vandalism, petty theft, and drugs, more and younger teenagers are turning to armed robbery, kidnapping, aggravated assault, and murder.

"There really is no nomenclature for kids like this," said Dr. Chris Berry, the Durango psychologist who examined Billy on the day after the murders. "Probably the closest word would be *unattached*. They are not attached to human beings. They have little empathy. They can't feel what other people feel, so they go out and abuse them and kill them, whatever, it doesn't matter."

The number of violent juvenile offenders had increased so rapidly that by the time Billy arrived at the CAT Center, the Colorado Division of Youth Services had plans to build five similar facilities to give the state a total of 192 beds for violent juveniles. Like the CAT Center, many of the new programs were being designed to provide treatment exclusively for violent juvenile offenders. Authorities had little doubts that the beds would be filled. The upsurge in juvenile delinquency had forced other states to take similar action.

Yet with the alarms sounding over a lost generation, an important statistic is often overlooked. Studies have shown that as few as 6 percent of all delinquent juveniles, mostly males, are responsible for the vast majority of violent crime committed by juveniles.

In a landmark study in Philadelphia of 10,000 delinquent males born in 1945, fewer than 7 percent were found to be responsible for more than half of all juvenile crimes and over two thirds of violent juvenile crimes. Similar studies were repeated with males born in the 1950s, 1960s, and 1970s with little change in the results. Many of the juvenile offenders reported having committed ten or more serious crimes for every one for which they were arrested.

These are the violent few, the rare juveniles who frighten the average citizen on the streets and shock communities like Bayfield. This group comprises less than 1 percent of America's youth, yet it demands a disproportionate share of time, money, and resources from the institutions that deal with its members. They overwhelm the juvenile justice system, clog foster care and social service programs, and overcrowd youth correctional institutions everywhere.

What do these violent few have in common? What traits did Billy share with his bunkmates at the CAT Center?

Unfortunately, these youngsters do not share attributes that could serve as certain warning of their impending violence. They do not follow predictable patterns of behavior. They arrive from every end of the socioeconomic spectrum and each of them brings a unique mix of emotional, physiological, genetic, cultural, or familial problems that may or may not cause violent tendencies. Some are repeat offenders and some first-time offenders. Some are arrested at early ages, others are "older" delinquents of sixteen or seventeen. Some start with petty crimes, while others proceed directly to their crime of violence. The only rule when predicting chronically violent offenders is that there is no rule. Only their crimes serve to identify them.

"If you are looking for a single cause, forget it," said Jonathan Hough, assistant director of the CAT Center. "You can deal with the various theories of crime: economic, sociologic, psychological. You can go through the criminology and sociology books and come up with a dozen theories, and they all have some validity, and they all answer some questions, but none answer all questions. You can trace similarities, but you are never going to find a causal factor."

The theories about the cause of violent delinquency range from lack of infant bonding, to child abuse, to cultural decay, and more recently, to pornography, rock music, and television. Some studies even suggest that the junk food diet of the average teenager aggravates violent tendencies.

Delinquency has been tied to violence in the home, genetics, malnutrition, hypoglycemia, and abnormal levels of chemicals and hormones. Studies suggest that deficiencies of vitamin B_6, ascorbic acid, niacinamide, and other vitamins aggravate violent behavior. The male hormone testosterone can cause sexual frustration and strong aggressive behavior in teenage males.

Violent youths many times are diagnosed as having neurological problems and learning disorders, some of which result from brain injuries inflicted in beatings by parents and others. Other teenage delinquents suffer from psychological disorders not limited to juveniles, such as paranoia and schizophrenia.

Most of these explanations, however, suggest that delinquency is a disease, mysteriously guided by fate, destined to strike some and bypass others. Another school of thought argues that, rather than a consequence of nature, delinquency is a consequence of nurturing—or rather a lack of it.

Many infants, neglected or left alone for days with only minimal care, miss the critical bonding stage that is the foundation of all later human development. This bonding involves the consistent repetition of a fundamental cycle of need, rage, gratification, and trust. The cycle must be repeated consistently throughout early childhood and particularly during the first three months of life. If the cycle is broken, infants become "trust bandits," as they are called, and later find it extremely difficult to bond to parents, society, and friends, and even to establish personal goals and aspirations.

"If bonding doesn't happen, we know it will never happen down the line. Without bonding you can't have a conscience," said Dr. Berry.

Even if early bonding is successful, many delinquents are the children of alcoholics or drug abusers and learn quickly enough the painful lessons of distrust and abandonment. Many more children are raised in dysfunctional families, where there is little communication or emotional exchange between family members.

This erosion of the family is often cited as a prime cause of delinquency. An increasing number of latchkey kids are growing up in one-parent households or with two parents absorbed with their careers. The extended family, which provided children with a variety of role models, is vanishing. If teenagers spend a lot of time with friends, often a new family hierarchy emerges, taking the place of the traditional family. The peer leader becomes the dominant role model, the lord of the flies.

Perhaps the greatest provocation for delinquency is sexual or physical abuse. Nothing is more devastating to a child than consistent or brutal violation by a parent, stepparent, or stranger. The damage caused is still being assessed, but everyone agrees that the damage is profound and widespread. Victims of sexual abuse have a far greater tendency to become abusers themselves. The National Center for Juvenile Justice reports that among thirteen- and fourteen-year-olds accused or rape, the greatest common denominator is sexual abuse.

Others blame delinquency on our fast-lane culture

with its banal messages of materialism and immediate gratification that contradict fundamental values. Religion, which once served as society's spiritual infrastructure, finds its influence crumbling, and schools no longer are accorded respect or the luxury of discipline. The influence of the community is also on the decline as families become more mobile and neighbors grow reluctant to reach out and introduce themselves to the strangers next door.

Society has also given teenagers heavy metal music, horror films, and prolific violence on television. Some studies show that by the age of sixteen the average child in the United States will have seen 200,000 acts of violence on television, including 33,000 murders. Experts are still debating whether these forms of entertainment promote violence, but many agree that watching an act of violence can serve as a model when the offender is ready to commit the crime.

There is also boredom to blame. Twenty-five percent of all teenagers drop out of school at some time in their lives. Teenage unemployment, particularly among minorities, is always high. Without school or meaningful work, teenagers have little to occupy their time, and society has few suggestions for them. Perhaps for the first time in history, an entire age group of the community has been disenfranchised. Teenagers have nothing to do.

The availability of drugs and weapons—and the criminal subculture that thrives on them—certainly fuels juvenile violence as well. And, of course, others blame the children themselves and their "me first" attitude.

Despite all the explanations for delinquency, experts are at a loss to explain why some juveniles become chronic delinquents and others don't. "You can blame it on the social history, or childhood tragedy," Hough said, "but there are millions of kids out there on the street with rotten home lives and learning disabilities that caused them to drop out of school, kids who have been abused and raped, on drugs. But they do not rape and murder. There is something else going on, and that something else is a choice. You have to get back to the point where you and the kid can define that choice point together and then work from there.''

One reason why it is so difficult to isolate the cause of delinquency is because causes are rarely isolated in individuals.

Like Billy, most delinquents are a tangle of problems.

Billy arrived at the CAT Center in mid-July. Instead of being the lone monster of the county, as he was in Durango, here Billy was just one of five resident juvenile murderers, ten child molesters, and an assorted mix of teenagers with records of aggravated assault stretching back to before their birthdays were measured in double digits.

Though Billy did not possess the illustrious histories of some of his peers, in his early years he exhibited many of the behaviors common to the group, such as frequent temper tantrums, physical attacks on others, cruelty to animals, chronic lying, vandalism, and fascination with weapons.

Parents, like Billy's, often excuse such behavior as a passing stage or as the caprices of youth. They are far from passing fancies, according to the staff at the CAT Center. They are the symptoms of troubled youths calling out in the only way they know how. The language is universal. Now, Billy had been heard and, even as he unpacked his bag, the CAT Center staff began the process of trying to rescue and reform this boy-killer.

16

Long after Kristy and Sherry were buried and the media vanished, long after the children of Bayfield fell in love with the heart of summer and Billy was ordered to rehabilitate himself at the CAT Center, the Jansons were left to navigate an emotional roller coaster that would neither stop nor slow down long enough to provide them even a temporary reprieve.

The ride jarred them with pangs of guilt for leaving the girls alone and vulnerable. Shame because they were chosen to live while their daughters died. Confusion over the meaning of their lives, now that they were no longer Mommy and Daddy. Outrage over Billy's sentence, that he would be free, perhaps to kill again, before he was eighteen. Disbelief that everyone did not scream their objections to laws that allowed thirteen-year-olds to murder with impunity. There was animosity toward those who believed in Billy's innocence. Bitterness toward the Keenans for the way they had raised their son. Despair over their long, desperate hours of solitude. Sorrow for the others who wept over Kristy and Sherry. And utter remorse over the unfulfilled joys that rightfully belonged to their children but had been taken away.

They passed through the agony of each emotion once, then returned again and again.

Occasionally the grief slowed, and the two were able to breathe, sleep, eat, kiss. Then a fleeting image or emotion abruptly started the engines again. It didn't take much: the impact of the club; the wounds; the spilled blood; the last phone call; the crowd of police cars; the dizzying moment of realization. There were hundreds of such moments, and with each the pain penetrated again, suddenly, physically, so that Joe and Vickie felt often as if they were the victims of Billy's attack.

The most vivid impression for Vickie was the image of Sherry at the sliding glass door watching in horror as Billy beat and stabbed her sister. Then, Billy turning his blank stare at Sherry and the little girl's realization that she was the next victim. This image would assault Vickie unexpectedly, at the most vulnerable moments or just as she felt she was finally emerging from despair. The familiar trembling would revisit. Often Vickie implored death for a reprieve, but it never came.

Then there were the material reminders. When Joe and Vickie returned to their house, they were faced with the children's belongings. Some items even smelled like the girls. Vickie found a roll of film that included pictures taken the day before the murders. They found an old Valentine's Day card made by Sherry, with little red hearts and a small bird on it. It read simply: "To Mom and Dad and Kristy, Made by Sherry, Love Sherry."

Vickie also came across a letter Kristy wrote three weeks before her death:

To my parents on Easter of '83

These past few days I've thought about Easter. I now know that it is much more than waking up Easter morning and finding a chocolate bunny and a basket full of candy. I always knew that there was something more to it. I know you've told me what Easter is all about but it never really sunk in. But now I think I understand. When Christ arose from the dead he brought new life to everything. It seems to all fit together. Easter has always been in the spring when life is just new.

But more and more lately I've noticed that no one seems to realize the true meaning of Easter anymore. This Easter though has really made me think. I really learned a lot. I sure am glad God talks back.

Have a joyous Easter.

Love,
Kristy

The parents felt blessed by these small discoveries. But, invariably, the darkness would enshroud them again and the light would dim and fade and cease. For Vickie, it didn't take much.

Ever since that evening in April on the Keenans' porch when Joe delivered the news, Vickie had wavered on the edge. She wept ten thousand tears and she felt as if each tear were a mere token of the pain inside.

Joe, on the other hand, would not allow emotion to overtake him. He had to hold tough for Vickie, he told himself. She needed his shoulders straight and strong. But soon he found himself living outside his body, growing more detached each day. Soon he no longer knew when he was feeling pain and when he was not. He found his actions becoming mechanical. His heart numb.

When he did take time to feel, the overriding emotion was anger, anger focused completely and exclusively at Billy. To vent it, Joe worked in his garage forging a large, metal, double-headed ax. It was not a simple wood-cutting ax, but a weapon. Joe imagined using it to kill Billy. He shaped the ax head, ground the edges exactingly, and fitted the handle. But the ax remained unused. It was nothing more than an icon to Joe's anger, a physical object to which Joe could transfer his unbounded hostility.

After he was home for some time, the anger finally transformed into grief, and Joe broke down into spells of crying that lasted for days. It had welled up for so long that nothing could hold it back. Protecting Vickie had protected him from having to deal with his own pain.

Now it was Vickie's turn to be strong, to let her man lean on her. The two would switch places many times.

Something else happened. For the first time since the killings, Vickie became obsessed with the details of the murders. At first she had not cared; the details were either too much to bear or unimportant in the spiritual scheme of things. Now she wanted to know it all: the method, the order, the suffering.

But after Vickie discovered some of the details and they sent her spiraling downward again, her interest faded.

Still, she felt a need to physically mark the deaths of the girls, to build a tangible memorial to the moment they were taken away. So at the spot where Sherry died in the woods, the parents placed a small plaque set in stone. It read: "Our daughter Sherry met our Lord Jesus on this spot April 25, 1983."

Except for a few close friends, most people went to great lengths to avoid the bereaved parents. Friends stopped calling and dropping by. No one dared invite the couple to social gatherings. In town, acquaintances darted down supermarket aisles or walked across the street to avoid the Jansons. People acted as if they didn't know who Joe and Vickie were or as if they didn't see the couple from the corner of their eye. Joe and Vickie were the parents who lost their children. They were cursed, suffering, diseased, and no one dared tempt contamination.

Those who wanted to approach the Jansons were not quite sure how to do it. What do you say? How do you express your feelings? It was so easy to say the wrong thing, to make matters worse, that for many it was simpler to bear the guilt of avoidance than to experience the shame of a blunder.

Joleen Stephenson, Sherry's teacher, avoided the Jansons for some time. For months, she had held on to Sherry's school project, the decoupage hot plate Sherry had made as a Mother's Day present. Sherry finished it in class on the day she was murdered. Joleen didn't know what to do with it. Should she keep it or take the chance of disturbing the Jansons? Finally she thought that if her children had been killed she certainly would want anything, everything connected with them. She decided to give Vickie the hot plate. Vickie noticed Joleen's hesitation and made sure she understood that the gesture was appreciated.

There were those who persisted with kindness. Friends and even people the Jansons did not know who called to express their condolences, listen sympathetically, and offer assistance. Joe and Vickie appreciated their concern. It helped somewhat. But the Jansons knew that no one could comprehend the depth of their grief. At times it felt as if the worst punishment was the isolation. There was Joe and Vickie, and then there was the rest of the world.

Friends directed the couple to the several organizations that catered to bereaved parents: the Compassionate Friends, in Oak Brook, Illinois; Families of Homicide Victims, in New York; Survivors of Murder Victims, in Walnut Creek, California; and perhaps the largest organization of all, the vividly named Parents of Murdered Children, with chapters throughout the country. Joe and Vickie thought it was a sad commentary on society that so many organizations existed based on the saddest of all common denominators.

Parents of Murdered Children sent the Jansons a list of tips for bereaved parents. Though Joe and Vickie found truth in the literature, they found little solace in commiserating with those who also had lost their children.

If there was solace to be found anywhere it was in several certitudes to which they held tightly: The girls were not dead, they were living in the presence of Jesus Christ. The spirit of Satan had captured Billy's heart and forced him to kill the girls. The killings were the will of the Lord, and Joe and Vickie need not carry the weight of the "why" on their shoulders. It was the Lord's will that the Jansons lived, and like Job, they had no business questioning God's authority. Vickie took to writing her thoughts in a daily diary.

I see both Kristy and Sherry as passing over all the steps that we must go through to reach heaven with all the pure happiness that we can obtain there. As it is impossible for little children to even imagine the happiness that a mother feels when her child is born, so it is impossible for us to imagine their happiness. I must live the remaining years of my life here confined to this body and all that goes with it in this world, resting assured that both Kristy and Sherry are ecstatically happy and that I shouldn't worry about them.

As far as Billy is concerned, I really still do love him. I still love him because he, I do not believe, is the one who really murdered the girls. I believe that he was possessed by some evil being, some demonic spirit that took his rage and magnified it into something uncontrollable and my daughters were the recipient of that anger. I know that there are things of the spirit world that we do not understand, things of God and things of Satan . . . I therefore believe that I can make the separation of the two in Billy. I also believe that he may be the product now of that evil possession and not at all the Billy we knew. Whether he ever will be again, only God knows.

Vickie had an easier time than Joe forgiving Billy and the Keenans. Around Thanksgiving, Vickie felt strong enough to write Phyllis Keenan a letter.

Dear Phyllis,

As Thanksgiving Day is at hand I am reminded of all I must be thankful for. I know the Lord has brought you and Ed to my heart to add to my list.

I am reminded of the friendship we have enjoyed these past years (including our children's friendship), and I feel joyful and blessed having shared so much together. It was our friendship and love for one another that brought Ed to me hurriedly that day our worlds fell apart. It was that friendship and love that caused you to reach out and hold my hand during that long, long trip to your home, not knowing what we were headed for.

I am thankful also as I remember the many good times we spent together in friendship. That kind of friendship can never be whisked away in a moment, no matter what has transpired. It does however need healing.

I pray that we can meet soon.

Peace & Love in Christ,
Vickie

Vickie never received a reply.

Each day, with their beliefs growing stronger, Joe and Vickie felt more compelled to share their experience with other evangelical Christians. They began by testifying at fundamentalist churches throughout Colorado and the Southwest.

One of their favorite episodes to recount was their return home to Hill Hollow Ranch. Vickie first told the story from the pulpit of her church, the Foursquare Gospel Church in Durango.

She wore a blue chiffon dress and white high-heeled shoes for the occasion. With her coiffed hair and dainty appearance, she looked the embodiment of Christian motherhood. She held the microphone in her hand and paced behind the pulpit. She spoke in a hesitant voice that grew stronger as she talked.

"We stayed with our friends for a month, we didn't go home. You see, our children were murdered at our home, one in our home, the other out in the forest. But we knew that we needed to get back to our home if we were to continue on with our lives. I felt that God did want me to live on. We had spent many years designing the home. We just did so many things on our own there. Our heart is there. And I knew that the Lord did not want us to just run away from it. And even though we were told: 'You can't go back there, how could you go back there? You might as well just leave town.' But that is not what the Lord wanted us to do, and we knew that.

"So we tried to go back home. We were there for fifteen minutes and we ran in fear. There was an evil presence there. It was so heavy and dark and cold. Then we tried another day. We tried for a half hour. But that didn't work. We had to run in fear again.

"So we decided that, if the Lord says in the Word to go out and preach the Gospel to all the nations, to heal the sick, to raise the dead, to cure the lepers, and to cast out demons, that he meant that. He meant that for all of his people to do that.

"Knowing the evil was there, the only way to reclaim our house was to cast the evil out. Well, how do you do that? That was the question.

"Well, you just do it. You take the name of Jesus and the authority and the power that he has given you and you just do it. So we stopped at the top of our driveway. It's eight hundred or nine hundred feet long. It's pretty long. And we felt that we needed to cast Satan out of our home and all the property around it. Because he had possession of it, very definitely. So we stopped at the top of our driveway on the strength of our belief. Joe and I had arm in arm, and we said: 'By the authority that Jesus has given us, in the name of Jesus, Satan we bind you and cast you away from here.'

"And the first step was shaky, and the second step was shaky, and the third step was shaky. But the farther we got down that driveway, the bolder and bolder and stronger we got. Pretty soon we were yelling, 'Satan, I bind you! Cast you! You have no authority over here! We are children of the King! This is holy ground!'

"We have ten acres of ground. We did not go over all of it. We went all over the place where we knew the children played, where everything had happened. It was tough. It wasn't easy. And we got to the house, and we opened up the door and it was really bad. We went through every room in the house, touched everything, and it's a holy place. We reclaimed it in the name of Jesus. And that was the real step to come back and to begin our lives once more."

After Vickie spoke, Joe took the pulpit. His booming voice rarely needed the microphone. He often wore wild and bright ties to show people, he told the congregation, that it was all right to laugh.

"Pain, horror, fear, confusion, despair. Who does that sound like? That's the devil. He wants you to think of death. I think he is the one who created the word because that word doesn't exist in God's vocabulary. The state that we live in, here in our flesh on the earth, that's the state that Satan wants us to remember and hang on to. All the pain and the garbage, he wants you to just dwell on that. That was what was happening to us, constantly.

"You know, I was thinking of this the other night. The Holy Spirit came down to me a number of times during those first two or three days. I don't know whether it was a gift of understanding or knowledge, maybe the pastor can straighten me out on that. But the Holy Spirit led me to understand that Sherry, when she was running through the woods, when the boy hit her from behind, Jesus Christ was standing right there going 'Got you,' and he grabbed her. Think of it as a door, if you would. Jesus Christ physically stood on that property.

"We can think about death all we want to, but they just passed over into a new life. Don't get me wrong, that realization didn't just cheer us over, and we went on. We still fight with that because we are in the world. We still walk around on the ground and the rain still falls on our head. But we know the girls are in heaven waiting for us.

"A lot of guys have come up to me and asked: 'What are you going to do about Billy?' And there are a lot of you macho guys out there that have probably asked yourselves what you would do if someone killed your kids.

"I don't know if you realize it or not, but the distance between the sun and Pluto is three billion, six hundred and sixty-six million miles. That's a long way. It takes five and a half hours for light to travel that far. Now, let's talk about eternity for a minute. If you took grains of sand, started at the sun and went all the way to Pluto, you could take each grain of sand and think of that as a lifetime. And the whole line of sand is eternity. What I do during the little grain of sand that is my own lifetime is going to affect the time of the whole line. Understand what I mean?

"So I can go over and do all sorts of neat Rambo stuff to this kid. But that jeopardizes my life with my children for the whole time. And I'm not going to do that. A lot of us think that we can cheat on our income taxes or chase a good-looking girl down the road, but all of that stuff affects our lives with Jesus and the eternal life that he says he will give us without reservation. And if he wants me to forgive that boy, I'm going to forgive him.

"I'm going to have a certain phrase put on my headstone. And that phrase is: 'Oh, Death, where is Thy sting? Oh, Grave, where is Thy victory? I go to my children who are with Jesus.'

"And I am looking forward to that.

"If I would tell you one thing from our experience that I have learned, it is to take the time now, today, to hold on to the people that you love. Tell your kids how important they are to you. I was the perfect example of a father that didn't tell his kids that he loved them all the time. Oh, I did, but never enough. Something might happen and it could be a long time before you see them again. You *will* see them again. But it will be a long time.''

17

In the weeks and months following the murders of Kristy and Sherry, no question was asked more frequently yet answered with less certainty than "Why?" Why had Billy found it necessary to slaughter the girls so savagely?

For the fundamentalist friends of Joe and Vickie, the answer was solid black. Satan, invisible yet ever present on this earth, found a little lost boy and manipulated him as he manipulates so many human puppets in his eternal play to bring chaos and suffering upon the world. Billy did not have the benefit of knowing Jesus as his personal savior and therefore could not deploy His glories to shield himself against Satan's treachery.

For Dr. John Nagel, the psychiatrist who hypnotized Billy, the boy suffered from one or more of a jumble of psychiatric ailments: "Adjustment reaction of adolescence, unsocialized aggressive behavior, possible acute hysterical dissociative reaction related to atypical dissociative disorder, and or brief reactive psychosis."

The diagnosis did little to impress the Jansons or many of the townspeople who appreciated clearer answers to life's questions.

Dr. Chris Berry, the psychologist who examined Billy the morning after the killings, attempted a hypothesis in more human terms. "I think it was symbolic," Berry said shortly after the murders. "I don't think he was killing the Janson kids. I think he was killing something else or somebody else. It could have been his mother. It could have been society. It could have been women in general. The girls just happened to be the target that day. If it hadn't been them, it probably would have been somebody else. And if it hadn't happened when he was thirteen, he would have been eighteen or twenty-six or some other age.''

The philosophic Captain Nick Boyd saw an even larger picture. ''I think they knew he had problems and was not a happy kid, but I don't know if anyone is happy in this society anymore. It shows that society is not dealing with life, that we are not a happy people with all our wealth, technology, and freedom. We don't live well. If we valued our children so much, and if there had been a parent home in both of those houses when they were back from school, theoretically it would not have happened. But Billy would have had to sit down and tell his parents. He would have had to been able to talk with them and tell them 'I am not happy, I'm frustrated,' even before this event.''

To Billy's defense attorney, the explanation was more pragmatic. ''Have you ever driven down a road,'' said Dave West, ''and thought, just *thought* about crossing the double yellow line and hitting the car coming the other way? You might even inch your car over in that direction. But at the last second, you pull back because, though you may think about it, you can never do it. Billy Keenan did more than think about killing the girls. He crossed that line. He never pulled back.''

For many of Billy's schoolmates there was no answer and it was foolish to search for one. Billy did it, and Kristy and Sherry were dead. It's a fact, just like there was Adolf Hitler and there was a big war. It happened, you grow up and you move on, hopefully away from Bayfield. Sometimes you think about it, sometimes it goes away for a long time, but it always comes back. And you don't ask why because there isn't an answer and there never was. It just is.

The assembly of staff workers at the CAT Center who

poked and prodded at Billy's motivation were compelled to arrive at a workable diagnosis if they were to help him with treatment. Dr. Nagel's labels were helpful in describing the symptoms but did little in explaining the cause. If Billy was to change, the staff had to discover what caused the "brief reactive psychosis" or whatever it was that allowed him to kill with impunity.

They started with a battery of educational, vocational, and medical tests. Delinquency is often aggravated by physiological factors, but no serious problems were discovered with Billy. An EEG and CAT scan ruled out any organic problems as well. After several therapy sessions, the staff concluded that Billy's problems were purely psychological.

The first symptom was the most obvious: despite his admission in hypnosis and his confession before the judge, Billy still denied killing Kristy and Sherry. He would not take responsibility. He could not say "I did it."

Staff workers called authorities in La Plata County and requested photos of the dead girls' bodies. They also called the Jansons and asked for photos of the girls when they were alive. The photos were brought out in therapy sessions and pinned on the walls of Billy's room as constant reminders that here, at least, he could not escape his deeds.

Staff noted that Billy was also a chronic liar and lied whenever it was to his advantage. They wrote in an evaluation that he was "particularly adept at covering his tracks and withholding thoughts and reactions to situations." They found that the more Billy knew about the staff and his peers and their expectations, the more proficient he became at lying to them.

He was also found to be "self-centered and self-indulgent." He was irresponsible, acted immaturely when it was in his best interest, and responded positively only when he felt that it would lessen punishment or help him obtain special privileges. With staff he was at times "overly compliant" to mask "manipulated and

calculated efforts to protect himself from consequences." Consequently, "he sought out others whom
he perceived as powerful and went to great lengths to
ally himself with them." The relationships he formed,
however, were nothing more than "superficial, self-
serving attachments."

He suffered from very low self-esteem, and whenever he got in trouble or felt threatened he waited for
someone to rescue him, as he had with his dad back
home. He portrayed himself as the victim of everything
that happened to him and used his victimization as an
excuse for his behavior, however inappropriate.

Billy also played "power thrust" games, as they were
called at the CAT Center, each with its own idiomatic
expressions, such as "get-backs," "me-firsts," "guilt
trips," "superior behaviors," and "put-downs."

Furthermore, Billy displayed what the psychologists
labeled as "serious cognitive distortions." He perceived events differently than as they happened. He particularly distorted the motivations of others.

Finally, the staff found that on a day-to-day basis
Billy displayed few social skills and few alternatives for
dealing with problems and difficult situations he en-
countered. He overcontrolled his aggressions and believed he was unable to exert any control over his
environment. He compensated by "an inflated sense of
self-omnipotence, by projecting omnipotent powers to
significant others, and by excessive dependency."

In short, Billy exhibited contradictory symptoms. He
was at the same time a helpless victim and the all-
knowing, all-seeing Billy. He was both the bully and
the victim, the controller and the controlled. He
switched back and forth between the roles like a waif
looking for a home.

In conclusion, the staff found that Billy was a "cold
narcissistic youth with many of the emotional characteristics of a criminal personality."

Some psychologists speculated that Billy's narcissistic tendencies resulted in part from his home life, where

he and his troubles always seemed to take center stage. His mother doted over him, made excuses for him, gave him whatever he wanted. His father did the same. But from his father came something more.

Discipline.

For that Billy feared and admired his father tremendously. At the CAT Center, the staff found that Billy allied himself with powerful peers and "projected omnipotent powers to them," only to play himself in a position of excessive dependency. So it was at home with his father. His father was everything, possessed all powers, and defined Billy's very sense of being. The man held all the strings to Billy's self-esteem. "Inconsistent management with harsh discipline," the book called it. Billy perceived his mother as weak, soft, passive. But his father was strong, dominant, assertive. And Billy was in awe.

Like Billy, many of the CAT Center's worst delinquents were not necessarily former residents of housing projects or broken homes. They were "middle-class murderers," young, white boys with angelic faces and sweet smiles who came from "normal" households in the suburbs. They would feel right at home on the golf course next door. Billy was one of these "cherubs," as they were called by the staff.

"There are the kids who feel they're entitled to be treated as the center of the universe," Dr. Vickie Agee, the creator of the CAT Center program, told reporters. "They react with violence when they go into a narcissistic crisis—when they realize everything's not going their way."

Billy's fellow inmate, Drew, was a prime example. The dark-haired fourteen-year-old had lived with his thirty-five-year-old mother in a suburban town house until the day they got into an argument. Drew's mother told him that she didn't want to buy him a waterbed. When she turned to leave his room, Drew picked up a bar from his weight set and struck her over the head. He hit her again and again.

She was able to stagger out the door and down the stairs, but Drew caught and choked her. Still she wouldn't die. So Drew pulled his mother back upstairs, grabbed a hunting knife, and stabbed her. Then he dragged her to a bathtub and held her under water until her body went limp. Court records showed that through it all her only words were "I love you, Drew." She said it over and over.

In court, the public defenders argued that Drew's mother had psychologically abused her son because of her infatuation with her career in real estate. The judge disagreed and sent Drew to the CAT Center. "Even if she was a rotten mother, she didn't deserve to die," Dr. Agee told reporters.

Mark was another CAT Center cherub. The fourteen-year-old kid with the Hollywood face was caught shortly after he pumped a hail of bullets into the body of a thirteen-year-old friend on the grounds of the local junior high school. He used a handgun his parents said they didn't know he owned. Mark was tried for first-degree murder and sentenced as an adult to twelve years in prison. Because of his age, his first stop was a four-year stint at the CAT Center. Mark received lots of letters and cards from girls who thought he was cute and had saved newspaper clippings about him. Late in his stay he was puzzled by their motivations and asked Dr. Agee why they acted like this. "Mark," she told him, "it's your face."

For these cherubs, the symptoms were there to recognize: a narcissistic life-style underscored by lying, stealing, truancy, running away, destruction of property, physical cruelty to animals and people, use of weapons, and fighting.

Yet if narcissism alone is benign, when do the symptoms indicate a fatal disease? The three boys at the CAT Center were not unlike millions of teenagers in this country who have learned society's lessons well. Plenty of youngsters are narcissistic, steal, lie, and cut school. What turned these selfish kids into killers?

For Billy, staff workers believed they uncovered at least a partial explanation during a series of intense family therapy sessions spread out over the first few months of his stay. Billy revealed that several months before he killed the girls he had been sexually molested by a male friend of the family. No charges were ever filed for the abuse, and the identity of the abuser remains unknown outside the therapy session walls.

Psychologists concluded that it was Billy's narcissistic focus, along with anger at his abuser and the teacher who confronted him the day of the murders, that helped provoke the killings.

"Sexual assault," one staff worker wrote of Billy, "generally creates feelings of powerlessness which, for a narcissistic youth, can be experienced as a catastrophic event. The degree of violence exhibited during the murders is partially attributed to rage reactions."

As Dr. Berry had diagnosed from the very beginning, Billy was angry, but not at the Janson girls. He was angry at life, at his victimization, at his powerlessness, at reality for failing to reflect his delusions of grandeur. His self-perception, already abject, was further diminished by the sexual abuse. Billy was angry and miserable because his self-centered universe was falling apart. And on the day of the murders, when Billy cringed at the thought of telling his father about his run-in with Mr. Winter, Billy feared the greatest loss of all, the admiration of his father.

With his bravado, Billy seemed desperate to emulate his father. He idolized him and dreamed of running away with him, psychologists learned. Now he was failing miserably. He had bragged about his hunting, his knives, and his fearlessness in the woods. But someone had abused him and he had been powerless to stop it. He was the hunted, the captured, the victim. He had tried so hard to prove his worth. Now he was failing in school and his thin facade of worthiness was crumbling. Others were aware that he wanted desperately to possess the power and security of manhood. But his weakness was apparent for all the world to see. Billy was sinking lower and lower. He could feel the bottom. Smell it. Touch it. The feeling was unbearable.

But as low as Billy was feeling, there were a few things he considered more despicable than himself. In the world Billy created, according to psychologists, those things were women, animals, and children. He loathed them because he loathed himself and they were more vulnerable than he. If he deserved punishment certainly so did these creatures. If he deserved to hurt so did the little animals. The Janson girls.

How might it have happened? It is all speculation, but at some point the pain becomes too much to bear. Perhaps it is when the intolerable Mr. Winter threatens Billy with failure, or when the girls tease Billy in class by holding up silly dress patterns to him.

Then something snaps. Conscience stretches until it becomes transparent. Anguish alters reality ever so slightly. Killing doesn't mean what it did. It becomes a cry, an act necessary for self-definition. Consequences vanish. Existence is defined in terms of retribution. There is Billy and the world. Billy hurts and the world must hurt, too.

The situation is right. There are two unwary victims. Something is said, some mild provocation that releases the well of anger. For one split second there is no substance but rage.

And the first blow comes.

It feels good.

The hurt subsides because someone else is hurting, too. Another blow, then another.

It feels so good. Anguish relaxes its suffocating grip. Release; every blow is release.

Billy is in total control again. It is bliss. There is no Mr. Winter. No sexual abuser. No Mr. Janson.

Billy is the conqueror, the abuser, the one with the power to threaten failure, and these little creatures have inherited his pain. It no longer belongs to Billy.

There is silence in the woods. One of the girls is

crying. Billy hits her again. In the kitchen he finds a knife. He toys with the girls, their bodies, their faces. Every thrust is power. Every penetration is revenge. There is no Kristy and Sherry, only two repositories of anger. He satiates himself with his domination. He wallows in it just as he had wallowed in his self-pity moments before. Billy is king. Billy is brilliant.

But then, a noise. A car. Has someone heard? Has someone seen? God, no. A new emotion overwhelms him. Fear. He can feel it in his fingers, his tongue, his scalp.

What if Mr. Janson finds out? What is his father finds out? What if he gets caught? What if they punish him?

Panic. Don't panic.

Suddenly the universe made so elementary by death is complicated again with signals of consequence, alarm, dread.

There must be no little Sherry or Kristy to tattle. They cannot speak. They must go away. They must die. Please die. Take this knife and die.

It is over.

The girls no longer move. The fantasy comes crashing down. He runs home. He calls Daddy. Daddy, rescue me; Daddy, rescue me.

Billy talks to the police. They believe him. His story is good. It's working. Hours go by. He is almost home. It will be over soon. Hang on.

But something happens. The officers start yelling. You did it. We know you did it. We have evidence. You did it.

What's going on? They know. But how could they know? They must know. Their power is overwhelming.

Where's his dad? He's got to speak to his dad. But Dad cannot help. The police are more powerful than his dad. They want to hurt him. God, no.

He is taken away. Save me, Dad. It is cold and dark in the squad car. Where are you, Dad? The handcuffs squeeze his wrists. Dad. His hands throb. Please, Dad.

The jail smells and the light glares. The men are so big. They have guns, uniforms. Please, Daddy, please.

He trembles. He is cold. He sweats. He rocks. The room swirls.

His mind goes blank. The deed burrows underground, under consciousness. It exists in another reality.

There is no knife. There is no club. There are no murders.

Morning comes. He is asked questions. He can answer in only half sentences. It's hard to talk. Hard to think. Hard to listen.

Billy's world has shattered. A billion pieces lay on the jail cell floor and Billy isn't even one of them.

Three months go by and Billy has restored the shattered pieces, but the vessel is still not right. It is cracked and fragile and unbalanced. He is just one more "cold narcissistic youth" like Drew and Mark, no different, no more disturbed, no more in need of help than his twenty-five fellow inmates at the CAT Center.

If there is a difference it is that he has good chance of recovery. The pieces may be misaligned but they are all there. He does not suffer from physiological or learning disabilities. He is bright, and despite his troubles in school, fairly well educated. Most important, his family is willing to enter into therapy with Billy.

By all accounts, the Keenans' anguish is sincere and deep. They are concerned parents. Perhaps they had made mistakes. Perhaps their relationships with one another had not been healthy. Perhaps they had ignored the symptoms of Billy's problems. Whatever their error, it was not the result of not loving him or one another. Like most parents, they had wanted a life of happiness for their children, nothing more. They too suffered a terrible loss and, like the Jansons, suffered long after the crimes vanished from the front pages.

The CAT Center encouraged their cooperation. Many of the parents of CAT Center teenagers refused to enter therapy with their children. Billy was lucky. His family was with him.

Billy also had the benefit of the CAT Center's competence. In its first seventeen years, nearly two thirds of its graduates never got into trouble again. Of the one third that did, many were convicted of much lesser crimes than the crimes that had landed them in the CAT Center in the first place. There were those, of course, who continued their criminal behavior and ended up in prison, or worse, on the streets. Nevertheless, the CAT Center took the worst of the worst and rehabilitated two out of three. The center was one of a handful of pioneering programs aimed at rehabilitating the violent juvenile offender. If Billy was to find salvation, it would be here.

Teenagers familiar with the workings of Colorado's juvenile system glorify the CAT Center because they know it is reserved for the very worst offenders. New inmates bring with them a certain pride for having "made it" here. They are the baddest of the bad and proud of it. Their crime had earned them a look inside the infamous CAT Center.

Since the facility is closed and placement is long-term, CAT Center residents have little opportunity to inform their peers on the outside of what really happens inside the squat brick building near the golf course. The foolish pride of the new inmates doesn't last long.

When most juveniles arrive at the CAT Center, they are bent on destruction, either of themselves or others, anything to get them out of the program. This tactic has worked before. Some new inmates are so disturbed that they will defecate, urinate, and vomit voluntarily over themselves and others in search of release. It may take months before they learn that their assaultive behavior will not get them transferred to another program. Lesson number one is that the CAT Center is the end of the line.

Even those who behave well upon arrival come with serious problems. They care little for others, often little for themselves, and only a few have a conscience worth noting. The only relationships they have known have been destructive. All they bring are bizarre histories and tales of horror buried deep within their subconscious. The average length of stay is between one and two years. In that time, the staff must try to reverse a lifetime of self-destructive behavior, violence, and aggression.

To the juvenile it may seem otherwise, but his stay is orchestrated from the moment he arrives to his final good-bye. Every moment of every day, every activity, from recreation to education, is used as a tool for therapy.

The second lesson an inmate learns is that his life, his behavior, his past is hung out on the line for everyone to see. There are no secrets, no places to hide. Everyone in the program is informed publicly of each inmate's crimes and behavior patterns. Every reaction is open to discussion.

Twice daily, each inmate is graded on a simple point system assessing his behavior in seven areas: adult interactions, peer interactions, personal hygiene, participation, work quality, impulse control, and honesty. Good behavior earns points. Bad behavior loses points. The more points accrued, the more quickly the inmate can move up levels and earn privileges, such as cigarettes, two-hour baths, phone calls, extended hours in the evening. When points are lost, privileges are lost. The inmate always knows where he stands and soon learns that he is the master of his fate.

Like all new inmates, after a short stint on the Entry Level Team, Billy skipped Team One and was afforded all the privileges of Team Two. The move is designed to show new arrivals that, if they can handle it, they will be treated as responsible, mature adolescents. As a Team Two member, Billy could wear personal clothing, eat all desserts and snacks, and correspond by mail without restrictions. If he continued to earn points on Team Two, Billy could earn more privileges, such as visits with his family outside of therapy and permission to decorate his room.

As often happens, inmates can't handle Team Two, and they are quickly demoted to Team One, where they must wear institutional clothing, are forbidden to talk during meals, and perhaps worst of all, must be in bed with lights out one hour before Team Two members.

In his first few months, Billy was demoted twice to Team One, once for lying and another time for "negative behavior."

There is one level lower than Team One. It's called Monad, and it has only the most elementary privileges. Billy was demoted to Monad twice, once for verbally threatening a peer and a second time for hiding a laundry bag rope in his room. Each time he was demoted, Billy quickly moved up again to the next team. He seemed to understand the system and appreciate its fairness.

The next lesson that each inmate is taught is that bad behavior is dealt with immediately. For some, it is the first time in their lives that they had to suffer prompt repercussions for their actions. If the inmate is "acting up," insincere, lying, cheating, or behaving in any other manner deemed inappropriate by peers or staff, privileges are revoked. If the bad behavior includes violence, then a demotion is probable.

To the utter astonishment of new inmates, they also learn they are held responsible for the behavior of their peers. If someone "acts up," everyone near the offender is obliged to write him a ticket—or "book 'em," as it's called. If a nearby inmate does not book a peer who is behaving badly, he is booked also. Offenders are then brought before a tribunal of peers and staff. If they are guilty, punishment is meted out right away. There's no way out.

Soon inmates realize that they have to watch out for their fellow inmates if they don't want to get into trouble themselves. At some point during their stay, this vigilance turns into caring, and the beginnings of constructive friendships take form. Unlike other programs that attempt to disband peer pressure, the CAT Center program uses peer pressure as the driving force for rehabilitation.

Behavior modification, however, is just the beginning. It is not enough to teach offenders that their bad behavior solicits immediate penalty. It doesn't work that way in the real world, where these teenagers are headed. They must dig deep into their hearts, take responsibility for their crimes, grieve, and only then can they begin to change.

The centerpiece of the program is therapy. Every day, for at least two hours, inmates break into groups and are motivated to reveal themselves and to confront one another on their feelings, attitudes, and distortions. The groups are led by staff members, though the motivation comes from the peers themselves. If the group isn't producing results it is forced to stay in session until the cause of the insincerity is rooted out. Some groups have stayed in session for days. Billy was placed in a special "murderers group."

The delinquents soon discover that there is no way out of the building, no way out of therapy, and no way out of their behavior. They can't run away, assault, steal, or lie their way out. They have no choice but to deal with themselves and each other, and the pain is often excruciating. This is the end of the line, and that is the program's trump card.

Especially for the sex offenders and murderers, the first goal is to get them to take responsibility for their crimes. Some teenagers take months before they admit their guilt. All their lives they have learned to blame others for their actions: "He was going to kill his parents, I was just trying to stop him." "She wanted it or she would have fought harder." "I was high at the time, I didn't know what I was doing."

Getting them to say "I did it," and mean it, is the first milestone to recovery. And it's a very hard step to take. It took Billy months.

When a juvenile finally admits his guilt, "it's an extremely emotional experience," writes Dr. Agee. "Like lancing an emotional boil, the youth is unable to control his expression of sorrow and shame . . . No matter how convincing their initial facade, the response is always the same, an outpouring of horror and shame." One youth spent many hours rocking, sobbing and moaning in a semifetal position at the moment he admitted responsibility for raping a woman in front of her children.

"There may be some youths," Agee said, "who are indeed the cold, unfeeling, hardened killers or rapists described in the media, but [I] have yet to experience one."

The next step is to encourage and amplify the inmate's grief. It's a long, cruel process where the youth is expected to express anger at himself, his victim, his family, society. Grief hurts, and the youth longs to return to the time when he wasn't forced to take responsibility for his crime. But the therapy group won't let him regress. They confront him until he has no choice but to grieve some more, to analyze his behavior, to understand his nature, until he becomes completely vulnerable.

At this critical juncture, the inmate's ego is stripped down to nothing. He is no longer what he once was. His slate has been erased as clean as the mind will allow.

Then the rebuilding starts. He must learn new habits, new behaviors, new attitudes based on the behavioral and therapeutic cheerleading of his peers and staff. He has reached the third and final phase of therapy.

By now, many months have passed and new juveniles have joined the group. The new inmates don't want to accept responsibility for their crimes. But the older peers, who have journeyed through the hell of self-exploration, will confront them. The older peers are helping their brothers and sisters, and for many it is the first constructive action they have experienced in their lives. In helping others, they help themselves build their self-esteem. Peer pressure works again.

At the same time, the older inmates are learning new skills, some as simple as balancing a checkbook or learning how to date, shop, have fun. They may earn a GED degree, or learn vocational skills. If their behavior is sincerely improved, they can take a job in the community and begin the gradual process of reentering society.

Inevitably, it's time to leave. Some juveniles stay just a few months at the CAT Center, others four or five years. When it is time to emerge, the teenagers are faced with the seductions of society. At every street corner lurk opportunities and inducements to revert back to their lives before the CAT Center. There are old friends to deal with. Family members to confront. Drugs and alcohol. Easy money and easy sex. The world hasn't changed much. It is the same old place filled with uncaring people and disappointment.

And then the "ifs" begin. If the juvenile has truly changed his behavior. If his insight is keen enough to probe and reveal his problems. If he has sincerely learned to feel that strange new emotion, remorse. If he can live through the guilt. If he can forgive his parents. If he can persevere. If he can make peace with himself. And if he can find salvation through sanity.

If all these things happen, if he can sustain them, then, perhaps, he has a chance to succeed in the world outside. And perhaps he may know happiness for the first time in his young life.

18

On a cold day in late January nine months after the murders, Joe and Vickie sat nervously in the antechamber of a hearing room in Denver's gold-domed Capitol Building. In a few minutes they would be asked to testify before the state Senate Judiciary Committee. The legislative body was debating a bill that would toughen Colorado's Children's Code, a compendium of laws that the media was calling "among the weakest in the nation."

If passed, Senate Bill 127 would create a new class of "aggravated juvenile offenders," consisting of delinquent twelve- and thirteen-year-olds charged with first- or second-degree murder. Children in this new class would face a sentence of up to five years in a juvenile facility. Then, if the delinquent was found to be "incorrigible or was not being helped by treatment," he or she could be transferred to the state penitentiary at the age of eighteen.

An additional amendment under debate would ensure that once in prison, juveniles would receive time off for good behavior calculated only on the time they actually spent in the penitentiary, not based on their entire sentence.

The bill would give authorities the power to send twelve-year-olds to prison if need be. It was, if not landmark legislation, then certainly a bold move toward tougher handling of delinquents. The bill was one of seven aimed at clarifying the Children's Code that were under consideration by the two houses of the Colorado legislature. The highest state in the union, like so many others, were undergoing the formidable task of revamping its juvenile laws.

The Jansons quietly rehearsed their testimony as they awaited their turn to speak. Though they knew today's hearing would have no bearing on their case, they had waited a long time for this moment. Joe and Vickie were testifying for the benefit of the unknowing victims of future juvenile murderers. They planned on telling the lawmakers that they opposed the bill. It wasn't harsh enough. They wanted the punishment to fit the crime regardless of age.

"The law has blown it," Joe told a reporter for the *Denver Post.* "Why should there be a difference in the degree of sentencing between a juvenile and an adult when there is no difference in the degree of death of the victim?"

Joe had distilled his argument to thirty words. The *Post* reporter liked that. The quote played high up in the paper's story on the bill and was picked up by the Associated Press and printed in several regional papers.

Supporters of the bill saw the heavy coverage as confirmation that the press and public were sincerely interested in toughening juvenile justice laws. They were also aware that the sensational aspects of the Jansons' case would greatly help their cause, regardless of the Jansons' stance. Who couldn't sympathize with parents who had lost their children and also had lost the opportunity for peace of mind because the killer was twelve days shy of his fourteenth birthday? Supporters of the bill knew they couldn't ask for a better publicity vehicle.

If the Jansons found themselves in the spotlight, it was exactly where they wanted to be. Their spiritual beliefs had helped them cope with the death of their children but did little to help them rationalize the injustice of Billy's sentence. His punishment was the work of man and therefore, the couple believed, required their earthly attention. And so, during the late summer and early fall months after the deaths of Kristy and Sherry, the Jansons set out to toughen the state's juvenile laws. They began by circulating petitions in Durango and Bayfield and later in Denver, Grand Junction, and Colorado Springs. With the help of friends, in a matter of weeks they gathered 2,683 signatures. The petition read:

A juvenile as described by this petition is *anyone* under the age of 18.

1. As concerned citizens for juveniles who commit violent crimes, we ask for tougher laws for Class I Felonies (murder and attempted murder).

2. We feel that in the case of Class I Felonies committed by a juvenile, the courts should be allowed to hand down a sentence based on the severity of the crime and not the age of the convicted juvenile felon.

3. Juveniles should be placed in a juvenile detention center until the age of 18, then serve the remainder of the sentence in an adult facility.

Many people refused to sign the form. They were troubled by the notion of sentencing children to long prison terms. What if a ten-year-old child committed a murder, or an eight-year-old? If a five-year-old discharges a gun in a moment of anger, do you shackle him, put him on trial, and whisk him away from his parents for the next twenty years? If society begins punishing five-year-olds as it does adults, what does that say about society? How can you teach children the value of life if you don't value their lives?

Those who penned their names to the petition believed that the rare case of the eight-year-old killer should not make it easy for older delinquents to get away with violent crime. These kids knew very well the difference between right and wrong. They must be punished for their actions, otherwise society would be overrun with children free to carry out any mischief they desired. Society had changed a lot since the days when a delinquent was a kid who came home late at night. The laws had to be amended to reflect that change.

Two months after the Janson murders—and partially in response to them—Governor Richard Lamm established the Commission to Review the Colorado Children's Code. Cases like the Jansons' had convinced many politicians and law enforcement officials that the Children's Code needed revising. Lamm had other problems with juveniles aside from a crazed killer in the far corner of the state. Well-organized youth gangs were operating freely in Denver and Colorado Springs and other smaller cities throughout the state. They specialized in robbery, assault, drugs, and prostitution. The towering Rocky Mountains to the west and the monotonous plains to the east did little to protect the pristine state from the societal ills that pained states on the coasts. Colorado was no different. Its courts were seeing fifteen-year-old repeat offenders as big and hardened as many older criminals. Every day the courts dealt with thirteen-year-old prostitutes and twelve-year-old drug runners. And the courts did so with a hodgepodge of juvenile laws ill-designed to handle this new wave of delinquency. Colorado was caught in the same time warp that trapped most other states in the union: modern youth and antiquated laws.

When juvenile laws in the United States first distinguished between juveniles and adults in the early nineteenth century, violent juvenile crime was rare.

The first major ruling on juveniles came during an 1838 Pennsylvania case in which a minor, at the request of her mother, was incarcerated as "incorrigible." Her father wanted her released, however, and petitioned the court. He argued that she had not been granted the benefit of a trial due to her age.

The Pennsylvania Supreme Court denied the father's

appeal, concluding that the Sixth Amendment right to "a speedy and public trial by an impartial jury" did not apply to minors. Furthermore, the court ruled that the state had the right and duty to intervene as a "substitute parent" when the parents were "unequal to the task."

This landmark case established the doctrine of *parens patriae*, which served as the foundation for all juvenile law to come. Under this philosophy, a child was brought before the court for protection rather than for prosecution. Other states quickly affirmed this rehabilitative philosophy and structured laws accordingly. In 1899, the state of Illinois established the first juvenile court. The new court was given the mandate to "consider the child in need of care and protection of the state."

By 1920 nearly every state in the country had established a juvenile court based on this rehabilitative philosophy. And since the nascent juvenile courts made great pains to separate themselves from their criminal counterparts, a new nomenclature emerged, as well. The offender's wrongdoing was no longer considered a crime, rather the "cause for delinquency." The term "defendant" was displaced by the more innocuous "respondent." Indictments were referred to as "petitions." The simple trial became the "adjudicatory hearing." Words like *guilt* and *innocence* became obsolete; a juvenile could either "agree to the finding" or "deny the petition." Finally, whatever the outcome, it was to be referred to as a "commitment" and by no means a sentence.

Since juvenile cases were civil and not criminal cases, it followed naturally that there was no need to worry about the constitutional protection due defendants, nor the stringent regulations concerning warrants and evidence gathering, nor any of the other rigid standards that applied to adult criminal cases. The court's sole objective was to determine if the state should exercise its right of *parens patriae*. If so, then the state would decide what recourse was best for the child, whether it be treatment, supervision, guidance, or, as the last resort only, punishment. The process was not considered even remotely connected with the criminal justice system.

That all changed in 1966 when the United States Supreme Court heard its first cases involving juvenile justice.

Morris A. Kent, Jr., was a sixteen-year-old with a history of burglaries and purse snatching. On September 2, 1961, he entered the apartment of a woman in the District of Columbia and robbed and raped her. Three days later Kent was taken into custody by police and was interrogated over a two-day period without his parents or a lawyer present. He admitted his involvement in the offense and volunteered information about similar offenses he had allegedly committed. Since he was sixteen, he was subject to the jurisdiction of the juvenile court and was detained without petition for over one week.

Later, the juvenile court judge waived his jurisdiction and sent Kent to criminal court. Kent subsequently was tried and convicted of burglary and robbery and sentenced to thirty to ninety years in prison, though he was found not guilty by reason of insanity on the rape charge. His lawyers appealed his conviction on several grounds, all of which involved alleged violations of due process.

The Supreme Court heard the case and agreed with Kent's lawyers. They ruled that even though "the juvenile court should have considerable latitude" to determine whether a juvenile's case should be waived to criminal court, "it does not confer upon the juvenile court a license for arbitrary procedure. . . . There is no place in our system of law for reaching a result of such tremendous consequences without ceremony—without hearing, without effective assistance of counsel, without a statement of reasons."

In short, the Supreme Court ruled unequivocally that

juvenile procedures must measure up to the essentials of due process and fair treatment.

There was, however, more to come. One year later the Supreme Court ordered changes in the juvenile justice system that state legislatures are grappling with still.

The case concerned a fifteen-year-old Arizona juvenile named Gerald Gault who was taken into custody with a friend after the two allegedly made lewd phone calls to a neighbor woman. Two hearings were conducted before a judge without transcripts, recordings, or memorandums being made of the proceedings. The complainant never signed a sworn statement or filed official charges. Nevertheless, the judge committed Gault to the State Industrial School ''for the period of his minority [until age twenty-one].'' Because Gault was fifteen years old, he effectively received a sentence of six years. Had he been an adult convicted of making lewd phone calls, the maximum punishment would have been two months in jail and a $50 fine.

In the Gault case, the Supreme Court ruled that both a juvenile and his parents must be notified early and in writing of the charges against him, that juveniles must be notified of their right to counsel, and that, like adults, juveniles should be afforded protection against self-incrimination and the right to cross-examine witnesses against them. Finally the Court ruled that there was to be no distinction between adult and juvenile cases in the areas of the confession and sworn testimony.

It was a landmark decision. The Gault ruling provided juveniles with many of the protections of due process previously reserved for adults.

Subsequent rulings further clarified the juvenile's right to due process, stopping short, however, of requiring jury trials for juveniles.

With its decisions, the Court forced states to move away from the rehabilitative model they had relied on for years and edge closer toward the adversarial model of criminal courts. Many states, faced with rising delinquency and growing popular support for law and order, were quite ready to make the changes.

However, changing a system as steeped in tradition as the juvenile justice system is an arduous process. As drafters of the Colorado bill discovered, it was nearly impossible to draft legislation that would clear the books and create a new system. Instead, they found it easier to make changes slowly, as problems or opportunities developed.

For Republican Senator Jeff Wells of Colorado Springs, sponsor of Senate Bill 127, the problem was the young aggravated offender, the twelve-year-old or thirteen-year-old who unquestionably had embarked on a career of criminality and for which the law had no recourse. Though his bill also addressed procedural problems, the young offender was its primary focus.

Joe Janson, however, was not interested in the history of juvenile justice or the complexities of drafting legislation. He was interested in getting killers like Billy off the streets forever. For him the bill didn't go far enough. And that was what he planned on telling the lawmakers today.

It was just before lunch when the Jansons were called up before the committee. As soon as the couple took their seats, the bright lights of the television crews lit up and the tape recorders began whirling. The morning had been filled with testimony from bureaucrats and experts. This was the media's first chance to infuse the story with emotion.

Joe Janson cleared his throat. He set down his stack of signed petitions before him. Vickie took out a pad and pen to take notes.

"We have a number of very strong questions to ask this board this morning," Joe began. "In our case, which I only refer to simply because it's so paramount in our lives, the young man was twelve days shy of being fourteen years old, and he is as big as I am. I have a real problem trying to figure out why the juvenile law sets up a difference in degree of sentencing for

Class One Felonies for juveniles than for adults, when there is no difference in the degree of death for the victims. I don't understand why we have put a limit on the amount of people somebody has to kill before they say 'You've gone too far and now you have to pay a penalty that's more than two years.'

"Why doesn't the governing body of this state leave the sentencing to the courts and base the sentencing on the severity of the crime and not on the age of the perpetrator? We've addressed this to our local people down in the southwest corner of the state and I have about three thousand signatures on a petition here that would ask that we would do that—try to get the courts back some muscle in this type of situation. I don't think that you can honestly tell me that five years is sufficient in a case like Charles Manson, for example. What's the difference between his victims and the victims of a thirteen- or fourteen-year-old kid?''

Joe leaned back. He was familiar with the glare of the media lights.

The bill's sponsor, Senator Wells, replied. ''I agree with mostly everything you said. The fact, however, is that this bill will make it stronger than the existing law. This bill may not go far enough from your perspective, but it does go further and it is stronger. It does allow now for a commitment for five years, which is substantially more than the two. I guess I can't explain what the philosophical reasoning has been in this state for having the age fourteen as the minimum age for trial as an adult, and I'm not trying to address that. This bill addresses a new option.''

"But you haven't answered the question,'' Joe said.

''I said at the beginning,'' said Wells,'' I have no way of answering that. The age is something that for some reason this General Assembly philosophically stuck in years ago.''

Now Vickie leaned forward. ''For myself and many other people in our area, the fear of a known felon returning back to the area from which he came, and putting all of us in a very difficult situation, is very real. I believe that the lawmakers are wrong to put law-abiding citizens in that situation."

Joe was beginning to grow angry. "What if this boy had killed the governor and his entire family?" he asked the senators. "I mean, let's really look at it for a minute. My job is to build specialized tooling for mentally and physically handicapped people. I've worked at it for six years now, and I'll tell you something, they don't get better in two years. So, I guess what we would like to ask is to add a section to this bill to address Class One felons and give the courts the power to sentence not based on age but on the severity of the crime. I don't understand why there should be a problem with that."

"I'm not sure," Senator Wells responded, "we want to rewrite the law for an aberration. And in your case it *was* one and it *was* an unfair result. There is no question that the two years is an unfair result in this case. This bill more than doubles the penalties. I don't know of any other case where there happened to be a thirteen-year-old that committed a murder in this state. It's an unusual circumstance. If we want to address that, I would rather do that in a separate bill."

The clerk turned to Joe Janson. "Do you have some more to say to the committee?"

"No," Joe said. "I would like to present you with these petitions that we were able to get and we ask that you review what we've asked."

Joe and Vickie stood up and were led to the rear of the chamber. They sat in the gallery as the next witness was called to testify.

It was Cathy Franks, the mother of Mark, the pretty boy at the CAT Center who had shot and killed his thirteen-year-old playmate. Mark was fourteen at the time of the murder and had been tried as an adult and sentenced to twelve years. His mother read from a prepared statement.

"I come before you today in a dual role, foremost

as a mother and also as a very concerned citizen. Two years ago this April, my fourteen-year-old son, Mark, took a gun, an antique gun, from my father's home and a few days later he shot and killed a fellow classmate—a tragic, needless waste of a precious young life. The worst of nightmares cannot compare to what transpired on that day and since. I learned in one split second that your life can change to a degree never before imaginable. This was my son in the headlines, *my* son, not someone else's, but mine. How could this be? No gun, not even a toy one, had been allowed in our household. And yet this. What in God's name had happened? These issues and many others, I'm still grappling with today.

"The issue at hand here is revision of the juvenile code, whereby society as well as justice may be served. We must have some other way of dealing with escalating juvenile offenders than our present Colorado code allows. I believe the bill before you is a step in the right direction.

"Every aspect of our society and most of its laws reflect that until the age of majority is reached one is a child, and therefore protections are guaranteed to that child. How then, I ask you, can a single act, no matter what it may be, suddenly catapult a child into adult status? For serious offenders the current juvenile code is inappropriate. It requires revision both to serve society and to save the children involved. Judges have had little leeway in their sentencing of serious juvenile offenders. They were either given a token sentence of two years or sentenced on an adult plane. Both, in my opinion and my experience, are terribly inadequate. The former is only a token and the latter is a senseless waste of these children. No child, and I repeat, *no* child, should be sentenced as an adult.

"I am convinced had my son gone to prison as was originally decreed, he would no longer be alive today. The present system as it stands creates a dual tragedy, a loss of two precious lives, the victim and the child offender. Do two wrongs make a right? . . .

"The bill before you affords a more reasonable approach to the issue at hand. It would allow for a penalty more appropriate for serious offenders, and yet provide for meaningful and constructive treatment within the juvenile system. The only thing I would change in this bill would be to make it mandatory. . . ."

The testimony by the Jansons and Cathy Franks offered lawmakers a microcosm of the two camps battling it out in the juvenile justice arena. Joe sought a punitive response toward delinquency and the eventual abolition of the juvenile courts altogether. Franks embraced a rehabilitative model that offered society protection while giving the serious offender an opportunity to rehabilitate. In effect, the parents disagreed over who should have control of the system. The Jansons argued for control by the legal system, which specializes in rendering judgments. Franks preferred the social welfare system, designed to accommodate and rehabilitate.

For nonserious offenders, most states now recommend deinstitutionalization and diversion to community treatment programs. For serious offenders, however, most states have toughened their stance. New York, for example, has mandated criminal court jurisdiction for juveniles as young as thirteen accused of any of a wide range of offenses. In Illinois, all youths convicted of a range of designated offenses and having been twice convicted of prior felonies are sentenced to the state department of corrections without eligibility for parole for a period running to the twenty-first birthday. Delaware automatically excludes juveniles accused of murder from juvenile court jurisdiction. Washington has established a point system with clearly defined penalties. In other states, the prosecutor has been awarded greater power to decide who goes to adult court and who does not.

The Colorado senate committee was debating lower ages and increased commitments for violent or homicidal offenders. At the same time, the bill hoped to deter juveniles from crime by dangling before them the threat of incarceration in adult facilities. Colorado was entering the twentieth century.

As testimony continued, committee members were surprised to find that both the state's District Attorney's Association and the American Civil Liberties Union favored the bill. Agreement between the two groups rarely occurred and few senators were ready to pass on the opportunity of pleasing both. The press reacted favorably to the bill, as did most constituents. For the politicians, it would sound good come election time: "I toughened juvenile laws."

The bill passed the committee on a four-to-one vote. It was later passed by both houses with little controversy and only minor revisions. Governor Lamm signed the bill into law effective January 1984, one more incremental change in society's changing attitude toward juvenile delinquency and justice.

Epilogue

James Childress, the presiding judge in the Keenan affair, sifted through his morning mail on April 16, 1986, and came across a letter from Billy Keenan. The four-page letter was handwritten in a childish script with a slant that shifted haphazardly backward and forward. It is reproduced here, complete with misspellings and errors in grammar.

Judge Childress,

I am writing to explain to you what I have done since I have been in [the Closed Adolescent Treatment Center]. Also what I plan on doing from here on out. When I came to CAT Center I was 13 and acted about four. I was very cold when I murdered Kristy and Sherry and only thought of myself. Because the way I thought was so messed up I didn't see just how violent and how much I hurt and affected people when I murdered Kristy and Sherry. For the first year or so I messed around and played games and didn't deal with what I needed to. After that I had to make a decision as to whether or not I was going to change. That took a bit longer than it should have.

I decided, first, I would work on insucurities and how I used my feeling low as an excuse when I murdered Kristy and Sherry, and hurt other people. I needed to accept that I wasn't the only person in the world with insecurities and that the only person who was messing with me was my self. I also had to deal with my self centardness which also goes into being real cold. I acted like a little kids does, if I wanted something and it didn't go my way, I would act like a kid and wine or throw a timper tantrum. I also had to make a decision on whether or not I wanted to grow up. I have done a lot of victum awareness since I have been here. For one I had to own to myself that I had hurt someone very badly and nothing means more than life and I had taken from Kristy and Sherry. When I went over the pictures of Kristy and Sherry I finally realized what a violent and sick thing I had done to them. I don't think I will ever understand how much I hurt Kristy and Sherry and their parents totally. I feel like I understand much much more than I did before. I believe their was no reason for what I did because their is no reason for taking someones life. I feel very badly for what I have done and deserve to have the same happen to me that I did to Kristy and Sherry. I owe more than I can ever give back!

I have gone over in my head what I have done and wonder whether or not I deserve to do what I need to do to grow up and go on. I have come up with as good an answer as I can. No, I don't deserve to do that but that is what is going to happen, and I need to remember that and use that never to hurt anyone ever again. To remember my crime, and what I did to Kristy and Sherry is something for me to be scared of. When I am scared of something, I am more on top of it and make sure it does not happen. I know I will not hurt anyone again because of that all. I also know that in words that does not mean much and I will be proving that the rest of my life. That is the biggest way I must give back, by being straight as long as I am alive. This doesn't even cover what I owe.

I am trying to apply all that I have learned in the CAT Center to situations out there. I have learned alot in family therapies and have dealt with issues that I needed to. My family has dealt with these problems too, even though I am not living with them I feel I am much closer to them now. We are doing family interaction passes once a month, so that even if family therapies are completed we can continue to build our relationships. The interaction passes are to put what we have learned into situations in society. I have planned to do things out there and to be able to come back here and talk about whatever I may need to. I have a lot of fears about my not knowing exactly how people work in society, or how anything else works. I feel like I see things alot differently than I did when I was free. I also feel more equipped to deal with what I need to. But for me it is always scary to do something I don't know about or is real unpredictable and new. But, at the same time, I feel like I must do all that, and I feel good about it. The things I have set up are:

1. I have a part time job on grounds now.

2. I will be starting a full-time job off ground's working for an Outward Bound Warehouse.

3. I will go on Outward Bound, May 16th for 23 days, I will be back on the 7th of June. I want to earn all the money for this on my own that's what the jobs are for.

4. When I get back from Outward Bound I plan on starting school on June 12th.

Number four is a big one. I will start in my junior year and get a diploma and graduate. All my plans are set up in steps so I can work into being out there again. My plans also give me time to process and deal with what ever may come up. To me all this is a big part of growing up. I am writing and telling you this so I can get your opinion about it. Mainly around my going back to school. I would appreciate hearing what you think about my plans, and look forward to hearing from you in the near future.

Sincerely,
Billy Keenan

The timing of Billy's letter was no coincidence. Billy had spent nearly three years at the CAT Center. He had risen in rank from a disruptive rookie to a polished client enjoying the privileges reserved for higher team members. He had grown to become a handsome young man, with well-developed biceps and a disarming smile. Preparations were under way for his release within a year, perhaps sooner.

Billy's counselor at the CAT Center also wrote a letter to the judge concerning Billy's inevitable discharge.

"Billy," she wrote, "has demonstrated consistent progress . . . He has developed a values system and empathic responses to others to the extent that he no longer gives himself permission to injure others . . . He has developed impulse control which is internally motivated and has developed a significant amount of remorse."

The counselor explained that Billy had stopped his aggressive outbursts, and had been in only one altercation in the previous year after being called "baby killer" for two weeks by a youth attempting to engage him in a fight.

Billy had ceased his chronic lying, the counselor reported, and had "maintained an open, honest stance during family therapy when difficult issues were explored.'' Billy also had ''given up major aspects of his narcissistic orientations. He treats others as though their rights were equal to his, is able to compromise situations, has developed patience, and accepts delayed gratification or denial of his wants.''

The counselor concluded that Billy was ''aware that there is no way to atone for the murders and has shared concerns about what rights he has, since he took so much away. He has reached the conclusion that what he can give back is to change, to maintain the change and help other youth whose offense is murder to change.

''I would like to close with a personal note,'' the counselor wrote. ''Given Billy's initial characteristics, he has far exceeded my expectations. I have worked in mental health agencies and this unit for a total of twenty years and I have never worked with a youth who had effected such a major characterological change.''

Was Billy's makeover real or a brilliant charade? It was not uncommon for a client in any program to learn the right things to say and bluff the desired responses without making significant changes. Lesson one in criminology is that criminals are born con men. Even though the CAT Center program was designed to minimize the possibility of fraud, its creator admitted that there was always that chance. Billy had lied his way through situations before. He did a splendid job of lying the night of the initial murder investigation, and when he entered the CAT Center, staff described him as ''particularly adept at covering his tracks and withholding thoughts and reactions to situations.'' Had he succeeded now in beguiling his counselors or were his changes sincere?

The question, though intriguing, was irrelevant. Billy's term was coming to a close. In 1985, his initial two-year commitment had been extended an additional two years without objection by the Keenans. Time passed quickly. By the time Billy penned his remorseful dispatch to the judge, he had only one year of his four-year sentence left to serve, and the paperwork for his release was being prepared. The staff had little choice but to hope for the best. Ready or not, Billy was soon returning to "the outside."

If Billy was faking it, he was doing a good job. His Outward Bound trip went without a hitch. Under direct staff supervision, he made several excursions into the community without incident. He worked hard at his job on the compound. He attended classes at nearby Bear Creek High School and socialized well. He excelled in emancipation classes. Soon he was allowed unsupervised meetings with his parents and ultimately was granted overnight passes from the CAT Center.

In fact, Billy was doing so well that the staff decided to release him eight months early. Instead of release in June 1987, Billy was looking at freedom in October of 1986.

Then something happened.

In May 1986, while on a day pass, Billy was caught stealing a video cassette from a convenience store. Billy was hauled before a judge in Jefferson County, sentenced to two days in jail, and ordered to pay $70 restitution. Though the offense was treated seriously at the CAT Center, it delayed Billy's departure only two months.

Freedom came on December 22, 1986, as sort of a Christmas present for Billy and his family. Billy was welcomed home by his parents, who had since moved to the Denver suburb of Aurora. Billy was seventeen years old and had served forty-two months for the murders of Kristy and Sherry Janson. He was big, strapping, and eager to resume where he had left off when he was just a child of fourteen. It seemed so long ago.

The only problem with Billy's release was that no one told anyone in La Plata County.

Joe Janson was the first to uncover the detail. Joe had called the CAT Center to check on Billy's status while preparing for a radio talk show.

Authorities told him that Billy had been released a month earlier. Joe couldn't believe what he was hearing. He phoned Vic Reichman, who had been elected district attorney the previous year. Reichman immediately boarded a plane for Denver and caused a stir that ended with the *Rocky Mountain News* running an editorial citing the Keenan case as an example of why the Division of Youth Services needed to alter its near-maniacal bent for secrecy.

It seemed that authorities were so intent on protecting Billy from his past that they had failed to alert top officials at Billy's high school of his crimes. Though the school principal knew Billy was living at the CAT Center, he found out that Billy was a murderer only after reading the newspaper accounts of his bungled release. "It all came as a surprise to me when I heard it. I had no clue," said the principal of Bear Creek High. "I'd at least want to be on guard and take whatever preventive action that I could."

Reichman argued with authorities that he and the Jansons should have been updated on the boy's treatment or, at least, been asked to comment on his parole conditions. Reichman was particularly disturbed that he wasn't shown the final disposition report written by Billy's counselor. He said it was the first time he had been in a situation where he had not been kept apprised of a defendant's progress by either the treatment facility or the court.

"His counselor didn't have to go out and look at the bodies or suffer the stress the Bayfield community did," Reichman told reporters. "There was a presumption that the judge and the district attorney couldn't be trusted with the information. I would have liked to have had input. So would the victims' family. He's two murders up on the rest of us. He killed two human beings. In my judgment he'll always be a danger to society."

Reichman argued his case before the director of the Division of Youth Services and Billy's parole officer. He convinced them to at least bar Billy from La Plata

County for the length of his probation and to increase Billy's contacts with his parole officer, which had been scheduled for every two weeks.

Reichman was also shocked to learn that the parole agreement made no provision for psychological treatment. Billy would have the right to decide whether he wanted to continue therapy. "That's too much responsibility for a seventeen-year-old," Reichman complained to authorities.

Not a month had passed after the uproar over his release when Billy was in the news again. It seems that while on a weekend pass a month before his parole, police had caught Billy slashing a car tire, a mimicry of his previous crimes. Billy did not tell the officer that he was a resident of the CAT Center and lied when asked if he had a criminal record. The police officer ticketed him and let him go.

Billy hid the encounter from the staff and his peers at the CAT Center. He later lied to his parole board about the offense. It was only after he was let out that, by chance, a policeman recognized Billy's name on a report and the tire-slashing offense was brought to the attention of Billy's overseers.

The incident prompted another round of outrage and publicity, and Billy's parole was revoked on February 17, less than two months after his release.

"Taking a tape and slashing a tire doesn't seem like major-league stuff," Reichman said, "but we're talking about Billy doing those crimes. Nobody is looking to ruin Billy's life, but he committed two more crimes and obviously needs more supervision."

As it turned out, the outside didn't suit Billy very well, anyway. In the short time he was out, Billy dropped out of high school, began working full-time in a fast-food restaurant, and started hanging out "with the wrong elements," according to authorities.

Staff members at the CAT Center were disappointed in Billy's behavior, but not surprised. Delinquents, they said, often got into minor trouble upon release. Compared with a structured environment, the real world feels anarchic to newly released delinquents. They need to test limits. All the staff could hope for was that their former clients would find the limits quickly.

Because Billy was still a minor at the time he committed his misdemeanors, he was recommitted to another juvenile residential program for "an indeterminate time to two years." Billy the freed man was Billy the inmate again.

The intake counselor at Billy's new home, the Lookout Mountain School in Golden, was not as impressed with Billy as had been his outtake counselor at the CAT Center. "Billy shows many signs of being institutionalized," wrote his new counselor. "He talks openly about being more comfortable in the structured institutional setting than being in the community. Because of his strong need for acceptance, he found he was more easily accepted by negative peers in the community and that he gravitated to the negative culture and illegal activities . . . Billy doesn't seem to have a wide range of emotions or much depth to his emotions."

Still, Billy's assessment was not all bad. "He adjusted easily to the program," the counselor continued, "got along well with peers and staff, and exhibited appropriate behaviors. His group skills were well above average. He handled anger appropriately, was assertive, patient, exhibited little narcissistic tendencies, and was generally a responsible person."

Once again in a structured environment, Billy shined. While at Lookout, Billy received his high school diploma following successful completion of a GED course. He also found full-time work as cook and dishwasher at a local restaurant. The months passed quickly.

For the second time, authorities were contemplating an early release for their star inmate. "Billy has consistently worked more than forty hours per week," wrote the Lookout Mountain counselor in a later report. "He walks to work and back every work day, and has handled his time in the community in a responsible manner. His current supervisor states that he is a most valued employee. This is one example of how Billy has been able to channel his strong need for acceptance and his ability to work into a positive experience.

"Since our last report, Billy has made consistent progress in the transition program. He had completed work sheets on emancipation skills such as banking services, job search skills, nutrition, transportation, job applications, and interviews. In October, he began attending our weekly community reentry group, where problems in the community are discussed by residents and former residents."

The only trouble Billy found during his stay at Lookout Mountain was driving a friend's car without a license. Otherwise, his behavior so impressed the staff that they saw no reason for him to fulfill the last thirteen months of his two-year sentence for the shoplifting and tire-slashing charge.

In August, in anticipation of Billy's second early release, Ed, Phyllis, and Laura moved to Southern California, back from whence they came.

In November, Billy was released from Lookout Mountain. He served two days in the Jefferson County jail for the shoplifting charge, then was flown out of Denver's Stapleton Airport to live with his parents on the coast. For the second time in eleven months, Billy would attempt to make it in the real world.

Southern California was the perfect location for a family with a history like the Keenans. Few people in the fast-lane culture would care to slow down long enough to ask probing questions. Here in the capital of narcissism, Billy would be safe, surrounded by the culture that created him. The Keenans found a little house near a park in a residential neighborhood and started once again from scratch, all the while keeping vigilance over Billy. Always Billy.

The state of California agreed to supervise Billy's parole with stipulations. First, Billy was to provide the local sheriff's office with up-to-date mug shots. And he was prohibited from possessing or using weapons, alcohol, narcotics, or dangerous drugs, including marijuana. He was also expected to find full-time employment and seek outpatient counseling. To date, Billy has done all that was required of him and has not been in trouble since.

Back in Colorado, in their chalet-style home surrounded by tall pines, the Janson were left to reconcile a series of contradictions in their beliefs. The first was that Billy was forgiven by the grace of Jesus yet at the same time had not been punished adequately. The second, that their girls were better off in heaven yet missed so terribly on earth. The task was not an easy one, and more and more Joe and Vickie sought refuge within the indomitable beliefs of evangelical Christianity.

As the couple's confidence grew, Joe and Vickie enlarged their circuit of testimony. Where once they testified in small-town fundamentalist churches with half-filled auditoriums and poor sound systems, now they praised the Lord before millions on cable television on shows such as "The 700 Club." They had good material: the murder of their children, salvation through Christ. It made for busy pledge lines.

The format was always the same, Joe and Vickie sitting on two comfortable chairs next to a comfortable preacher. The preacher would ask questions, pray to God, become outraged over Satan's dastardly work in the world, ask more questions, beseech the mercy of the Almighty, hold hands, pray, then ask the viewing audience to call a toll-free line that flashed on the screen.

In Durango and Bayfield, the couple was rarely singled out by passersby anymore. Slowly, the townspeople who had avoided Joe and Vickie found occasion to reacquaint themselves. Life went on, and in the minds of most, other crimes and calamities had taken the place of the Janson murders. For them, time worked its healing powers.

More than half of the families living in the Homestead subdivision moved away, either to Durango or away from the area entirely. Bayfield High School graduating ceremonies for Billy and Kristy's class transpired without mention of Billy or Kristy. The graduates privately talked a lot about getting out of Bayfield for good.

Joe took the liberty of visiting the CAT Center once while Billy was still a client there. Joe met with its director, Dr. Vickie Agee. She asked him why he had come.

"To make sure you're talking care of Billy," Joe answered. "He's sick, he's killed my children, and I want to make sure you are doing the best for him so that he doesn't do it again."

Agee said that she was doing the best she could. "I have a daughter, and I'm dealing with Billy for the next two years. If he's let out early, who do you think he's going to come after?" Agee said. Then she added, "What would you do if you saw Billy walking down the street?"

"I'd blow his head off. What do you think I would do?"

"You realize if you did that, they would lock you up for murder, too," Agee said.

"I'm one of the guys who designed the motors to put the man on the moon, and you are giving me two years to figure out how to blow somebody away?"

Agee didn't have an answer.

As the years passed, Joe found that he was losing his memory of the girls. He had difficulty remembering certain adventures the family had together. He remembered them only when he and Vickie looked through the family photographs together. It bothered him tremendously. "You shouldn't have to look at a bunch of pictures to remember your kids."

Vickie has taken on some wrinkles and her face has saddened. Even her warm smile cannot hide the traces of her loss. She keeps busy in the community. Her medical billing service is very profitable. Church activities take up a good portion of her time. The couple spends their evenings at home together or with friends. Through the grace of Jesus, they enjoy periods of sincere happiness.

The photos of the girls still hang on the hallway walls, even the pictures that include Billy. Vickie prepares dinner nightly on the spot where Kristy was killed. Tubby, the fluffy black dog Billy came to return that day, remains penned up outside the house and barks with excitement at approaching visitors. The path to Sherry's last moment on earth is covered now with pine needles and dust. Joe has since painted the house brown and built a two-car garage and a body paint shop near the house. Joe likes to keep busy.

He also designed and built a houseboat, something he had always promised the kids he would do. Joe and Vickie often take the boat to Lake Powell and other lakes in the region. They travel frequently. Once they visited the town in California where Billy lives. Vickie didn't realize until she was back in Bayfield that she might very well have bumped into Billy or any of the Keenans on the street, she had distanced herself so much from him.

Joe and Vickie rarely visit Sherry's and Kristy's graves. There is no need. The girls don't reside there. Their spirits are elsewhere. Safe. Joe and Vickie know because the girls returned in visions to comfort their parents.

For Vickie, the apparitions came late one night when Joe and Vickie were visiting Joe's family in Houston.

"We were lying on the floor on a mattress," Vickie remembered. "The TV was behind us. It was cold out. We had prayed as a last resort for the Lord to heal me because I had this terrible headache. I remember it was in the wee hours of the morning. I was asleep but not really asleep. I remember it so distinctly.

"I was almost awake. Kristy was kneeling right here, not like she was there, but just almost there. She was kneeling. Sherry was down right at my feet. Kristy had her hands out. I didn't see her lips move or anything.

But she said to me, 'Mom, it's going to be okay.' I heard it, but I didn't see her lips move.

"I know she said it. I *know* without a doubt that they both were there. I saw Sherry and I saw Kristy. Then I realized what I was experiencing. I tried to awaken, to realize what I was looking at. All of a sudden, they were gone.

"I said, 'Joe, I have to tell you just what happened to me right now.' I told him the whole thing, and then there was such an incredible comfort and peace and warmth. It felt so peaceful.

"The thing that I needed the most was to know that they were still alive up there. I didn't ask for this. I never asked for this. But to now know something that I believed by faith, really, it was a blessing.

"When I woke up, my headache was gone and I just thanked the Lord. I could have gone the rest of my life without that moment, but I'm glad I don't have to. It was so extra-special. It was just like a little gift from God. I *saw* them.''

Joe had his experience sometime later. "I haven't seen both of them," he said, "but I have seen Kristy. It was really weird. Kristy used to be a sleepwalker. Once, when she was alive, I heard the front door open in the middle of the night. It was a terrifying sound. I came out. The front door was wide open.

"I saw this nightgown going out into the woods. I went out and took Kristy's hand and turned her around and led her back to bed. She never knew she did it. After that, I put flip locks on the door.

"Still, Kristy would come down some nights. I'd be sound asleep, and all of a sudden I would realize someone was standing beside my bed. It's enough to scare the life out of you. Most of the time I would ask her, 'How are you? Who are you? Spell your name.' She would spell her name and come out of it.

"One night I was lying there and I was aware that she was standing beside the bed. I said, 'Are you okay?'

She said, 'Yeah.' I said, 'Well, you can go back to bed now.' And she walked out of the room.

"Only this was about two years after she died. She heard me talking to her. She was standing right there.

"I don't know why this has happened to us. I can't say that I would like to have everybody know that we have had those visits from the kids because those are very personal things. They serve no purpose except to us because we can't verify them in any way, and some people think we're kooks. But they are comforting and we feel very comfortable about where our girls are. We've made our peace.

"I find that so many people who have been through tragic times in their lives don't have a real desire to keep on, to keep growing. They just give up. That is the worst thing. It's common knowledge that so many elderly mates die within a certain time of the other's death. They are lonely and just give up.

"I have a friend who lost his son and once a week he goes up to his grave and eats lunch up there. He hasn't let it go. That's wrong. I remember I had a phone call from a relative who was pregnant and wanted to know if she should have an abortion because of what happened to the girls. That got me so mad. I said, 'For heaven's sake, don't stop living.'

"If there is one thing that we've learned it is that people give death too much credence. You must never surrender to death.

"Never."